Threshold Concepts in

This innovative and user-friendly book uses a design thinking approach to examine transformative learning and liminality in physical education (PE). Covering theory and practice, it introduces the important idea of 'threshold concepts' for PE, helping physical educators to introduce those concepts into curriculum, pedagogy and assessment.

The book invites us to reflect on what is learned in, through and about PE – to identify its core threshold concepts. Once identified, the book explains how the learning of threshold concepts can be planned using principles of pedagogical translation for all four learning domains (cognitive, psychomotor, affective and social). The book is arranged into three key sections which walk the reader through the underpinning concepts, use movement case studies to explore and generate threshold concepts in PE using design thinking approach and, finally, provide a guiding Praxis Matrix for PE Threshold Concepts that can be used for physical educators across a range of school and physical activity learning contexts.

Outlining fundamental theory and useful, practical teaching and coaching advice, this book is invaluable reading for all PE teacher educators, coach educators, and any advanced student, coach or teacher looking to enrich their knowledge and professional practice.

Fiona C. Chambers is Head of the School of Education and Senior Lecturer in PE and Sport Pedagogy at University College Cork, Ireland a Hasso-Plattner Institute-certified Design Thinking Coach and Programme Director of the new PGDip in Innovation through Design Thinking. Her teaching, research and civic engagement focuses particularly on the areas of physical education and sport pedagogy, mentoring and social innovation. She is an Invited Member of UNESCO Scientific Committee for Physical Activity, as well as Secretary General for the Association Internationale des Écoles Superiéure d'Éducation Physique (AIESEP), and a founder and co-convenor of the European Educational Research Association (EERA) Network on Research in Sport Pedagogy. She is the founder of the Global Design Challenge for Sport and Physical Activity which uses design thinking to crowdsource ideas for incubation in and beyond the pandemic.

Anna Bryant is Director of Teacher Education and Professional Learning at the Cardiff School of Education and Social Policy (CSESP), Cardiff Metropolitan University, UK. Anna has made a significant contribution to Health Physical Education, specifically, in the area of physical literacy and 'Health and Well-being.' She has project led Cardiff Metropolitan University's Sport Wales Physical Literacy Consultants and was an international panel member for the Australian Sports Commission's Physical Literacy Project (2016–2017). Anna has been involved in providing academic consultancy to the Welsh Government on the new Health and Well-being Area of Learning and Experience (AoLE) and has played a central part in Cardiff Metropolitan University's Welsh Government National Professional Enquiry Project (NPEP).

David Aldous is Senior Lecturer in Cardiff School of Sport and Health Sciences, Cardiff Metropolitan University, UK. The focus of his current research, innovation and teaching interests lies in using forms of sociological theory to develop critical understanding of how education, sport and community-based organisations are able to creatively respond to the reform of education, sport and health policy. He is currently lead for the Physical Health Education for Lifelong Learning (PHELL) research group at Cardiff Metropolitan University. Future research will continue to contribute towards interdisciplinary approaches that support local communities in understanding and addressing the social, environmental and health problems facing society in the early 21st century.

Threshold Concepts in Physical Education

A Design Thinking Approach

Edited by
Fiona C. Chambers, David Aldous
and Anna Bryant

Routledge
Taylor & Francis Group

LONDON AND NEW YORK

First published 2021
by Routledge
2 Park Square, Milton Park, Abingdon, Oxon OX14 4RN

and by Routledge
52 Vanderbilt Avenue, New York, NY 10017

Routledge is an imprint of the Taylor & Francis Group, an informa business

British Library Cataloguing-in-Publication Data
A catalogue record for this book is available from the British Library

Library of Congress Cataloging-in-Publication Data
A catalog record has been requested for this book

ISBN: 978-0-367-35845-7 (hbk)
ISBN: 978-0-429-34226-4 (ebk)

Typeset in Goudy
by KnowledgeWorks Global Ltd.

The language used in this book is that of editors and does not necessarily reflect the views and opinions of Taylor & Francis

For those who have inspired me to be a physical educator:

Mary George, Padraig Griffin, Joanne Moles, Jacinta O'Brien (RIP), Pat Duffy (RIP), Mary Purcell, Michael Darmody (RIP), Arthur Twomey, Julia Walsh, Kathy Armour, John Evans, Liz O'Riordan, Uwe Püshe and Rachel Sandford
(Fiona Chambers)

For my family & friends - Ni yw y byd
(David Aldous)

For my family, Mark and Lili and to the super Sport Physical Education and Health Programme Team at Cardiff Metropolitan University.
(Anna Bryant)

Contents

Contributors

Lisa M. Barnett, Institute of Physical Activity and Nutrition, School of Health and Social Development, Faculty of Health, Deakin Unuversity, Australia.

Jane Bellamy, Cardiff School of Sport and Health Sciences, Cardiff Metropolitan University, UK.

Marc Cloes, Department of Sport and Rehabilitation Sciences, University of Liège, Belgium.

Rosalie Coolkens, Lecturer and Researcher at PXL-Education, PXL University of Applied Sciences and Arts, Belgium.

Donna Duffy, Department of Kinesiology, University of North Carolina at Greensboro, USA.

Lowri Cerys Edwards, Cardiff School of Sport and Health Sciences, Cardiff Metropolitan University, UK.

Håkon Engstu, Lecturer, Department of Sports, Physical Education and Outdoor Studies, University of South-Eastern Norway, Norway.

Orlagh Farmer, PhD Candidate, Sports Studies and Physical Education Programme, School of Education, University College Cork, Ireland.

Nathan Hall, Department of Kinesiology and Applied Health, Faculty of Education, University of Winnipeg, Canada.

Oliver Hooper, Loughborough University, UK.

Hannah Jarvis, Secondary School Teacher, UK.

George Jennings, Lecturer, Cardiff School of Sport and Health Sciences, Cardiff Metropolitan University, UK.

Joanne Moles, University of Limerick (retired), Ireland.

Wesley O'Brien, Sports Studies and Physical Education Programme, School of Education, University College Cork, Ireland.

Yoshinori Okade, Professor, Faculty of Sport Culture, Nippon Sport Science University, Japan.

Amy Rees, Cardiff School of Sport and Health Sciences, Cardiff Metropolitan University, UK.

António Rodrigues, Laboratório de Pedagogia, Faculdade de Motricidade Humana e UIDEF, Instituto de Educação, Universidade de Lisboa, Portugal.

Rachel Sandford, Loughborough University, UK.

Christophe Schnitzler, Senior Lecturer/Associate Professor, Faculté des Sciences du Sport, Université de Strasbourg, France

Kazuhiro Shibata, Professor, Faculty of Health and Sport Science, Ryutsu Keizai University, Japan.

Rebecca Straker, School of Sport and Health Sciences, Cardiff Metropolitan University, UK.

Gareth Stratton, Applied Sports, Technology, Exercise and Medicine, Swansea University, UK.

Nicolas Vanhole, Parkour influencer, Physical Education Teacher, and Performer and Teacher in parkour at the Circus school in Leuven, Belgium.

Mathilde Wassner, Université de Strasbourg, France.

Introduction

Fiona C. Chambers, David Aldous and Anna Bryant

Introduction

This seminal book (and e-book) is an innovative, yet user-friendly *practical and theoretical* guide for PE teacher educators. This is a teacher education book for physical educators who work across the continuum of teacher education i.e. Initial Teacher Education, Induction and Continuing Professional Development. This edited book uses a design thinking approach to interrogate liminality (transformative learning) in physical education and furthermore to develop threshold concepts for physical education and supporting curriculum, pedagogy and assessment approaches to support learning of these threshold concepts for physical education.

It invites us to pause to reflect on what is learned in, through and about physical education, i.e. to identify its core threshold concepts. Once identified, the learning of threshold concepts can be planned overtly using 'rich learning outcomes' (Dennehy & Chambers, 2019) that stretch across all four learning domains (cognitive, psychomotor, affective and social).

Why use design thinking?

Design thinking adopts a user-centric approach beginning with compassion. The user in this case is the learner. The design thinking process involves the *'development of idea stages, applying an iterative process that forces designers to move back and forth between inspiration, ideation and implementation'* (Borja de Mozota & Peinado, 2013, p. 1). This attitude is characterised by empathy, integrative thinking, optimism, experimentalism and collaboration (Brown, 2008, p. 87). It is a process that employs abductive reasoning (Martin, 2010). This helped us to interrogate the seven movement case studies at the core of this book leading to the identification of threshold concepts for physical education.

Brown (2008) coined the term 'Design Thinking' to encapsulate the phenomenon when design was not merely construed as a physical process but as a way of thinking. Further, Brown and Martin (2015) asserted that Buchanan's (1992) article 'Wicked Problems in Design Thinking,' made very clear and concrete links to how design thinking might be used to tackle fluid, assiduous and obstinate challenges. Devitt (2014) describes three types of problems (a) simple (lack of data) (b) complex (lack of data, unknown algorithm and (c) wicked (stakeholders' disagreement, interconnected system, unclear goals, poor understanding, no algorithm possible and data uncertainty). Wicked problems are:

> Not stable but are continually evolving and mutating; have many causal levels; have no single solution that applies in all circumstances and where solutions can only be classed as better or worse, rather than right or wrong (Blackman et al. 2006, p. 70).

Identifying the threshold concepts for physical education could be deemed a wicked problem. Hassi and Laakso (2011) concluded that the design thinking process is itself complex as it is based on a three-dimensional framework where a set of practices interact with cognitive approaches and a specific (abductive, divergent and open) mindset. This encourages abstract solutions to concrete problems (Goligorsky, 2012). The design thinking framework adopted in this book is a multi-stage iterative process, e.g. (1) Compassion, (2) Ideate, (3) Prototype, (4) Implement & Evaluate (Chambers, 2018). It is intended that by learning the design thinking approach, physical educators can make sophisticated choices about the curriculum, pedagogy and assessment used to deliver threshold concepts for physical education. In this way, physical educators can be seen as the designers of bespoke learning experiences for each learner. This is possible because designers (educators) are trained in observation techniques, experimentation and the continuous testing of their ideas in what are often unstable learning contexts. Designers (educators) are risk-takers who learn how to manage uncertainty via prototyping, based on observation and user-awareness and testing (Borja de Mozota and Peinado, 2013, p. 1). Design thinking begins with a problem statement (Liedtka, 2015), which focuses on the end-users i.e. the physical educator and the learner. Therefore, the problem statement at the heart of this book is:

Problem Statement:

> *Description:* As a profession, we do not appear to have an agreed matrix of threshold concepts for PE.
> *Learning Need:* PE educators need to identify threshold concepts for PE so that they can plan implement and assess learning in and through PE.
> *Insight:* The absence of agreed threshold concepts in PE leads to ambiguity and a weakening of the perceived value of PE in the curriculum and also impacts the status of our profession.

In sum, this book has found solutions to this central problem statement. The writing pods for each movement case study used design thinking to generate (a) proposed threshold concepts for physical education and (b) proposed curricular, pedagogical and assessment approaches that promote learning of their proposed threshold concepts for physical education.

Organisation of the book

There are three key sections which (a) walk the reader through the underpinning concepts, (b) use case studies to explore and generate threshold concepts in physical education using design thinking approach and finally and (c) provide a guiding Praxis Matrix for PE Threshold Concepts that can be used for PE educators across a range of school and physical activity learning contexts.

Section 1: Core concepts

In this section, we will present dedicated chapters to unpack the key concepts. In Chapter 1, *The languages of/for Movement in 21st Century Physical Education*, we interrogate the notion of movement as it pertains to physical education navigating concepts such as physical activity, physical literacy, fundamental movement skills, functional movement skills, motor competence and skill acquisition. In Chapter 2, we turn to the concepts of Threshold, Liminality and Flow, in a general sense and then linking it specifically with physical education as an interdiscipline. This section closes with Chapter 3: Design Thinking: Pedagogy, Process, Mindset and Space, which details the theory of design thinking, all of which is showcased by outlining the planning, implementation and outputs of the 2020 AIESEP Design Thinking Workshop on 'the Pedagogy of Physical Literacy.'

Section 2: Movement case studies: A design thinking approach

In this section, seven movement case studies are interrogated. Each chapter has a writing pod comprising academics and practitioners. The seven exploratory case studies used the Chambers (2018) design thinking approach to address the design challenge to identify threshold concepts (and their supporting pedagogies) for physical education. Writing pods, comprising academics and practitioners examined the following areas of human movement: gymnastics, dance, parkour, outdoor education, martial arts, Gaelic games and netball. Writing pods drew on their (a) research, (b) experiences of teaching children and young people and (c) educating current and future PE teachers. These contributions were also shaped by writing pod authors' own biopedagogies (Armour & Fernandez-Balboa, 2001).

Section 3: Lessons learned: Threshold concepts for physical education

The last section comprises three chapters. Chapter 11 outlines the process of dialogic and discourse analysis of the seven movement case studies. It then presents four threshold concepts for physical education – Corporeal Reflexivity; Corporeal Aesthetics, Self-actualisation through Human Movement and Eudaimonia through Human Movement. In Chapter 12: Threshold Concepts for Physical Education: From Conceptual Possibilities to Pedagogical Realities, the four

threshold concepts in PE are translated to praxis guided by a set of pedagogic principles of translation within a design thinking framework. In closing, Chapter 13
Endnote: Final Thoughts and Future Directions considers the journey of curiosity
and where it might lead to next in putting forward future considerations.

References

Armour, K. M. & Fernandez-Balboa, J. M. (2001). Connections, Pedagogy and Professional Learning. *Teaching and Teacher Education*, 12(1), 103–118.

Blackman, T., et al. (2006). Performance assessment and wicked problems: the case of health inequalities. Public Policy and Administration 21, 66–80.

Borja de Mozota, B. & Peinado, A. (2013). New Approaches to Theory and Research in Art & Design lead Educational Programs – Can "Design Thinking" spark new answers to old problems? Annual Conference of the College of Art Association (CAA) New York.

Brown, T. (2008). Design thinking. *Harvard Business Review*, 86(6), 84–92.

Brown, T., & Martin, R. (2015, September). Design for action. *Harvard Business Review*, 93(9), 58–64.

Buchanan, R. (1992). Wicked Problems in Design Thinking. Design Issues. The MIT Press 8(2), 5–21.

Chambers, F. C. (ed.) (2018). *Learning to mentor in sports coaching: A design thinking approach.* Oxon, Ox: Routledge.

Dennehy, N. & Chambers, F. C. (2019). Connected Curriculum: Principles of Assessment. University College Cork: 10.

Devitt, F. (2014). Design Thinking Workshop. IRDG Conference, Leopardstown Racecourse Pavilion 14th October.

Goligorsky, D. (2012). Empathy and Innovation: The IDEO Approach. *Lecture*, Harvard Business School, Boston, MA.

Hassi, L. & Laakso, M. (2011). Design Thinking in the Management Discourse: Defining the elements of the concept. 18th International Product Development Management Conference, Innovate through Design. Delft, The Netherlands.

Liedtka, J. (2015). Perspective: Linking Design Thinking with Innovation Outcomes through Cognitive Bias Reduction. *Journal of Product Innovation Management*, 32(6), 925–938.

Martin, R. (2010). Design thinking: achieving insights via the knowledge funnel. *Strategy & Leadership*, 38(2), 37–41.

Part I

Core concepts

Chapter 1

The languages of/for movement in 21st Century physical education

David Aldous, Anna Bryant and Rebecca Straker

Introduction: The continued transformation of Physical Education

Much continues to be written, discussed and debated about the ability of physical educators to respond to an eclectic range of globally significant economic, social, political and technological challenges of the 21st Century (Organization for Economic Cooperation and Development (OECD), 2018). As evidenced by the title of this book, one of the most enduring challenges, past, present and future has been the role of physical educators in the construction and practice of movement (Laker, 2002; Brown & Payne, 2009) and preparing young people for lifelong physical activity (PA) in the hope of addressing a plethora of health outcomes (Evans et al., 2004; Sperka et al., 2018). In addressing these issues, physical educators have continued to draw upon an eclectic range of conceptual and pedagogical positions, perspectives and ideas (Evans & Davies, 2002; 2012) that have been historically constructed across the hierarchical and horizontal knowledge structures (Bernstein, 2000; Moore & Maton, 2001) comprised of philosophy, science and pedagogy (Kretchmar, 2008; Tinning, 2008).

Echoing the thoughts of Evans & Davies (2011, p. 276), students and practitioners of physical education (PE) in the conceptualisation and practice of movement are too frequently 'required to speak particular social and theoretical languages ... and tend to become socialised deeply into the underlying codes and modes (or more particularly, their teachers perspectives).' Indeed, drawing upon the thoughts of Bernstein (1977, p. 167) physical educators are often 'told and socialised into what to reject but rarely told how to create.' In many respects such tendency for conceptual rejection prohibits teachers from engaging with what Kirk (2010, p. 129) has previously illustrated as a 'radical agenda for PE'; one that necessitates both the convergence and divergence of different perspectives that are generated from an eclectic range of theoretical and practical languages.

Such aspirations for the discipline of PE are not as utopian as once perceived (Quennerstedt, 2019). Indeed, readers will be familiar with how the transformation of PE curricula towards health, lifelong PA and movement continues to be seen across a number of different global contexts. For example, within our own context of Wales, the transformative education agenda outlined by the Welsh Government (2017) and the renewed focus on health and well-being offers potential for Welsh physical educators to contribute to a holistic, progressive agenda for lifelong engagement with PA (Aldous, 2018). Nevertheless, translating such a position into practice necessitates that scholars and practitioners within 21st Century PE continue to challenge what Evans & Davies (2011, p. 276) term 'research fundamentalism' and move across the rigid boundaries of existing conceptual positions. Doing so necessitates that practitioners are provided with the skills and knowledge to move beyond positions of 'acceptance' and 'rejection' of ideas, values and practices to one in which they are able to create new *languages of and for movement* that enable the continued transformation and evolution of PE through the 21st Century.

With this in mind, in this chapter, we begin outlining how such a process of language/concept creation might be achieved. In line with Tinning's (2008) argument for a 'languaging' of the terms pedagogy and sport pedagogy about the meanings of such terms, we are also keen to focus on how *practices* of and for movement are informed by certain *languages* and ways of seeing the world that encourages practitioners to engage with further reflexive, critical thinking and practice within PE. In foregrounding this, we shine a light on the underlying generative principles of existing movement languages, with the intention of providing a starting point from where we might offer forms of support to practitioners in the creation of their own movement languages and pedagogies. We now outline the influence of Bernstein's concept of languages of description (Bernstein, 1996; 1999; 2000) on our understanding of 'languages of movement.'

Articulating the languages of movement within PE: The contribution of Bernstein's sociological theory

Research within the intertwined fields of education and physical education has continued to be enriched by the contribution of Bernstein's sociology of and for education (Morais et al., 2001). Such contribution is particular notable in the ways Bernstein's concepts have been utilised in the construction and implementation of curricula in which the practice of movement is strongly emphasised through particular discourses (Penney & Evans, 1999; Penney et al., 2009; Brown & Penney, 2017). Yet, whilst much of this important utilisation of Bernstein's principles has focused on how movement is constructed within forms of curriculum and pedagogical practice, our use of his work aims to contribute to the field by offering a slightly different conceptual angle. To do so, our position draws extensively on Bernstein's concept of the languages of description (Bernstein, 1996; 1999; 2000), which places focus on:

> what is to count as an empirical referent, how such referents relate to each other to produce a specific text and translates these referential relations into theoretical objects or potential theoretical objects (Bernstein, 1996, p. 136).

Resonating strongly with Chomsky's work on surface and deep grammar (Moss, 2001), Bernstein's concept enabled a stronger, more enriched and dialectical understanding of how languages within the field of education are transformed and how this transformation leads to the creation of new, empirically informed understandings of the pedagogical context in which they are practiced (Ivinson, 1997). This relationship is wonderfully illustrated within the work of Morais and Neves (2001, p. 186) who advocated using Bernstein's principles to develop a model in which the 'theoretical and empirical are viewed dialectically' to provide a conceptual structure that is 'diagnostic, predictive, descriptive, explanatory and transferable' (Morais & Neves, 2001, p. 187). In adapting these principles, we have attempted to illustrate some of the existing languages that inform the practice of movement within contemporary PE.

Importantly, our adaptation exemplifies how the use Bernstein's language of description provides an illustrative account of how PE as a discipline is comprised of three elements that describe the dynamic interplay between theoretical concepts and empirical research. The first describes an internal language of description that is comprised of concepts (e.g. experimental, sociological, psychological and pedagogical) that enables articulation of 'the perspectives and activities of its members, the kinds of things that are defined as 'problems,' the ways in which problems will be typically dealt with'(Moore & Muller, 2002, p. 630). The second element outlines the external language of description (Bernstein, 1999) and focuses on the structure of *specialised* approaches and frameworks (such as Laban's Movement Analysis, Fundamental Movement Skills or Physical Literacy) how they are classified, maintained and insulated to produce empirical data. The third element then outlines the social relations of the pedagogic activity, where the two languages, are expressed. Commonly, Bernstein postulated how this might be within textbooks or contexts such as classroom activities.

Significantly, for our own work, the principles outlined in Figure 1.1, offers a means from where to understand the complex, dialectical relationships that lie between (i) the construction of languages of description (as outlined within the internal languages component); (ii) those languages of movement where there is a focus on external language of description (specialised knowledges with an empirical focus) and (iii) the social contexts in which those languages are expressed and acquired within practice (and also through texts) in PE. What is also interesting is how the dialectical position offered by Bernstein's model resonates with some of the thoughts of Arnold (1979, p. 103) who asserted that language is not a static entity, 'but something that evolves in response to a need to identify and refer the pertinent phenomena in a more economic and/or illuminating way.'

In adding a further layer of analytical sensitivity, Bernstein also made a distinction between those languages that have a strong/weak internal grammar *and* those that have a strong/weak external grammar (Bernstein, 1999). Those disciplines that are comprised of languages with weaker internal grammars might include sociology, philosophy, social anthropology and cultural studies. Importantly, with languages of description that are comprised of weaker structures, particular within the internal language of description, there is more onus on the knower (e.g. within the focus of our work academics and practitioners) to translate the internal language into

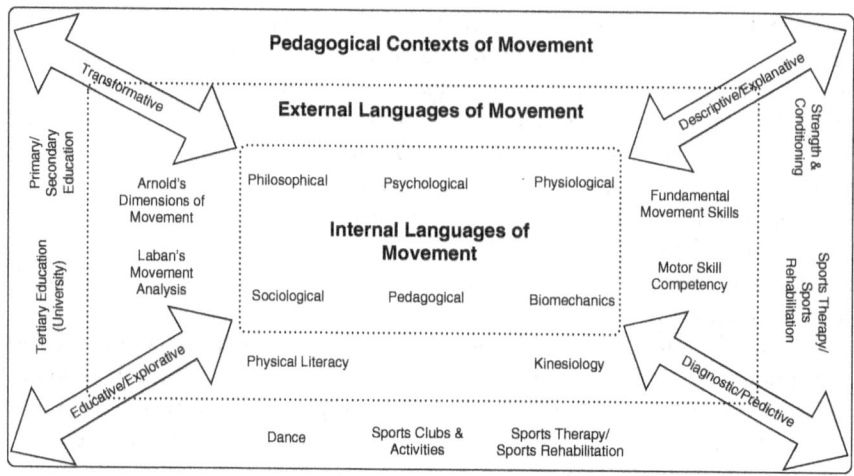

Figure 1.1 Diagram to illustrate the languages of description within the context of contemporary Physical Education.

Source: Adapted from Morais & Neves, 2001.

their own context. It also demands that they be responsible for the transferability, description and explanation of models and concepts within the pedagogical activities in which these languages are expressed (see Figure 1.1 above).

Contrastingly, those languages of description that can described as having a strong grammatical element consist of languages that have a 'explicit conceptual syntax capable of 'relatively precise empirical descriptions and/or of generating formal modelling of empirical relations' (Bernstein, 1999, p. 164). As a consequence, those languages characterised with an explicit conceptual syntax generate analytical and conceptual power by *restricting* their empirical gaze to a very narrow focus on particular elements of movement, such as skill. Within the context of PE, it may be argued that disciplines such as biomechanics, physiology and to a degree cognitive psychology are all disciplines comprised from languages of description with strong and explicit grammatical syntaxes that continue to be prominent in shaping understanding, measurement and practice of movement. Interestingly, their prominence is particularly notable since the onset of university degrees such as 'sport and exercise science' and 'kinesiology' (Kirk, 2010; Silk et al., 2014; Aldous et al., 2016).

With these examples in mind, we would argue that Bernstein's language of description offers a unique set of heuristic principles from where PE scholars and practitioners can become more sensitised towards a range of languages that enable the conceptualisation, analysis and practice of movement. In this way they may both interrogate the accepted reproduction of existing discourses of health and PA *and* begin to aspire to the creation of movement languages, created through a unique set of analytically distinguishable grammatical properties. In what follows, we provide illustrative examples of some of the current languages that have contributed to the development of movement practices within PE.

The role of philosophical and socio-educative focused movement languages

Despite the continued influence of scientific orientated languages within PE, there remains a strong re-orientation towards the recontextualisation and translation of languages that can be illustrated as having a philosophical and socio-educative focus. Such re-orientation, rather than radical creation, towards these historically situated languages is not surprising given how reading of these positions of the past offers the starting point of how concepts may be developed in the future (Kirk, 2010; Hickey et al., 2014). One of the most prominent examples of the re-orientation towards philosophical and socio-educative languages of movement can be seen in the attempted implementation of Peter Arnold's seminal work on 'in, through and about movement' (Arnold, 1979; 1988).

Example One: Arnold

Generated to overcome what Arnold felt was a disproportionate focus on cognitive development, Arnold's much vaunted work attempted to reposition personal meaning of movement as central to the experiences of individuals within forms of PE (Brown, 2013). Such focus was constructed through orientation towards three interrelated dimensions: Education in movement; education through movement and education about movement.

These principles are illustrative of a language of movement that has an internal language of description that has a weak grammatical syntax. It places emphasis on a form of enquiry about movement that draws upon an eclectic range of sub-disciplines (biomechanics, sociology and philosophy) to provide explanation and practice of movement. However, more prominent to Arnold's treatise are the influences of phenomenology and existentialism, particularly through the work of scholars such as Sartre, Merleau-Ponty and, later, the work of Dewey. Such a weak grammatical internal and external language has enabled Arnold's work to be translated across a number of across a number of different global contexts and has seen a renaissance amongst policymakers and curricula designers.

One prominent example of this application of Arnold's work can be seen within the context of Australasian curricula design (Brown & Penney, 2012). Here, the explicit re-orientation towards movement is clearly evident within the propositions of the Health and PE curriculum, particularly in the proposition titled 'Valuing learning in and through and about movement' (see Australian Curriculum, Assessment and Reporting Authority (ACARA), 2012). Yet, as noted by the valuable work of Brown (2013, p. 144) despite 'sound knowledge of the language of 'in, through and about movement,' the concepts, in their original entirety have often not been entirely translated into practical and pedagogical context. This is also evident within the work of Culpan (2000), who notes how the translation of the philosophical principles within the New Zealand curriculum were presented as generic statements of movement that emphasised more about the learning of movement skills rather than a focus on the meaning of movement. Again, this example is indicative of the key challenge in how the conceptual power of philosophical languages of movement can be retained as they are translated into policy and pedagogical contexts. Similarly, Stolz & Thorburn (2015) also raise powerful questions regarding the need for further work on the translation of philosophical principles to be further developed and importantly further engaged with by practitioners. Arguably, for this to be achieved, practitioners must engage with what Stolz & Thorburn refer to as the 'complicated historical development' of philosophical languages by returning to the internal languages of description.

Example Two: Laban

Another example of a philosophical language can also be seen within the work of Laban. Whilst retaining strong resonance with the principles of phenomenology and monism, Laban Movement Analysis (Laban, 1980) is characteristically described as a multifaceted framework (Schwartz, 1995; Payne, 2017) from where there is a conscious attempt to reflect on the meaning generated from the dynamic interaction between body and mind. To do so, Laban's analysis focuses on four movement elements; body, effort, space and shape (Tsachor & Shafir, 2017; Payne, 2017). What is immediately evident in the reading of these elements of the framework is again the focus on fluidic and transferable principles that aim to understand the interconnections between the body, mind and space. As illustrated by Schwartz (1995, p. 26), LMA framework represents:

> An open system. It is a dynamic and evolving set of principles which provides a language with which to describe and direct movement experiences. It focuses attention on dynamics of movement, spatial range, and principles of physical development.

The illustration provided by Schwartz strongly alludes towards a framework that like the Arnoldian dimensions of movement, is conceptually focused around an internal language of description that has a weak grammatical syntax. As a consequence, such weak grammatical structures enable the possibility of translating highly abstract philosophical meanings regarding the body, space and mind into a text that made explicit to practitioners' ways of understanding and practicing movement. For example, LMA has been used by dance practitioners to develop forms of curriculum that move away from a sole focus on skills to one that encompasses intention, imagination and, importantly, centralises the body within these processes. When construed as a language comprised of a weak grammatical syntax, LMA does not so much represent a framework but a set of *heuristic principles* that were evidently designed to be applied, transformed and practiced across many cultural contexts and disciplines.

Yet, similar to Arnold's principles, what is evident within the context of PE is how Laban's language of movement has continued to be refined and reduced from a reflexive language constructed from philosophical principles to become more focused on generating a more prominent external language of description that is strongly orientated towards very specific pedagogical elements of the movement process. For example, whilst the original work of LMA placed a stronger focus on the role of imagination in movement, within other later examples, such as evident within the work of Payne (2017), Laban's principles have been translated in reference to the assessment and diagnosis of, for example personality disorders. Whilst evidently extreme in their translation, such psycho-therapeutic work offers examples of a wider movement that has resulted in Laban's work becoming evolved from a philosophical position, to one that strongly aligns with conceptualising movement within strongly framed external languages of description. Whilst undeniably powerful, the stronger orientation towards diagnostic and prediction has inevitably reduced the possibility of creative boundary crossing between each of the components of the Laban framework.

Example Three: Physical Literacy

Our final example of how the philosophical languages of movement have continued to evolve is illustrated through the continued development of the concept Physical Literacy. Despite more prominent focus within literature and practice, the concept of Physical Literacy has a long and historical influence on the understanding and practice of movement (see Cairney et al., 2019). Whilst earlier manifestations of Physical Literacy have always existed, the concept has become again more prominent and popular with policymakers and practitioners in the fields of PE, sport and physical activity. As many readers will acknowledge, central to the re-emergence and prominence of Physical Literacy has been the seminal work of Whitehead (1990; 2001). This work has several strong features that illustrate Physical Literacy as a concept with an internal language comprised of weak grammatical characterisations:

> Physical Literacy, on the contrary, focuses on the lived body, the embodied dimension of human existence. Nurturing this aspect of our being is seen to make a distinctive contribution to human life, through enriching experience and assisting in the realisation of our full potential (Whitehead, 2007, p. 283).

Resonating strongly with other theorists of movement such as Arnold, early manifestations of Whitehead's development of Physical Literacy placed strong focus on the role of 'lived embodiment' within an individual experience of PE. Here, similar to the work of Arnold, there is a notable orientation towards the existentialist and phenomenological writings of Sartre and Merleu-Ponty. This strong and prominent focus on such theorists within the internal language of description reinforced perhaps the original proposition of Physical Literacy as a language that *refutes* descartian dualisms and could explain how an individual moves with 'poise, economy and confidence in a wide variety of physically challenging situations' (Whitehead, 2001, p. 131). Yet, similar to the other philosophical languages outlined within the chapter, the abstract nature of Whitehead's earlier conceptualisation of PL has continually transferred into a pedagogical context that is increasingly reliant on diagnostic and predictive languages. This makes retention of her original concepts more challenging. Thus, there is a danger that unless languages of movement with weaker internal grammatical syntaxes are able to generate empirical understanding, they remain nothing other than what Bernstein (2000, p. 133) describes as 'something good to think with.'

As a result, what is evident since Whitehead's introduction of the term Physical Literacy, is *a re-evolution* of the concept by a range of theorists and practitioners determined to ensure that these principles are transferable into a micro-level, classroom-based context. Such has been this process of evolution that there are now multiple ways in which the Physical Literacy language is both constructed and transformed away from its original internal language of description (Young et al., 2019). In some respects, this is not that surprising. Like all languages, concepts are cultural and contextual derivatives of the core principles (a lovely example is how many derivatives of Welsh and Gaeilge there are). As such, it was always inevitable that if Physical Literacy was to be used across a number of different sport, PE and physical activity contexts that there would naturally be multiple translations of the external language of description.

Such an evolution of the concept is illustrative within the significant increase of the term within the contexts of PE, sport and physical activity (Dudley et al., 2017; Edwards et al., 2017; United Nations Scientific and Cultural Organizations [UNESCO], 2015). What is notable within Edwards et al. (2017) comprehensive review is that through every iteration of the term, Whitehead's definition of Physical Literacy has slowly evolved to become focused on describing key elements of movement, which are articulated as 'the motivation, confidence, physical competence, and knowledge and understanding to value and engage in physical activity for life' (International Physical Literacy Association (IPLA), 2019; Whitehead, 2019, p. 8). Whilst these examples still outline an orientation towards the internal language of description, comprised of weak grammatical syntaxes such as monist and phenomenological principles, it is evident that the external language of description has become less focused on retaining an orientation towards the core philosophical principles (Edwards et al., 2018).

As a consequence, what has recently emerged is a form of Physical Literacy that places further significance on a more scientific, diagnostic and explanative language of movement (Keegan et al., 2019; Barnett et al., 2019). Whilst undoubtedly politically and scientifically powerful, the work originating from such examples represent an interesting evolution away from the original internal language of description that focused on the application of what can be broadly described as monist philosophical principles. Thus, what these later examples of Physical Literacy represent are a lessening of the (necessary) volatility between internal languages comprised of philosophical concepts with weak grammatical characteristics (Bernstein, 1999). For example, whilst the inclusion of addition of domains such as the social (see Mandigo et al., 2012; Keegan et al., 2019) may be regarded as an attempt to provide a more multi-dimensional version of Physical Literacy, doing so further strengthens the grammatical syntax of the internal language of description, re-orientating Physical Literacy as a conceptual language that is more orientated towards the measurement of movement within the pedagogical context. As a result, what we observe is the continued orientation towards movement languages that are generated from the natural and physical sciences.

The continued influence of 'scientific' movement languages

As has been documented elsewhere (Macdonald et al., 2002), the knowledge and practices of PE have been strongly influenced by what Kirk (2010, p. 89) refers to as the process of 'academisation, scientisation, specialisation and fragmentation.' Such processes, in existence since the 1970s (when degree-level qualifications became more prominent), have led to an increased value and implementation of movement languages that are comprised of scientific principles that reflect wider discourses such as interventionism, efficiency, calculability, control and predictability (Macdonald, 2011).

The continued influence of scientifically orientated languages of movement within PE can be illustrated through the continued influence of languages such as motor skills and motor skill competency (Stodden et al., 2008). This is reflected within the early work of Clark and Whitall (1989, p. 183) who, in their work on outlining the history of these terms, note how the concept of motor development has evolved from an initial focus on process of motor development to a point now where there is stronger focus on the outcome. With this in mind, they offer a definition of motor skill development as being 'changes in motor behaviour over the lifespan and the process(es) which underlie these changes' (p. 194). What is interesting within this definition of Clark and Whitall is the orientation towards a scientific language of movement in which the internal language focus is comprised of concepts that place emphasis on the processes of motor skills and have their origin in biological, psychological and kinesiological systems. In Bernsteinian terms, such focus, strongly resonates with a conceptual language with a weaker grammatical syntax than may be first thought. Such languages contrast with those found within motor development research that has previously defined movement competency as 'the efficiency or optimisation of a performer to complete a goal-directed movement or task' (Robinson et al., 2015, p. 1274).

What is evident within both examples is the orientation towards diagnostic and predictability within the pedagogical context. Moreover, what is also important to recognise is how such diagnostic and predictability outcomes are predicated on a complex language of movement. However, due to the complicated nature of the biological system and its possible, multiple interactions with context specific tasks and environments (Newell, 1986; Renshaw et al., 2010), such language complexities have made it more difficult to determine what competency actually looks like within the pedagogical context of PE.

Yet, at the same time, through the use of these types of languages it may also be argued that understanding of the individual components of movement have become stronger, more powerful in their focus. As a result, it is possible to understand their popularity and increasing centralisation within forms of PE policy (National Assembly for Wales, 2019; UKActive 2019) that strives to make positive impact on the lives of the children it serves. Therefore, what these examples also demonstrate is how it is more appropriate to describe motor skill and motor skill competencies as *hybrid* scientific languages that are continually evolving in their perspective and application within PE. One such evolution of these languages has been the development and application of Fundamental Movement Skills (FMS).

Aligned to the increasing role of sport science within PE, the last 15 years has seen an increasing refinement of terms that reflect a focus on the advancement and measurement of movement skills. Much of this renewed focus has been generated through the continued aspiration to create a language that is predicative in helping to develop positive health outcomes that place focus on developing motor competences within contexts such as health-fitness, physical activity and weight status (Robinson et al., 2015). Yet, it is also evident from the literature (see Logan et al., 2018 for an excellent overview) how ambiguous the term FMS has become. As Logan et al. (2018, p. 781) note:

> The evolution of terms within motor development has created ambiguity in terminology within the literature and across the various disciplines and sub disciplines of human movement and there remain a variety of terms that are used to describe levels of movement skill.

The ambiguity that Logan et al. (2018) identify is illustrative of how scientific movement languages are increasingly characterised with an internal language comprised of a weak grammatical that has enabled the conceptual evolution of the term FMS. For example, whilst the traditional Wickstrom (1977) definition conceptualised movement skills as being comprised of 'building blocks' such as running, jumping and throwing, more recent conceptualisations have continued to add additional categories such as balance and stability skills (see Rudd et al., 2015; Barnett et al., 2016). Importantly, due to FMS' weak internal language, a number of different external languages of description have been generated. For example, as well as fundamental movement skills as identified by Logan et al. (2018) and Hulteen et al. (2018) several terms have been used interchangeably in the understanding of movement skills, including foundational motor skills, gross motor skills and movement patterns.

As a consequence, what is seen within the contexts in which FMS is used is a very powerful language of movement that is increasingly used to predict and measure positive health outcomes. Furthermore, the strength of FMS has enabled it to become infused and dominant within other languages where the grammatical syntax is weaker. For example, the languages of Physical Literacy and FMS are now increasingly used interchangeably (Almond et al., 2013). Yet, despite the evident development and application of FMS, for many human movement practitioners both in and beyond PE, questions remain regarding the creation of scientific languages of movement that are able to offer more holistic solutions. Such questions include: (a) *within imaginative, creative and holistic understanding of movement what is the desired outcome in various contexts?* and (b) *what implications do the further evolution of these types of movement languages have on the future transformation and role of PE?* As illustrated by Gallwey & Kriegel there is a necessity for users of FMS to be further creative in their application of FMS' 'By discovery or by doing rather than thinking about doing' (Gallwey & Kriegel, 1977, p. 49). Thus, what practitioners require are the skills to be able to access and think critically with these languages so they can be applied in solving human movement problems.

As the above examples illustrate, concepts and practices within the discipline of PE continue to be influenced by *hybrid* languages that continue to enable the collation of experimental evidence by scientists and practitioners that have a strong explanatory focus. Because of their perceived visible explanatory power, it is understandable why there appears to be a dominant presence of languages of movement with strong grammars and visible explanatory power within PE at both a policy and practice level.

One of the possible (unintended) consequences of the prominence of such scientific movement languages is their role in reinforcing the necessity of philosophical languages. Scientific movement languages remain so powerful they often intimidate – they don't invite creativity or questioning. Therefore, practitioners are reluctant to 'play with them' through praxis and to generate further movement language theories through usage. This may have resulted in students' knowledge about movement becoming more formulaic (Quennerstedt, 2019) and less focused on being able to understand and practice movement using educative and philosophical languages.

Moving forward: The necessity of creation

The purpose of this chapter has been to illustrate how various movement languages are used to conceptualise, practice and assess movement have continued to evolve within PE. As the illustrations provided have highlighted, practice within 21st Century PE continues to be informed by an eclectic range of conceptual languages. Interestingly, these generate pedagogical contexts in which philosophical and scientific understanding of movement exist within dichotomised relationships. Such dichotomised relationships are mostly generated from the function of indirect and direct external pressures of the authoritarian vertical discourses of the market or the State itself (Bernstein, 1999; 2000). Building upon Bernstein's thoughts, it could be argued that such authoritarian discourses have resulted in forms of PE that reflect orientation towards the acceptance of 'pedagogic populism' rather than the translation and practice of more creative languages. Furthermore, what is also evident from the review of existing languages is that rather than being a linear process, the construction and application of languages within specific contexts has been somewhat fractal. In this sense, whilst the development of 21st Century PE can be charted through pockets of evolution on the use of languages that are characterised with philosophical orientations, the overall pattern of movement languages within PE remains one where external languages with stronger grammatical syntaxes still dominate understanding and practice of movement. As a result, continuing to build on the thoughts of Bernstein (1977) illustrated at the beginning of this chapter, the 21st Century PE *still* remains very adept at communicating and practicing what to reject/accept and rather less focused on how to create/generate ideas.

Yet, such a situation is not without hope. As this chapter has also illustrated, the understanding and practice of movement within 21st Century PE is increasingly informed by a return to what we have termed as more *philosophically orientated* languages. Although not necessarily creating new understanding, the return to these languages within both policy and practice is fundamentally important to the evolution of PE. Whilst highly abstract in their conceptual focus, such languages, characterised with weak internal languages of description focus on conceptualising not only what is evident but also tacit forms of knowledge; the intrinsic, underlying and often abstract processes that are crucial to practitioners being able to generate their own languages of description that enable depth and enriched understanding of movement. Yet, such a position also necessitates focus on how we ensure that teachers/practitioners are supported in the translation of a radical and pluralistic vision for PE, one that nurtures lifelong engagement with PA, into forms of what Green (1998) terms 'everyday philosophies and practices' within the micro-level of the classroom.

Given the relative power of such languages, questions remain as to why they are not easily translated into practice and further embraced by practitioners. Drawing upon the thoughts of Collins (1998, p. 787) communities such as PE have a historical tendency to raise the level of abstraction and reflexivity of their languages of description without necessarily looking at solutions for how these then might be translated into practice. As Bernstein (1977, p. 629) reminds us,

> In a subject where theories and methods are weak, intellectual shifts are likely to arise out of conflict between approaches rather than a conflict between explanations, for, by definition, most explanations will be weak and often non-comparable, because they are approach specific.

Later, Bernstein (2000) also comments on how 'the principles of description, although derived from the theory, must interact with the empirical contextual displays so as to retain and translate the integrity of the display' (p. 91). Such a position strongly resonates with those articulated by Stolz and Thorburn (2015, p. 387) who also note it is 'vital in the future that theory serves practice and practice serves and informs theory in better ways than is the case at present.' Thus, an internal language of movement is only valuable *if* it is able to interact with the pedagogical interactions that are generated from the use of language. Therefore, it is not a question of new languages of movement but how these existing languages are translated into forms of practice.

Thus, if the discipline of PE is to genuinely embrace this proposed transformative agenda what is required is the continued dialectical 'construction of an external language of description that consists of empirical categories that can unambiguously be translated into the conceptual categories of the internal language' (Moore & Muller, 2002, p. 634). It also requires the user of that language (i.e. the educator) to work at a deeper level of resemblance, to have the skills, willingness and time to reassemble knowledge in relation to the particularities of the cultural context in which they reside. Mastering the mechanics of the languages of movement enables practitioners to be more creative in the development pedagogies for movement and less reliant on accepting/rejecting positions that cause our understanding of movement to become dichotomised. For physical educators to embrace a truly radical and sustainable transformative agenda will not only require radical questions but also a commitment to *radical action* that is focused on the translation of concepts through practice.

Our position, which will be further outlined within this book is that there is still more to be done in supporting practitioners within the field of PE in their 'translation' of highly abstract philosophical ideas into forms 'everyday' practices within the micro-level of the classroom (Green, 1998). Echoing the thoughts of Ennis (2013) we believe that 'without a concerted effort to invite teachers to engage with us in this process, our implementation initiatives may not enhance the meaningful and educative process that these scholars envision for PE' (p. 115). However, for this to be actualised, it necessitates that practitioners to have the ability to recognise, generate and transform their practice through the development of their own languages of description (Figure 1.1). Without the space to engage and transform complex principles into practice, we might argue that nothing will be transformed or created and in the end all the discipline of PE will do is end up continually fueling its own echo chamber in which the discourses of acceptance and rejection are perpetuated instead of embracing the necessity of creation.

References

Australian Curriculum, Assessment and Reporting Authority [ACARA]. (2012). Australian Curriculum: Health and Physical Education, Foundation to Year 10. *Draft for consultation*. Sydney: ACARA.

Aldous, D., Miles, A., & Tong, R. (2016). Teaching and learning issues in sport and exercise science. *The Sport and Exercise Scientist, 47*, 26–27.

Aldous, D. (2018). Working towards understanding the possibilities and constraints of contemporary curriculum reform within Welsh Secondary Physical Education, *Oral Presentation to British Education Research Association (BERA) Annual Conference*. Manchester, UK, September 2018.

Almond L. (2013). Physical literacy and fundamental movement skills: An introductory critique. *International Journal of Sports Science and Physical Education, 65*(1), 81–89.

Arnold, P. (1979). *Meaning in Movement, Sport and Physical Education*. London: Heinemann.

Arnold, P. (1988). *Education, Movement and the Curriculum – A Philosophical Inquiry*. London: The Falmer Press.

Barnett, L. M., Stodden, D., Cohen, K. E., Smith, J. J., Lubans, D. R., Lenoir, M., … Morgan, P. J. (2016). Fundamental movement skills: An important focus. *Journal of Teaching in Physical Education, 35*, 219–225.

Barnett, L. M., van Beurden, E., Morgan, P. J., Brooks, L. O., & Beard, J. R. (2009). Childhood motor skill proficiency as a predictor of adolescent physical activity. *Journal of Adolescent Health, 44,* 252–259.

Barnett, L. M., Dudley, D. A., Telford, D., Lubans, D. R., Bryant, A. S., Roberts, W. M., … Keegan, R. J. (2019). Physical literacy in young people: Guidelines and recommendations for the selection of measures in schools, *Journal of Teaching in Physical Education (JTPE),* 38(2),119–125.

Bernstein, B. (1977). *Class Codes and Control, Towards a Theory of Educational Transmissions* (Vol. 3), London: Routledge and Keegan Paul.

Bernstein, B. (1996). *Pedagogy, Symbolic Control and Identity: Theory, Research, Critique* (1st ed), London: Taylor and Francis.

Bernstein, B. (1999). Vertical and horizontal discourse: An essay. *British Journal of Sociology of Education, 20*(2), 157–173.

Bernstein, B. (2000). *Pedagogy, Symbolic Control and Identity: Theory, Research, Critique* (2nd ed)., London: Taylor and Francis.

Brown, T., & Payne, P. (2009). Conceptualizing the phenomenology of movement in physical education: Implications for Pedagogical Inquiry and Development, *Quest,* 61(4), 418–441.

Brown, T. (2013). A vision lost? (Re)articulating an Arnoldian conception of education 'in' movement in physical education. *Sport, Education and Society,* 18(1), 21–37

Brown, T., & Penney, D. (2012). Learning 'in', 'through' and 'about' movement in senior physical education? The new Victorian Certificate of Education Physical Education. *European Physical Education Review,* 19(1), 39–61.

Brown, T., & Penney, P. (2017). Interpretation and enactment of senior secondary physical education: pedagogic realities and the expression of Arnoldian dimensions of movement. *Physical Education and Sport Pedagogy,* 22(2), 121–136.

Cairney, J., Dudley, D., Kwan, M., Bulten, R., & Kriellaars, D. (2019). Physical literacy, physical activity and health: Toward an evidence-informed conceptual model. Sports Medicine, 49(3), 371–383. https://doi.org/10.1007/s40279-019-01063-3

Clark, J.E. & Whitall, J. (1989). What is motor development? The lessons of history. *Quest, 41,* 183–202.

Collins, R. (1998). *The Sociology of Philosophies: A global Theory of Intellectual Change,* Cambridge, MA: The Belknap Press.

Culpan, I. (2000). Getting what you got: Harnessing the potential. *Journal of Physical Education New Zealand, 33*(2), 16, 29.

Dudley, D., Cairney, J., Wainwright, N., Kriellaars, D., &Mitchell, D. (2017). Critical considerations for physical literacy policy in public health, recreation, sport, and education agencies. Quest, 69(4), 436–445.

Edwards, L. C., Bryant, A. S., Keegan, R., Morgan, K., &Jones, A. M. (2017). Definitions, foundations and associations of physical literacy: A systematic review. *Sport Medicine,* 47(1), 113–126.

Edwards, L. C., Bryant, A. S., Keegan, R. J., Morgan, K., Cooper, S., & Jones, A. M. (2018). Measuring' physical literacy and related constructs: A systematic review of empirical findings. *Sports Medicine,* 48(3), 659–682.

Ennis, E. (2013). Implementing meaningful, educative curricula, and assessments in complex school environments. *Sport, Education and Society,* 18(1), 115–120.

Evans, J., & Davies, B. (2002). Chapter 2: Theoretical background. In Laker, A. (Ed.), *Theoretical background.* London: Routledge.

Evans, J., Davies, B., &Wright, J. (2004). *Body Knowledge and Control: Studies in the Sociology of Physical Education and Health,* London: Routledge.

Evans, J., & Davies, B. (2011). New directions, new questions? Social theory, education and embodiment. *Sport, Education and Society, 16*(3), 263–278.

Evans, J., & Davies, B. (2012). Embodying policy concepts. *Discourse: Studies in the Cultural Politics of Education, 33*(5), 617–633.

Keegan, R.J ., Dudley, D. A. Telford, D. Lubans, D. R. Bryant, A.S., Roberts, W.M., ... Barnett, L. M. (2019). Defining and operationalizing physical literacy: A modified Delphi method. *Journal of Teaching in Physical Education (JTPE), 38* (2), 105–118.

Gallwey, T., &Kriegel, B. (1977). *Inner Skiing,* New York: Random House.

Green, K. (1998). Philosophies, ideologies and the practice of physical education. *Sport Education and Society, 3*(2), 125–143.

Hickey, C., Kirk, D., Macdonald, D., & Penney, D. (2014). Curriculum reform in 3D: A panel of experts discuss the new HPE curriculum in Australia. *Asia-Pacific Journal of Health, Sport and Physical Education, 5,* 181–192.

Hulteen, R. M., Morgan, P. J., Barnett, L. M., Stodden, D. F., & Lubans, D. R. (2018). Development of foundational movement skills: A conceptual model for physical activity across the lifespan. *Sports Medicine, 48*(7), 1533–1540.

Ivinson, G. (1997). Book review: Pedagogy, symbolic control and identity. Theory, research, critique. *British Educational Research Journal, 23*(5), 673.

Laker, A. (2002). *The sociology of sport and physical education,* London: Routledge.

Logan, S.W., Ross, S.M., Chee, K., Stodden, D.F., & Robinson, L. (2018). Fundamental motor skills: A systematic review of terminology. *Journal of Sports Sciences, 36*(7), 781–796.

Macdonald, D., Kirk, D., Metzler, M., Nilges, L.M., Schempp, P., & Wright, J. (2002). It's all very well, in theory: Theoretical perspectives and their applications in contemporary pedagogical research. *Quest, 54*(2), 133–156.

Macdonald, D. (2011). Like a Fish in Water: Physical Education Policy and Practice in the Era of Neoliberal Globalization, *Quest, 63*(1), 36–45. DOI: 10.1080/00336297.2011.10483661

Mandigo, J., Francis, N., Lodewyk, K., & Lopez, R. (2012). Physical literacy for educators. *Physical Education and Health Journal, 75,* 27–30.

Moss, G. (2001). Bernstein's languages of description: some generative principles. *International Journal social research methodology,* 4(1), 17–19.

Newell, K.M. (1986). Constraints on the development of coordination. In Motor development in children. Aspects of coordination and control, ed. M.G. Wade and H.T.A. Whiting, 341–60. Dordrecht The Netherlands: Martinus Nijhoff.

Kirk, D., Macdonald, D. &Tinning, R. (1997). The social construction of pedagogic dis-course in physical education teacher education in Australia. *The Curriculum Journal,* 8(2), 271–298.

Kirk, D. (2010). *Physical Education Futures.* London: Routledge.

Kretchmar, R. S. (2008). The increasing utility of elementary school physical education: a mixed blessing and unique challenge. *The Elementary School Journal, 108*(3), 161–170.

Laban, R. (1980). *The Mastery of Movement.* (4th ed.). London: MacDonald and Evans.

Laker, A. (2002). The Sociology of Sport and Physical Education. London: Routledge.

Moore, R., & Maton, K. (2001). Founding the sociology of knowledge: Basil Bernstein, intellectual fields and the epistemic device. In A. Morais, I. Neves, B. Davies, &H. Daniels (Eds.), *Towards a Sociology of Pedagogy: The Contribution of Basil Bernstein to Research,* New York: Peter Lang.

Moore, R., & Muller, J. (2002). The growth of knowledge and the discursive gap. *British Journal of Sociology of Education, 23*(4), 627–637.

Morais & Neves, (2001). Pedagogic social contexts: Studies for a sociology of learning. In A. Morais, I. Neves, B. Davies, &H. Daniels (Eds.). *Towards a Sociology of Pedagogy: The Contribution of Basil Bernstein to Research.* New York: Peter Lang.

Moss, G. (2001). Bernstein's languages of description: Some generative principles. *International Journal social Research Methodology*, 4(1), 17–19.

National Assembly for Wales, Health, Social Care and Sport Committee (2019) or of Children and Young People. Retrieved April, 2019 from www.assembly.wales/SeneddHealth

Payne, H. (2017). The Psycho-neurology of embodiment with examples from authentic movement and Laban movement analysis. *American Journal of Dance Therapy*, 39, 163–178.

Penney, D., & Evans, J. (1999). Politics, Policy and Practice in Physical Education, London: Routledge.

Penney, D., Brooker, R., Hay, P., & Gillespie, L. (2009). Curriculum, pedagogy and assessment: Three message systems of schooling and dimensions of quality physical education. *Sport, Education and Society*, 14(4), 421–442.

Quennerstedt, M. (2019). Physical education and the art of teaching: Transformative learning and teaching in physical education and sports pedagogy. *Sport, Education and Society*, 24(6), 611–623

Organization for Economic Cooperation and Development [OECD]. (2018). *The Future of Education and Skills Education 2030*. Paris, France: Organization for Economic Cooperation and Development.

Renshaw, I., Chow, J.Y., Davids, K., & Hammond, J. (2010) A constraints-led perspective to understanding skill acquisition and game play: a basis for integration of motor learning theory and physical education praxis? *Physical Education and Sport Pedagogy*, 15(2), 117–137.

Robinson, L.E., Stodden, D.F., Barnett, L.M., Lopes, V.P., Logan, S.W., Rodrigues, L. P. and Hondt, E. D. (2015). Motor Competence and its Effect on Positive Developmental Trajectories of Health. *Sports Medicine*, 45(9), 1273–1284.

Rudd, J. R., Barnett, L. M., Butson, M. L., Farrow, D., Berry, J., & Polman, R. C. (2015). Fundamental movement skills are more than run, throw and catch: The role of stability skills. *PLoS One*, 10(10). doi:10.1371/journal.pone.0140224

Schwartz, P. (1995). Laban movement analysis: Theory and application. *Journal of Physical Education, Recreation & Dance*, 66(2), 25–26.

Silk, M., Francombe, J., & Andrews, D. L. (2014). Slowing the social sciences of sport: On the possibilities of physical culture. *Sport in Society: Cultures, Commerce, Media, Politics*, 17(10), 1266–1289.

Sperka, L., Enright, E., & McCuaig, L. (2018). Brokering and bridging knowledge in health and physical education: A critical discourse analysis of one external provider's curriculum. *Physical Education and Sport Pedagogy*, 23(3), 328–343.

Stoltz, S. A., & Thornburn, M. (2015). A genealogical analysis of Peter Arnold's conceptual account of meaning in movement, sport and physical education. *Sport, Education and Society*, 22(3), 377–390.

Stodden, D. F., Goodway, J. D., Langendorfer, S. J., Roberton, M. A., Rudisill, M. E., Garcia, C., & Garcia, L. E. (2008). A developmental perspective on the role of motor skill competence in physical activity: An emergent relationship. *Quest*, 60, 290–306. doi:10.1080/00336297.2008.10483582

Tinning, R. (2008). Pedagogy, sport pedagogy, and the field of kinesiology. *Quest*, 60(3), 405–424.

Tsachor, R. P., & Shafir, T. (2017). A somatic movement approach to fostering emotional resiliency through Laban movement analysis. *Frontiers in Human Neuroscience*, 11, Article 410. Retrieved from https://doi.org/10.3389/fnhum.2017.00410

UKActive. (2019). *Generation Inactive*, Retrieved February, 2019 from https://www.ukactive.com/wp-content/uploads/2018/09/Generation-Inactive_1_ukactive.pdf

United Nations Scientific and Cultural Organizations [UNESCO]. (2015). *Quality Physical Education: Guidelines for Policy Makers*. Paris: UNESCO Publishing.

Young, L., O'Connor, J., & Alfrey, L. (2019). Physical literacy: a concept analysis. *Sport, Education & Society*. doi: 10.1080/13573322.2019.1677586

Welsh Government. (2017). Prosperity for All: The National Strategy. Retrieved March, 2019 from https://gov.wales/prosperity-all-national-strategy

Whitehead, M. E. (1990). Meaningful existence, embodiment and physical education. *Journal of Philosophy of Education*, *24*(1), 3–14.

Whitehead, M. (2001). The concept of physical literacy. *European Journal of Physical Education*, 6(2), 127–138. https://doi.org/10.1080/1740898010060205

Whitehead, M. (2007). Physical literacy: Philosophical considerations in relation to developing a sense of self, Universality and Propositional Knowledge. *Sport, Ethics and Philosophy*, *1*(3), 281–298.

Whitehead, M. (2019). *Physical literacy across the world*. London, UK: Routledge.

Wickstrom, R. L. (1977). *Fundamental Motor Patterns*. (2nd ed.). Philadelphia, PA: Lea & Febiger.

Chapter 2

Physical education: Threshold concepts, liminality and flow

Fiona C. Chambers and Donna Duffy

Introduction

Learning is fundamentally about grasping concepts. There are three ways in which to define concepts: (1) **Word-like symbols in the language of thought** (Fodor, 1975), where thought mirrors language (Rowbottom, 2007). (2) **Abilities** (Brandom, 1994), that is, intellectual abilities and are described by Bonjour (1998) as:

> Possession of the concept of an X by a person is to be identified with that person's having a certain cluster of intellectual abilities: the ability to think of X's, to classify things as X's, and, in some cases at least, to recognize X's in appropriate circumstances (pp. 151–152).

(3) **Fregean or Abstract entities** (Peacocke, 1992). Which are non-mental and non-spatiotemporal objects of thought associated with names (Lowe, 1995) and where the same name can have a different meaning, for example, capital in geography versus capital in accountancy.

Perkins (2006) outlined that three conceptions of knowing could be found among teachers and students: (a) A *possessive conception*, where knowing is seen as knowledge to be retained and applied consistently in routine situations; (b) A *performative conception*, where knowing is seen as a capacity to talk and think about something in a personal way and to be able to use in a variety of situations; and (c) A *proactive conception*, where knowing is seen as applying knowledge actively, creatively and imaginatively in a variety of ways and where it forms the basis for further inquiry. There is a significant leap from performative to proactive conception. This aligns with Biggs & Tang's (2011) work on the SOLO taxonomy (Structure of the Observed Learning Outcome) recently applied to the context of physical education (PE) (Barnett et al., 2019; Keegan et al., 2019; and Dudley, Goodyear & Baxter, 2016). In the SOLO framework, it shows five key stages, with the significant leap from 'relational' to 'extended abstract.' What pedagogical intervention needs to be in place to help the learner to make that leap in learning across that Progression Threshold?

It is clear that negotiating this leap is a pedagogical transaction between teacher and learner. Within this, the learner needs to have a particular learning disposition, that is, to be open-minded, curious, concerned with evidence, to be alert and engaged and willing to venture beyond the comfortable and the known. The metaphor of climbing Everest can be used to capture the learning journey as there are moments in that climb when there is a demand on the learner to apply what they know to an entirely new risky situation, for example, climbing a sheer ice wall (Chambers, 2007). It is in such circumstances that proactive conception (Perkins, 2006) is tested. Clearly, every discipline has concepts which the learner must grasp, but there are some concepts which are key to a deep understanding of a discipline. It is the latter that is negotiated in the Extended Abstract zone (see Table 2.1). Meyer and Land (2003) distinguish between a concept, which could be a step increase in knowledge

Table 2.1 A quality and health optimising PE assessment framework

Progression	'Prestructural'	Unistructural	Multistructural	Relational	Progression Threshold	Extended Abstract
All Learning Domains	The acquisition of unconnected information, which have no organisation and make no sense	Simple and obvious connections are made, but their significance is grasped	A number of connections may be made but the meta connections between them are missed, as is their significance for the whole	The student is now able to appreciate the significance of the parts in relation to the whole		The student is making connections not only within the given subject area, but also beyond it, able to generalise and transfer the principles and ideas underlying the specific instance. Students have exceeded the cognition, affective, social or psychomotor, expectations of the developmentally appropriate standards
Learning Context	No apparent learning observed	Learning progression evident across all learning domains, with significant learning noted in Extend Abstract phase.				

Source: Adapted from Dudley, Goodyear, & Baxter, 2016, p. 328

and understanding (Prestructural to Multi-structural), and a threshold concept which gives access to transformed understanding (Relational to Extended Abstract). We will now interrogate how grasping a threshold concept might be considered transformative for the learner.

What are threshold concepts?

Threshold concepts

Every discipline has threshold concepts. When mastered, threshold concepts are what enable students to look at problems in completely new ways and to 'think, practice and talk' in the manner of scholars of a particular discipline (Davies and Mangan, 2008). Examples of threshold concepts in particular disciplines include: complex numbers in Maths; ambiguity in Design; precedence in Law; opportunity cost in Economics; equal temperament in Music and entropy in Physics. A **threshold concept** can be considered:

> as akin to a portal, opening up a new and previously inaccessible way of thinking about something. It represents a transformed way of understanding, or interpreting, or viewing something without which the learner cannot progress (Meyer & Land, 2003, p. 1).

Fundamentally, it unsettles what is known and involves a conceptual as well as an ontological shift (Cousin, 2006). According to Meyers and Land (2005) a threshold concept has eight key characteristics: Transformative, Performative, Irreversible, Integrative, Bounded, Troublesome, Reconstitutive and Discursive. We will deal with each in turn, drawing on further literature:

1 *Transformative*: It can lead to a significant shift in the perception of a subject. It is akin to a powerful insight which involves a change in identity, perspective, values, feelings or attitudes (Viscardi-Smalley (2018, p. 9).
2 *Performative*: It has a performative element which Bruner (1966) terms this as *enactive* concept. As stated earlier, this is where the learner can apply the concept to new situations by thinking and talking about it in a personal way and also enacting the concept in applied settings.
3 *Irreversible*: The idea that once a threshold concept is learned it takes considerable effort to unlearn it (if it is possible to do this). This also points to the fact that experts often find it hard to empathise with novice learners in a discipline, as they lack empathy or understanding, having already learned the threshold concept.
4 *Integrative*: It reveals the interconnectedness of a concept and the complexity of that concept.
5 *Bounded*: Possibly (often though not necessarily always) bounded in that any conceptual space will have terminal frontiers, bordering with thresholds into

new conceptual areas. It can also refer to the fact that threshold concepts may be attributed to certain disciplines.

6 *Troublesome*: 'Troublesome knowledge,' a term coined by Perkins (1999), indicates how threshold concepts can be conceptually difficult, counterintuitive or 'alien.' Learners often engage in mimicry, as they try to grapple with troublesome knowledge. There are two categories of such knowledge:

    a *Ritual Knowledge* – Perkins (1999) describes this as being routine and meaningless. Even if presented as a schematic, the learner may only see the surface meaning and not understand the complexity within the schematic.

    b *Inert Knowledge* – These can be knowledge bites that are retrieved only when needed but are never connected to other concepts to lead to the rich and complex threshold concepts.

    Perkins (2006) adds a number of other categories in his later work: conceptually difficult knowledge; the defended learner; alien knowledge; tacit knowledge; loaded knowledge; troublesome language

Latterly, Meyer and Land have augmented Perkins' (1999) six original characteristics of Threshold Concepts. They include two further attributes:

7 *Reconstitutive*: Rhem (2013) asserts that this links with the notion of Transformative and Integrative. This means repositioning oneself in relation to the content (White, Olsen, and Schumann, 2016, p. 53)

8 *Discursive*: Meyer and Land (2005) suggest that the crossing of a threshold will incorporate an enhanced and extended use of language:

    It is hard to imagine any shift in perspective that is not simultaneously accompanied by (or occasioned through) an extension of the student's use of language. Through this elaboration of discourse new thinking is brought into being, expressed, reflected upon and communicated. This extension of language might be acquired, for example, from that in use within a specific discipline, language community or community of practice, or it might, of course, be self-generated. It might involve natural language, formal language or symbolic language (p. 374).

White, Olsen and Schumann (2016, p. 53) assert that this is gaining language related to the content.

    This resonates with the work of John Dewey and his view that 'growth' is one of the aims of education.

Dewey, transformative learning and threshold concepts

Dewey's (1916) view of education as growth construed a **transformative** power rather than one of seeking to establish – or transmit – unquestionable metaphysical 'truths.' Dewey did not believe that all experiences led to growth. In fact, some restrict growth and can impede further growth and could 'tend to land him in a groove or rut' (p. 26). Being in a groove or rut links with the idea of **troublesome** knowledge (Meyer & Land, 2003). If such an experience arouses curiosity, it can open up horizons to create the conditions for further growth.

Armour, Quennerstedt, Chambers & Makopoulou (2015) highlighted that Dewey's 'growth' could not be understood as a finite achievement but instead is an on-going (continuous) process. This points to the fact that the learning is lifelong and life-wide. In fact, we contend that learner '*growth spurts*' occur when the learner has a profound learning experience having mastered a threshold concept. This learner trajectory continues throughout life, a point that Dewey emphasised when he said that 'life is growth' (1916, p. 43). Moreover, he asserted that change must be regarded as the norm for all individuals, irrespective of age, because we are always unfinished participants in an unfinished world (Dewey, 1938).

Interestingly, in terms of PE and its threshold concepts, Dewey's (1916) view of learning from experience is helpful: *an experience is capable of generating and carrying any amount of theory (or intellectual content), but a theory apart from an experience cannot be definitely grasped even as theory* (p. 118). Ideas (or concepts) are shaped by experience to help individuals to make sense of these and to develop increasingly diverse responses in dealing with the environment (Pekarsky, 1990). This is what Dewey (1916) called 'interdependence' of the learner and the environment: both the person experiencing and what is experienced have the potential for change. For Dewey, growth was captured as learners' plasticity (1916), that is, the power to retain from one experience something, which is of avail in coping with the difficulties of a later situation. Saury and Durand's (1998) notion of 'cognitive alchemy' is helpful here is describing learning, that is, flexible application of (social) rules, using deeply integrated past experiences' (p. 265). This means the power to modify actions on the basis of the results of prior experiences; the power to develop dispositions (p. 38) i.e. learner disposition that is comfortable with ambiguity. Rhem (2013) stated that self-efficacy is very much a requirement in helping students understand threshold concepts. This is because it places the student in a psychological frame of mind needed to overcome the threshold concept. This points to the learner grappling with troublesome knowledge, being empowered to overcome it, learn it and be metamorphosed by it. As Hodkinson, Biesta, and James (2008) posit, learning can change and/or reinforce that which is learned, and can change and/or reinforce the habitus of the learner. In these ways, a person is constantly learning through becoming, and becoming through learning (p. 41).

Dewey highlights the importance of bodily activities being understood as part of (or embedded in) the meaning-making processes to help learners to reach deep and rich understandings. In essence, thinking and doing are bonded together in a mutual and simultaneous dialogical relation (Armour et al., 2015). This reaffirms Land & Meyer's assertion that there is a **performative** element to learning where learning is an embodied experience. In 1874, Karl Marx argued for the unity of theory and practice, the doctrine of *praxis* or 'critical-practical activity.' This is a cornerstone of PE.

Threshold concepts and liminality

Todd (2014) posits that there is an urgency to ensure that educational experiences take account of not only the product of learning, but the process of learning. This encourages to discern the telic from the atelic, where telic is valued in terms of end point and atelic for their intrinsic value and the pleasure of doing them. For us, this is where liminality comes in. Liminal space comes from the Latin word limen meaning on a threshold or at a boundary and evokes a period of time/space 'in-between' typically during an individual's rite of passage (Turner, 1974). Van Gennep's (1960, 1909) theory states that this period of liminality is rife with uncertainty – it is transitory, temporary and can be an anxious time where, for example, known norms, behaviours and identities are suspended. Van Gennep's original work was developed by Turner who asserted that liminality was a state in which the individual was 'betwixt and between' a social position and/or identity, and as such could not be clearly defined. Turner also saw it as space for liberation from 'structural obligations' (Turner, 1982, p. 27) and where 'anything may happen' (Turner, 1974, p. 13). Many academic disciplines have used Van Gennep and Turner's conceptual framing of liminality, for example, education (Cook-Sather, 2006; Meyer and Land, 2005). It is often located within a temporal or spatial dimension – linked to a moment in times where an individual moves through a ritualistic passage (Thomassen, 2012). Land, Vivian & Rattray (2014) connotes the notion of liminality as a space. But what do we mean by a 'space'? Is it a space or is it a period of time? Or is it more a set of social relationships? Land unpacks this by focusing on two dimensions of liminality: the conceptual and the ontological. The idea of troublesome knowledge and getting stuck implies an intellectual, conceptual or cognitive endeavour. Land adds 'affective' to this (see Chapter 10 Sandford) the experiential element of learning and struggling through these difficult areas of learning; these stuck places. Shortt (2015) wonders if it useful to approach this in terms of ontological space and to consider what kind of 'threshold capital,' cultural capital or psychological capital students might need in order to negotiate that space well. This seems to link nicely with Rhem's (2013) assertion that learner disposition is important. Some work has been done on interrogating the concept of psychological capital which is defined by Luthans et al., (2007, p. 3) as 'an individual's positive psychological state of development.' It has the following characteristics:

1 Self-efficacy – having confidence to take on and put in the necessary effort to succeed at challenging tasks.
2 Optimism– making a positive attribution about succeeding now and in the future.

3 Hope – persevering toward goals and, when necessary, redirecting paths to goals in order to succeed.
4 Resilience – when beset by problems and adversity, sustaining and bouncing back and even beyond to attain success.

More recently, this work has been augmented by Merck (2018) in the compelling Curiosity Dimensions 2.0. These seem to give a clear outline the characteristics of the components of a learner's 'threshold capital':

a   *Openness to people's ideas*: Valuing people with diverse perspectives and ideas and intentionally seeing out different approaches...
b   *Joyous exploration*: The pleasure of recognising and seeking out new knowledge and information...and the subsequent joy of learning and growing.
c   *Stress tolerance*: The willingness to embrace the doubt confusion, anxiety and other forms of distress that arise from exploring the new and uncertain...
d   *Deprivation sensitivity* (recognising the gap in knowledge and pondering abstract or complex ideas to try to solve the problem and reduce the gap) The State of Curiosity Report (Merck KGaA, 2018).

It is clear that a learner needs such threshold capital, as when in a liminal state, the learner grapples with incorrigibles and failure as he/she negotiates the unfamiliar. Land (2018) also talks about liminality being a kind of flux which renders things fluid – as such it is a transformative state of transformative learning. Often, when transforming we have to relinquish something, our prior understanding – this has to be dislodged to make way for new understandings. In order to survive this, the learner may turn to mimicry or experience reality shock, to survive this fluid, uncomfortable and challenging learning experience. It is hard for the learner to let go of what we know or what we are good at – it links to a fear of failure... This is when the language at the heart of this learning encounter becomes so important (Vygotsky, 1978). Land (2018, n.p.) outlines the 'progressive function' of the liminal state as follows:

- A countenancing and integration of something new.
- A recognition of shortcoming of existing view.
- A letting go of the older prevailing view.
- A letting go of an earlier mode of their subjectivity.
- An envisaging (and accepting) of an alternative version of self through the threshold space (as a practitioner).
- Acquiring and using new forms of written and spoken discourse and internalising these.

In a liminal space, people are connected in a rite of passage or a common shared experience. Learning spaces are liminal spaces. Learners are supported to move through the liminal space and to grasp threshold concepts in order to move to

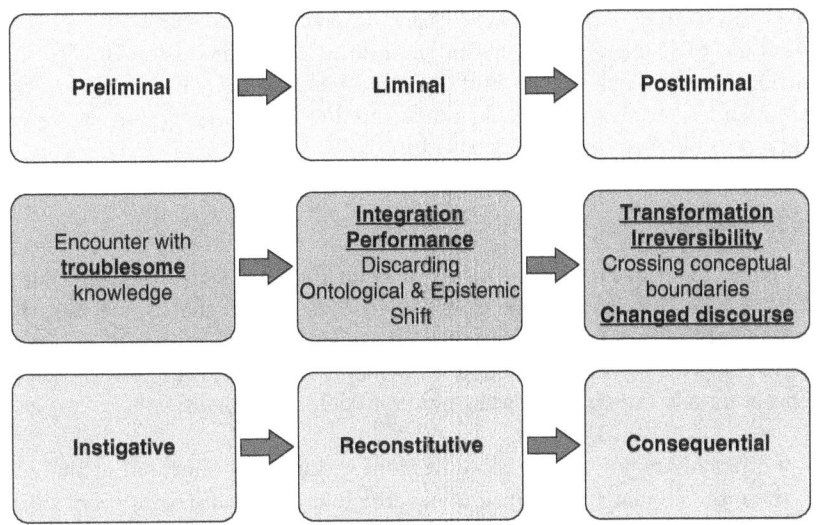

Figure 2.1 The features of learning a threshold concept.

Source: Adapted from Meyer, Land & Baillie, 2010, my emphasis.

the next state with a deep epistemic knowledge of their discipline. Land et al. (2005) describe how this process is highly iterative and messy. It involves learning a number of concepts (elements) to finally grasp the threshold concept (complex concept) (Raiker & Procter, 2012). Raicker and Procter (2012) used Pathfinder Associate Networks (PFNETS) software to map the elements or component concepts within the threshold concept of 'ratio.' They termed these 'knowledge maps.' The following schematic gives a sense of the progression pathway from preliminal to postliminal stages, which highlight seven (of eight) key features of learning the threshold concept with the concept of boundedness implicit in the diagram.

We pause to reflect on what is learned in, through and about PE, that is, to identify its core threshold concepts (Figure 2.1). Once identified, learning threshold concepts can be planned overtly using 'rich learning outcomes' (Dennehy & Chambers, 2019) that stretch across all four learning domains (cognitive, psychomotor, affective and social). These rich learning outcomes take account of the preliminal, liminal and postliminal states. By unpacking rich learning outcomes physical educators can identify the **threshold concepts** which the learner must attain to achieve this rich learning outcome. Finally, the manner in which each of these might be assessed is articulated.

Threshold concepts: Eudaimonia and flow through physical education

In order to be construed as physically educated and not simply a student of PE, we argue that every individual needs to learn the threshold concepts relevant to PE.

It is a concern that PE does not have clearly defined or agreed threshold concepts – This leads to ambiguity in our discipline and in our profession. It also may contribute to the (lack of) status of our subject area in schools. In the next part of the chapter, we investigate eudaimonia and flow as a starting point for perhaps finding possible threshold concepts within PE.

Eudaimonia and flow

Roumpou (2018) asserts that athletes (and all humans) strive for eudaimonia. Athletes have described moments of this in their career, that is, wherein they experienced a telic, uplifting feeling of skill mastery, mental happiness, enhanced self-esteem, a sense of intellectual enjoyment, transcendence, an ecstasy or euphoria state (Cooper, 1998). Murphy (1996) describes this as:

> a mystical and … unique place wherein execution is outstanding and continuous, automated and flowing. An athlete is able to disregard every all the challenges and demands and enable his or her body deliver the execution that has been learned so well (p. 4).

This is a phenomenon of being in flow, or the zone. Roumpou (2018) connects self-actualisation and eudaimonia as they appear to have the characteristics of cognitive states such as peak experience, mindfulness, flow and the zone (Csíkszentmihályi & LeFevre, 1989). Flow is highly correlated with eudaimonia (Csíkszentmihályi, 1997; 2000). When an individual proficiently engages in a stimulating activity, he/she is in flow and is at his/her most fulfilled. It must be a demanding activity which tests competences. Time and ego do not exist and if the individual loves the activity, he/she may experience a form of transcendence during it (Csíkszentmihályi, Abuhamdeh & Nakamura, 2005). Huta & Ryan (2010) describe how self-actualisation and eudaimonia are the catalysts for human endeavour. Eudaimonia involves an uplifted state which embodies wonderment, transcendence and motivation and a feeling of excellence. Chatfield (2012) describes it as human thriving and flourishing. Every child should attain this eudaimonic state in PE. In terms of human movement (and PE), performance flow is correlated with eudaimonia and self-actualisation –we will look at this phenomenon in the next section.

Performance flow

A flow state also commonly referred to as being 'in the zone,' is an optimal psychological state that people experience when there is a perceived balance between the demands/challenges of an activity and the skills/competencies they possess to perform that activity (Csíkszentmihályi, 1990). This perceived balance allows individuals to let go of concerns regarding performance outcomes because they believe that they possess the necessary skills to meet the challenges of the activity. A critical aspect of flow is therefore not the objective level of difficulty of the activity or the actual skill level of the individuals, but rather their perception of the activity's challenges and the skills they possess (Csikszentmihalyi, 1975). Allison and Duncan (1995) found that flow is described similarly among the sexes, people from different socioeconomic status, education levels and from cultural backgrounds. When the individuals have a perceived balance between challenges and skills, they will experience a state of heightened concentration and energised focus that enables them to become fully absorbed in the activity, which is conducive to productivity (Carter & Graef, 2016; Jackson & Roberts, 1992; Swan et al., 2018). However, there is no activity that inevitably elicits flow, since various variables, such as personality traits, play a role in the generation of flow. The term 'flow experience' was first used by psychologist Mihály Csíkszentmihályi in 1975 and in his seminal work on flow and the state of 'optimal being.' Csíkszentmihályi's work on flow stemmed from his early work on happiness and theorised that people are most happy when they are in a state of flow. Through extensive research on the subject, Csíkszentmihály identified nine defining characteristics of flow experience. The first is the perceived challenge/skill balance previously discussed. The second is the margining of action and awareness leading to automaticity. Third, is clear goals that provide a strong sense of what the individual is doing. Fourth, is unambiguous feedback, meaning there is immediate and clear feedback regarding the success of goals. Fifth, is total concentration on the activity being performed. The sixth characteristic is the paradox of control, which involves a sense of having control without actively trying to be in control. Seventh, is a loss of self-consciousness, where concerns for the self-dissipate and the individual becomes one with the activity being performed. Eighth, is the transformation of time resulting in a loss of time awareness. And finally, the ninth characteristic is an intrinsically rewarding experience (Jackson, 1996).

Flow and sport performance

Since Csíkszentmihályi coined the term 'flow experience,' and the concept is continually examined and applied in a variety of different environments where physical performance is required or necessary. In the sport world, flow has predominantly been studied in the context of peak performance among elite athletes (Swann, C. et al. 2016). Peak performance is a state of superior functioning resulting in optimal sport performance in which personal bests are achieved (Jackson & Roberts, 1992). However, despite years of applied research on flow, capturing the different variables and environmental conditions that make up a flow experience in sport performance remain elusive (Chavez, 2008). It is not possible to predict and plan for the flow state of performance. And, because flow just 'happens' during a performance, it is impossible to harness the moment and collect data; such an attempt would disrupt and end the flow state. Different quantitative (Koehn, Morris, & Watt, 2013) and qualitative (Chavez, 2008) studies have investigated how flow occurs in sport (Swann, Keegan, Piggott, & Crust, 2012). Qualitative methods (i.e. semi-structured interviews) have been used to understand athletes' perceptions and experiences with flow. However, this method has been criticised because it relies on memory of events and since one of the characteristics of the flow experience is a 'loss of consciousness' it is likely that important details of the athlete's flow experience cannot recalled. (Jackson & Kimiecik, 2008). In 1987, Csíkszentmihályi realised that capturing the flow experience in 'real time' was important in proving flow as a concept. To that end, Csíkszentmihályi, with his colleague, Larson, developed the Experience Sampling Method (ESM). The ESM is a strategy for gathering data from individuals in 'real time' as things occur. The ESM has been used effectively in other domains (e.g. learning environments) but less so in sports and competition given the dynamic nature of these environments. Additionally, several questionnaires have been developed in an effort to capture the flow experience. For example, the Flow State Scale-2 is designed to be administered soon after a performance, and Dispositional Flow Scale-2 which measures the frequency with which athletes experience flow (Jackson & Eklund, 2004). However, while these questionnaires are commonly used, they lack the detailed data of how flow occurs in specific, competitive performances. More recently, researchers have integrated the use of technology by using footage obtained from a head mounted camera with surfers, followed by an interview. This approach is promising in terms of collecting recent data about flow experiences using event-focused interviews. However, given that it is not feasible to use head mounted cameras in many competitive sports, this approach to data collection and understanding the flow experience is limited.

Flow in non-sport settings

Csíkszentmihályi suggested that most people experience flow while performing some type of structured work, rather than in their free time. While the concept of flow has been closely aligned with sport performance and competition, Csíkszentmihályi theorised that flow could emerge in any situation where there is activity/engagement and when a person is engaged in a task that meets a level of difficulty that is manageable and not overwhelming, including the musical performing arts. Chirico and colleagues (2015) believe that "*it is not unusual to experience a sense of total absorption, concentration, action-awareness, distortion of time and intrinsic enjoyment during an activity that involves music*" (p. 1). Empirical research on flow in music performance has increased significantly over the past decade, which led to a better understanding of how musicians of various abilities, experience flow during a performance (Chaffin et al., 2002; Lehmann et al., 2007; Marin & Bhattacharya, 2013; Wrigley & Emmerson, 2013). It is important to note that the flow findings for performance did not translate to a practice/rehearsal setting. Because a practice/rehearsal setting consists of many different stopping and starting points, while feedback is offered, is it not likely that a performer will experience the necessary autonomics of flow.

In learning environments, flow has been studied among students using digital technology and simulation games to conceptualise a theme/topic of a lesson.

A central task of educational research is to find ways to integrate technology to enhance learning and technology can be one method to achieve this outcome. A study by Chiang et al. (2011) found that the use of simulation games may facilitate a flow learning experience, regardless of the subject discipline. In this study, the students who had a flow experience reported a balance between the perceived challenge of the learning activity and their individual belief that he/she could solve the problem presented, for example. This may give some direction in how to understand 'flow' in the context of PE, that is the moment when the physically educated person enters the zone. A starting point for such deliberation needs to be an examination of the purpose of PE.

What is the purpose of physical education?

Over the past decade, there have been a plethora of debates PE, which have centred on the relative importance of physical prowess, wellbeing, gender, politics, status issues, health, motor/sports competence and/or a socially critical knowledge perspective. In Chapter 1, we interrogated the fundamental of purpose of PE from an epistemological and ontological standpoint. In this chapter, we build on points raised to grapple with the nature of PE as a discipline, what this means for learning in PE and how we might teach PE.

Physical education as an academic cross-discipline

A discipline is defined as an area of knowledge; a subject that people study or are taught, especially in a university (Oxford Dictionary, 2020). Henry (1978, 1964, p. 13) described that:

> an academic discipline is an organized body of knowledge collectively embraced in a formal course of learning; the acquisition of such knowledge is assumed to be an adequate and worthy objective as such, without any demonstration or requirement of practical application; the content is theoretical and scholarly as distinguished from technical and professional.

Tellingly, Henry described how in order for PE to meet the requirements of this definition, it must be structured as a cross disciplinary body of knowledge (p. 13). He argued that it was not possible for PE to claim that it was interdisciplinary; it must be developed as a series of courses organised horizontally as well as in-depth vertically (p. 14). Further to this, he outlined how PE as an academic cross-discipline does not include the application for the disciplines inherent within it. If this were the case, it would be a technical and professional discipline and not an academic cross discipline. Instead the study of PE centres on and links to basic knowledge concerning the human individual engaged in the motor activity that is an expression of being alive and functional (pp. 15–16).

Physical Education, Henry (1964) asserted:

> The scholarly field of knowledge that constitutes the academic discipline of physical education…(is)…constituted of certain portions of such diverse fields as anatomy, physics and physiology, cultural anthropology, history and sociology as well as psychology. The focus of attention is on the study of the human as an individual, engaging in the motor performance required in daily life and other motor performances yielding aesthetic values or serving as expressions of a personal physical and competitive nature, accepting challenges of one's capability to cope with a hostile environment and participating in leisure time activities that have become of increasing importance to our culture. (Note that it implicitly includes health, both physical and mental, in relation to physical activity; it implicitly includes motor learning, sport sociology and other areas of current emphasis).

Therefore, PE is not an academic discipline, it is an academic cross-discipline – Henry describes that as such:

> Cross disciplinary always refers to the appropriate part of a body of knowledge from another discipline that is related to the academic and scholarly aspects of physical education, with a concomitant development or tie-in with that relationship (p. 22)

In later work, Rosenfield (1992) interrogated the concept of cross-disciplinarity further. Disagreeing with Henry, he described a taxonomy of cross-disciplinary research: (a) multidisciplinary, (b) interdisciplinary and (c) transdisciplinary. In multidisciplinary and interdisciplinary settings, individuals work in parallel to address a common problem. In multidisciplinary settings, there is no integration of disciplines, while in interdisciplinary there is some integration of their respective disciplines. Of all, transdisciplinary is the most profound level of collaboration achieved by a team of different experts. In such work they may also be joined by a team of stakeholders with a vested interest in the issue and with local knowledge. In a transdisciplinary framework, researchers with varied expertise work jointly to address a problem they define under a shared conceptual framework; this approach essentially breaks down disciplinary boundaries as shared language and problem-solving approaches are developed (Rosenfield, 1992). In this taxonomy of cross-disciplinarity, PE is interdisciplinary.

PE is therefore highly unusual as it is a cross-discipline, and within this, an interdiscipline, reaching out to a number of disciplines to make sense of learning through movement. This means it has both discipline-centric threshold concepts from those disciplines that inform it (anatomy, sociology, history, motor development, psychology, sports medicine, adapted physical activity etc.) and then those threshold concepts which are found in the hybrid space, which only PE can claim and which are yet to be identified. The history of PE may help to make sense of this conundrum.

History of content and focus of PE

In 2013, Kohl & Cook described the trajectory of PE. Hackensmith (1966) described how PE became a subject matter in schools (in the form of German and Swedish gymnastics) at the beginning of the 19th century and its role in human health was quickly recognised. Weston (1962) commented that by the 20th century, PE curriculum also included personal hygiene, and exercise for health. It was Thomas Wood (1913) who pushed the curriculum toward an inclusive focus on fundamental movements and physical skills for games and sports as the major instructional content, and not health and hygiene which he deemed to be too narrow. Interestingly, PE seems to have come full circle with health and wellbeing being central to curricula in Canada, New Zealand, Australia, Scotland, Wales and Ireland. This means that we have moved to linking movement to its consequences i.e. physical activity and health (Kohl & Cook, 2013). Within this, we also continue to embrace Sallis and McKenzie (1991) view of PE as education content by using a 'comprehensive but physically active approach that involves teaching social, cognitive, and physical skills, and achieving other goals through movement' (p. 126). Siedentop (2009) corroborated this view – PE is education through the physical. In Aldous' chapter, the work of Peter Arnold is called out as being seminal, that is, viewing PE as education 'in, through and about movement' (Arnold, 1979;1988). Such focus was constructed through orientation towards three interrelated dimensions: education in movement; education through movement and education about movement.

Naming the cross discipline (interdiscipline)

Newell described how 'an overstatement to suggest that PE in higher education is in a state of chaos' (1990, p. 228). This was because in the United States, third level institutes in 1980s were using 100 different names for PE (Corbin, 1993, p. 85). It was Newell (1989) who put forward the idea that all should be brought under the title of kinesiology. His rationale for this bold move was five-fold: It was representative of the entire field; it sounded academic; it was succinct; it was neutral with respect to the major subdomain debates on each dimension; it was already established as the departmental title in a number of leading academic institutions. Fifteen years ago, Kretchmar (2015) offered an analogy for kinesiology to help us to visualise our cross-discipline, that is, as a river that changes as it flows with each contributing discipline working along some part of the riverbank.

Not everyone has embraced the term kinesiology. Different terms are used across the world: Health and Physical Education, PE and Kinesiology. For the purposes of this chapter, we will refer to PE and simply agree that it is an academic cross-discipline (with an interdisciplinary focus) and as such it draws on multiple disciplines to make academic sense of human movement.

Physical education and the third space

As an interdiscipline, PE has a third space. This metaphor was coined by Bhabha. It is an interstitial space. Engels-Schwarzpaul and Azadeh Emadi (2011, p. 1) observed: 'Bhabha's dynamic third space is an interstitial realm, like the threshold, which accommodates ambivalence, conflict, confusion, movement, change and notably, potentiality.' Bhabha (1994) claims that:

> It is held open by the tension between different spaces and temporalities and generates relationships in which both sides are changed through the negotiation of incommensurable strategies, rules and identities in cultural processes and practices (p. 218).

PE's third space is a place in which new threshold concepts can emerge; threshold concepts that can only be claimed by PE.

Conclusion

PE is a cross discipline which is categorised as an interdiscipline. This means that contributing disciplines offer threshold concepts. In addition to this, PE has an interstitial third space where all disciplines meet. This means that PE can offer its own unique threshold concepts. These have never been identified before. In Part II of this book, our case study chapters allow teams of practitioners and academics to work together to firstly identify concepts which are exclusive to PE and pedagogical approaches to perhaps teach these. We add these to our conceptual sandbox in Chapter 11 and put forward threshold concepts which can only be claimed by PE and the pedagogical approaches to foster these.

References

Armour, K. A., Quennerstedt, M., Chambers, F. C., Makopoulou, K. (2015). What is 'effective' CPD for contemporary physical education teachers? A Deweyan framework. *Sport, Education and Society, 22*(7), 799–811.

Arnold, P. (1979). *Meaning in Movement, Sport and Physical Education*. London: Heinemann.

Arnold, P. (1988). *Education, Movement and the Curriculum – A Philosophical Inquiry*. London: The Falmer Press.

Barnett, L. M., Dudley, D. A., Telford, D., Lubans, D. R., Bryant, A. S., Roberts, W. M., … Keegan, R. J. (2019). Physical literacy in young people: Guidelines and recommendations for the selection of measures in schools. *Journal of Teaching in Physical Education (JTPE), 38*(2), 119–125.

Bhabha, H. K. (1994). *The Location of Culture*. New York: Routledge.

Biggs, J. B. & Tang, C. (2011). *Teaching for Quality Learning at University*. Berkshire: Open University Press.

Bonjour, L. (1998). *In Defense of Pure Reason*. Cambridge: Cambridge University Press.

Brandom, R. (1994). *Making It Explicit: Reasoning, Representing, and Discursive Commitment*. Cambridge, MA: Harvard.

Bruner, J. S. (1966). *Toward a Theory of Instruction*. Cambridge, Mass.: Belkapp Press.

Carter J. E., & Graef, S. (2016). Mental skills for endurance sports. In T. Miller. (Ed.) *Endurance Sports Medicine*. Cham: Springer.

Chambers, F. C. (2007). *How do We Prepare Physical Education Teachers for an Unknown Future?* Cork: University College Cork.

Chiang, Y. T., Lin, S. S. J., Cheng, C. Y., & Liu, E. Z. F. (2011). Exploring online game players' flow experiences and positive affect. The Turkish Online Journal of Educational Technology, 10(1), 106–114.

Corbin, C. B. (1993). The field of physical education: Common goals, not common roles. *Journal of Physical Education, Recreation and Dance*, 6(1), 79–87.

Cousin, G. (2006). An introduction to threshold concepts. *Planet*, 17, 4–5.

Cook-Sather, A. (2006). Newly betwixt and between: Revising liminality in the context of a teacher preparation program. *Anthropology and Education Quarterly*, 37(2), 110–127.

Csikszentmihalyi, M. (1975). *Beyond Boredom and Anxiety* San Francisco: Jossey-Bass.

Csikszentmihalyi, M. (1990). *Flow: The psychology of Optimal Experience*. New York: Harper & Row.

Csikszentmihalyi, M., Abuhamdeh, S., & Nakamura, J. (2005). Flow. In A. Elliot &C. Dweck (Eds.), *Handbook of Competence and Motivation* (pp. 598–698). New York, NY, USA: The Guilford Press.

Csikszentmihalyi, M., & LeFevre, J. (1989). Optimal experience in work and leisure. *Journal of Personality and Social Psychology*, 56, 815–822. doi: 10.1037/0022-3514.56.5.815

Csikszentmihalyi, M. (2000). *Finding Flow: The Psychology of Engagement with Everyday Life*. New York, NY, USA: Basic Books.

Davies, P., & Mangan, J. (2008). Embedding threshold concepts: From theory to pedagogical principles to learning activities. In R. Land, J. H. F. Meyer, & J. Smith (Eds.), *Threshold Concepts within the Disciplines*. Rotterdam: Sense.

Dewey, J. (1916). *Democracy and Education. An Introduction to the Philosophy of Education* (1966 ed.). New York: Free Press.

Dewey, J. (1938). Experience and Education. New York: Touchstone.

Dudley, D., Goodyear, V., & Baxter, D. (2016). Quality and health-optimizing physical education: Using assessment at the health and education nexus. *Journal of Teaching in Physical Education*, 35(4), 324–336.

Engels-Schwarzpaul, A.-C., & Emadi, A. (2011). Thresholds as Spaces of Potentiality: Non-traditional PhD Candidatures in Art and Design. *Critical Perspectives on Communication, Cultural and Policy Studies*, 30(2), 1–14.

Fodor, J. A. (1975). *The Language of Thought*. Cambridge, MA: Harvard.

Gilmour Reeve, T. (2007). Kinesiology: Defining the academic core of our discipline: Introduction. *Quest*, 59(1), 1–4.

Hackensmith, C. W. (1966). *History of Physical Education*. New York: Harper & Row.

Henry, F. M. (1978). The Academic Discipline of Physical Education. *Quest*, 29(1), 13–29.

Hodkinson, P., Biesta, G., & James, D. (2008). Understanding learning culturally: Overcoming the dualism between social and individual views of learning. *Vocations and Learning*, 1(1), 27–47.

Huta, V., &Waterman, A. S. (2014). Eudaimonia and its distinction from hedonia: Developing a classification and terminology for understanding conceptual and operational definitions. *Journal of Happiness Studies*, 15(6), 1425–1456.

Jackson, S. A., &Roberts, G. C. (1992). Positive performance states of athletes: Toward a conceptual understanding of peak performance. *The Sport Psychologist*, 6(2), 156–71. https://doi.org/10.1123/tsp.6.2.156

Jackson, S. A. (1995). Factors influencing the occurrence of flow state in elite athletes. *Journal of Applied Sport Psychology*, 7(2), 138–66. doi: 10.1080/10413209508406962

Jackson, S. A. (1996). Toward a conceptual understanding of the flow experience of elite athletes. *Research Quarterly for Exercise and Sport*, 67(1), 76–90. https://www.tandfonline.com/doi/pdf/10.1080/02701367.1996.10607928?needAccess=true

Keegan, R. J., Dudley, D. A., Telford, D., Lubans, D. R., Bryant, A. S., Roberts, W. M., ... Barnett, L. M. (2019). Defining and operationalizing physical literacy: A modified Delphi method. *Journal of Teaching in Physical Education (JTPE)*, 38(2), 105–118.

Kohl II, H. W. & Cook, H. D. (Eds.) (2013). Approaches to physical education in schools. Educating the Student Body: Taking Physical Activity and Physical Education to School. Committee on Physical Activity and Physical Education in the School Environment, Food and Nutrition Board, and Institute of Medicine. Washington (DC): National Academies Press (US).

Kretchmar, R. S. (2015). Jigsaw puzzles and river banks: Two ways of picturing our future. *Quest*, 57, 171–177.

Land, R., Cousin, G., Meyer, J. H. F., & Davies, P. (2005). Threshold concepts and troublesome knowledge (3): Implications for course design and evaluation. In C. Rust (ed.), Improving Student Learning - Diversity and Inclusivity, Proceedings of the 12th Improving Student Learning Conference. Oxford: Oxford Centre for Staff and Learning Development (OCSLD), pp. 53–64.

Land, R., Vivian, P., & Rattray, J. (2014). A closer look at liminality: Incorrigibles and threshold capital. In Threshold Concepts: From Personal Practice to Communities of Practice. Proceedings of the National Academy's Sixth Annual Conference and the Fourth Biennial Threshold Concepts Conference, January 2014. Cork, Ireland: NAIRTL, pp. 1–12.

Land, R. (2018). Linkages to threshold concepts and troublesome knowledge 1: Linkage to ways of thinking and practising. *Threshold Concepts: Undergraduate Teaching, Postgraduate Training, Professional Development and School Education – A Short Introduction and a Bibliography from 2003 to 2018*. Retrieved on February 3, 2020, from https://nu2018.se/wp-content/uploads/2018/10/NU-2018-Ray-Land-....pdf

Lowe, E. J. (1995). The metaphysics of abstract objects. *The Journal of Philosophy* 92, 509–524.

Luthans, F., Avolio, B. J., Avey, J. B., and Norman, S. M. (2007). Positive Psychological Capital: Measurement and Relationship with Performance and Satisfaction. Leadership Institute Faculty Publications. 11.

Merck (2018). *The State of Curiosity Report*. Germany: Merck.

Meyer, E., & Land, R. (2003). Threshold concepts and troublesome knowledge: Linkages to ways of thinking and practising within the disciplines. Enhancing Teaching-Learning Environments in Undergraduate Courses Project, Higher and Community Education. Universities of Edinburgh, Coventry and Durham, TLRP ESRI. Occasional Report 4.

Marin, M. M., & Bhattacharya, J. (2013). Getting into the musical zone: Trait emotional intelligence and amount of practice predict flow in pianists. *Frontiers in Psychology*, 4: 853. doi: 10.3389/fpsyg.2013.00853

Meyer, J. H. F., & Land, R. (2005). Threshold concepts and troublesome knowledge (2): Epistemological considerations and a conceptual framework for teaching and learning. *Higher Education*, 49(3): 373–388.

Newell, K. M. (1989). Kinesiology. *Journal of Physical Education, Recreation and Dance*, 60(8), 69–70.

Newell, K. M. (1990). Physical education in higher education: Chaos out of order. *Quest*, 42(3), 227–242.

Peacocke, C. (1992). *A Study of Concepts*. Cambridge, MA: MIT Press.

Perkins, D. (2006). Constructivism and troublesome knowledge. in: Meyer and Land (2006).

Rhem, J. (2013). Before and after students 'get it': Threshold concepts. *National Teaching and Learning Forum Newsletter, 22.*

Rosenfield, P. (1992). The potential of transdisciplinary research for sustaining and extending linkages between the health and social sciences. *Social Science and Medicine, 35*(11), 1343–1357.

Roumpou, S. (2018). Aristotle's Entelechy and Eudaimonia in Sports. *Psychological Thought 11*(2), 62–74.

Rowbottom, D. P. (2007). Demystifying threshold concepts. *Journal of Philosophy of Education,* 1–8.

Sallis, J. F. & McKenzie, T. L. (1991). Physical education's role in public health. *Research Quarterly for Exercise and Sport, 62*(2), 124–137.

Saury, J. &M. Durand (1998). Practical knowledge in expert coaches: On-site study of coaching in sailing. *Research Quarterly for Exercise and Sport, 69*(3), 254–266.

Siedentop, D. L. (2009). *Introduction to Physical Education, Fitness, and Sport.* New York: McGraw-Hill.

Swann, C. et al. (2016). Psychological states underlying excellent performance in professional golfers: "Letting it happen" vs. "making it happen". *Psychology of Sport and Exercise, 23,* 101–113.

Swann, C., Keegan, R., Piggott, D., & Crust, L. (2012). A systematic review of the experience, 15 occurrence, and controllability of flow states in elite sport. Psychology of Sport and 16 Exercise, 13, 807–819. doi:10.1016/j.psychsport.2012.05.006

Thomassen, B. (2012). Revisiting liminality: The danger of empty spaces. In H. Andrews & L. Roberts (eds.), Liminal Landscapes: Travel, Experience and Spaces In-between. London: Routledge, 21–35.

Todd, S. (2014). Between body and spirit: The liminality of pedagogical relationships. Journal of Philosophy of Education, 48(2), 231–245.

Turner, V. (1974). *Dramas, Fields and Metaphors.* Ithaca, NY: Cornell University Press.

Turner, V. (1982). *From Ritual to Theatre: The Human Seriousness of Play.* New York: Performing Arts Journal Publications.

Van Gennep, A. (1960 [1909]). *The Rites of Passage.* Chicago, IL: University of Chicago Press.

Viscardi-Smalley, J. (2018). *What Music Industry Education Can Learn from Threshold Concept Theory.* International Summit of the Music & Entertainment Industry Educators Association. Los Angeles.

Vygotsky, L. S. (1978). Mind in Society. Cambridge, MA: Harvard University Press.

Wood, T. D. (1913). *The Ninth Yearbook of the National Society for the Study of Education (Part 1).* Chicago, IL: University of Chicago Press.

Wrigley, W. J., & Emmerson, S. B. (2013). The experience of the flow state in live music performance. *Psychology of Music, 41*(3), 292–305.

Chapter 3

Design thinking: Pedagogy, process, mindset and space

Fiona C. Chambers

Introduction

The fact that physical education (PE) does not have defined threshold concepts which are unique to it has caused issues for the status of both the subject and the profession. This is a complex problem, which could be construed as wicked. Rittel and Webber (1973) describe problems as 'wicked' if they lacked both definitive formulations and solutions and were characterised by conditions of high uncertainty and in Blackman et al.'s (2006) words 'no single solution applies in all circumstances' (p. 70). The common denominator in all cases is that developing human-centred solutions is a wicked endeavour. This is because linear analytical approaches are unlikely to successfully resolve them (Buchanan, 1992). According to Peters (2017) wicked problems have nine particular characteristics:

> difficult to define; no definite formation; no stopping rule; the solutions to wicked problems are good or bad, but not true or false; there is no immediate or ultimate test for solutions; all attempts for solutions come with a warning i.e. they may not be reversible or forgettable; they have no clear solution or set of solutions; each wicked problem is unique; a wicked problem may be a symptom of another problem; and there are multiple explanations for a wicked problem (p. 288)

Furthermore, wicked problems involve multiple actors and are socially *and* politically complex (Rittel & Webber, 2001). In trying to interrogate the issue of not having defined threshold concepts, an innovative approach which could handle this level of complexity (wickedness) is needed. This must be an experimental approach which explores multiple possible solutions. Design thinking appears to be such an innovative approach.

What is design thinking?

Design is the third area of human knowledge that fuses with humanities and science (Archer, 1979): a powerful interconnected triad. Design is ambiguous by nature – in fact ambiguity is the heartbeat of design. To tackle any complex design challenge, we turn to a particular genre of innovation i.e. design thinking (Brown, 2008). The defining pillars of design thinking are problem centeredness, nonlinearity, optionality, and the presence of uncertainty and ambiguity (Liedtka, 2015). Design thinking is universally used in innovation to solve intractable human-centred problems (Buchanan, 1992). In so doing, it engages creative multi-disciplinary, multi-stakeholder teams to use a *systematic and collaborative approach to identifying and creatively solving problems* (Luchs, Swan & Griffin, 2016, p. 2). Design thinking brings '*designers' principles, approaches, methods and tools to problem solving*' (Brown, 2008, p. 1). Lockwood (2016) asserts that the design thinking process '*emphasises observation, collaboration, fast learning, visualisation of ideas, rapid concept prototyping and concurrent business analysis*' (n.p.). Design challenges in the educational domain are typically wicked (complex) as it is 'not stable but continually evolving and mutating and had many causal levels' (Blackman et al., 2006, p. 70) and adding to this complexity, there are intergenerational, multisectoral and multicultural stakeholders with a range of philosophical views.

The ultimate solutions to such wicked problems are located at the sweet spot (design innovation) (IDEO, 2009) (see Figure 3.1). The sweet spot is the intersection of three aspects: (a) what is desirable from a human point of view (using design thinking) with (b) what is technologically feasible (agile development) and (c) economically viable (lean thinking) (Brown, 2016). Design thinking attends

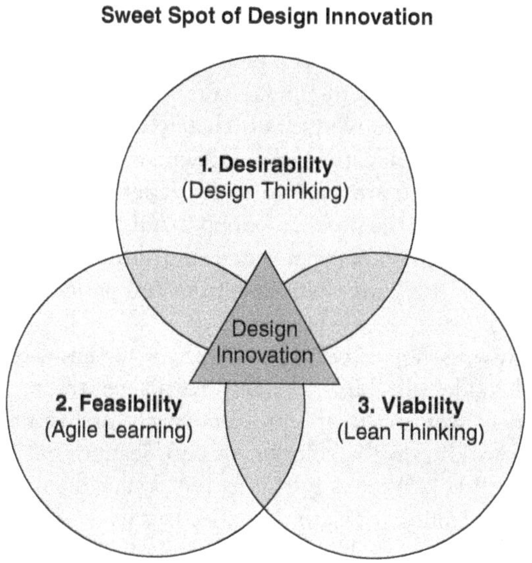

Sweet Spot of Design Innovation

Figure 3.1 Design innovation sweet-spot.

Source: Adapted from IDEO, 2009.

to the desirability aspect of the solution and is the first comprehensive process. Once a solution has been identified through design thinking, designers look to the feasibility using agile learning methods and then, viability of the solution using lean thinking.

Lean thinking (Womack & Jones, 2003) is a business methodology that aims to provide a new ways to think about how to organise human activities to deliver more benefits to society and value to individuals while eliminating waste. It uses the concepts of: (a) value; (b) value streams and (c) flow. Flow, in this context, is how people engage with the process from first step to last. The aim of 'continuous improvement is continuous improvement' (ibid), which means iteration and evolution of ideas and processes. Agile learning (Longmuß et al, 2016) is then employed to ensure that the solution can be scaled or delivered continuously. It is *based on the principles of inquiry-based learning on the part of the learner and a demand driven, empowering perspective of the learning coaches ("Give what is needed when it is needed")*' (ibid, p. 3).

To begin, we use design thinking to grapple with a design challenge. Design thinking comprises three key elements: design thinking process, design thinking mindset and design thinking space. Each of these elements will be described in detail in the forthcoming sections.

The design thinking process

The process of design thinking itself is a multi-stage iterative process that has been outlined by many different theorists (see Table 3.1). Despite the variety of nomenclature, there is agreement on empathy and/or compassion as the first step i.e. the human-centredness of the process and the need to begin there, to understand the actual problem. It fundamentally involves the 'development of idea stages, applying an iterative process that forces them to move back and forth between inspiration, ideation and implementation' (Borja de Mozota & Peinado, 2013, p. 1). These are referred to as 'design thinking spaces' (Brown, 2008), where: *Inspiration* is the problem or opportunity that motivates the search for solutions; *Ideation* is the process of generating, developing, and testing ideas; and *Implementation* is the path that leads from the project stage into people's lives (see Table 3.1).

In the case study workshop described in this chapter, we used the Hasso-Plattner Institute six-stage model (see Table 3.1). During this iterative process, 80% of the design time is spent working in the problem space (or Inspiration Space) and 20% of the time working in the solution space (Ideation and Implementation). The Design Council (2020) refers to this as the 'double diamond' a divergence–convergence model. Sammon (2016) describes this as a 'Figure of 8' where the designer oscillates between problem and solution spaces until a solution to the wicked problem in question has been innovated. Designers iterate from problem focus (exploring, understanding and defining), to solution focus (designing, building and evaluating) (see Figure 3.2).

Table 3.1 The Eight models of design thinking

Design thinking models	Design thinking spaces (IDEO, 2009)				
	Inspiration	Interpretation	Ideation	Experimentation	Implementation
The IDEO Model (IDEO, 2009)	Discovery		Ideation	Experimentation	Evolution
The d.school model (d.school Stanford, 2010)	Empathise	Define	Ideate	Prototype	Test
Design Thinking and Innovation Model (Goligorsky, 2012)	Clarification		Ideation	Development	Implementation
Designing for Growth Model (Liedtka 2015)	What is?		What if?	What wows?	What works?
Six Stage Model (Hasso-Plattner Institute, 2018)	Understand Observe	Point of view	Ideate	Prototype	Test
Figure of 8 (Sammon, 2016)	Exploring Understanding	Defining	Designing	Building	Evaluating
A Framework of Design Thinking (Luchs, Swan, & Griffin, 2016)	Discover		Define	Create	Evaluate
The Chambers' 4-Stage Model (Chambers, 2018)	Compassion		Ideate	Prototype	Implement and evaluate

Source: Adapted from Chambers, 2018

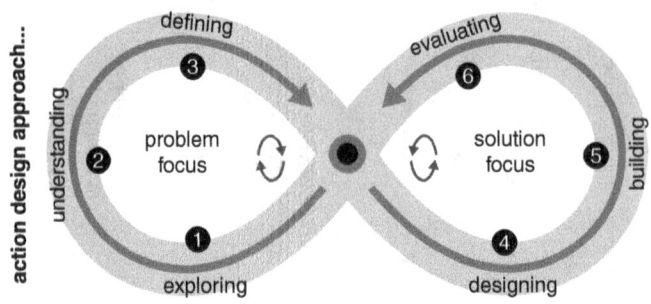

Figure 3.2 Action design approach.

Source: Sammon, 2016.

In design thinking, designers concentrate on products and/or services. The nature of the issue at the heart of this book has an education focus, and so this is a service design challenge. Service design is anchored in research, visualisation and a strategic, systems-oriented and approach. It can identify pain-points and build missing connections to improve systemic functionality. Services bring a value exchange to the provider and user, who collaboratively generate new flows of knowledge, care, emotions or other social units. Thus, the service-logic puts into perspective an individual's relational impact on others and their community. There are four key features of service design (Smirnow, 2017, p. 15): A strategic and systems approach that visualises and addresses complex issues with a holistic view; human-centred research driven by design ethics with high levels of empathy; value exchange and gain for all stakeholders through shared information flows; situational, interaction-based learning facilitated by design tools and mutual reflection. These inform six design thinking principles (Smirnow, 2017):

> **Design for transition**: To create engaging, safe spaces to critically reframe assumptions, beliefs and understanding during times of change, growth and transition, helping to overcome barriers that result from pre-established and deeply ingrained social roles, boundaries and hierarchies.

> **Accessible mutable system**: Not only the activities (but the system itself) should be accessible, open sourced and 'hackable' to tailor experiences to different contexts and levels of understanding/engagement.

> **Mutual learning through exploration**: Teachers, staff and students engage simultaneously in learning to generate data with values beyond the individual social context within the University (or in other jurisdictions).

> **Facilitated learning about oneself and others**: Moments that enable and encourage 'deeper learning' for all participants. A variety of resources offered (and a clear 'game plan') allow for self-directed reflection.

Multiple levels of intimacy: The scale of reflection on both levels, individual and group, plays an important role in building trust and processing the key takeaways about research contingencies.

At your discretion: Openness and mutual learning are encouraged but, the disclosure of sensitive information happens only according to the comfort level of each individual.

These features and principles, together with design thinking mindset, process and space, underpin the pedagogy of design thinking. In the next section, we will delve more into the design thinking mindset.

The design thinking mindset

Design thinkers have a particular mindset which enables them to tackle intransigent problems. In other words, they are comfortable with uncertainty – a threshold concept that all designers must possess (Meyer & Land, 2003). Acceptance of uncertainty is a prerequisite for the process of design, and so can be transformative and irreversible.

Within this mindset, there are three core areas to consider: Practices, cognitive approach and mindset, which converge under the notion of a 'design thinker's mindset.' Turning to the cognitive approach, an inherent feature of this is *abductive reasoning*. Shearer (2015) asserts that when using abductive reasoning, there is a need to understand how different kinds of conjectures might interact with one another during this part of the design development. The dictionary definition of conjecture asserts that this is a form, an opinion or supposition about something on the basis of incomplete information. By doing this, it helps provide a way to help multi-disciplinary design teams collaborate.

The design thinking activities, described in more detail later, were shaped by Shearer's (2015) taxonomy of conjecture i.e. starting points which stakeholders may use to begin the process:

Forms: What if we begin with a shape or form?
Objectives: What if we begin with an aim?
Vision: 'What if we begin with an ideal?'
Challenges/Opportunities: 'What if we begin with a material or an activity?'
Image of the World: 'What if we begin with one of our own core beliefs?' (pp. 130–133).
This taxonomy guided our tasks, particularly in the compassion and ideation phases.

As stated earlier, the process of design thinking involves the 'development of idea stages, applying an iterative process that forces solvers to move back and forth between inspiration, ideation and implementation' (Borja de Mozota & Peinado, 2013, p. 1). The design thinker must employ a range of skills to navigate this

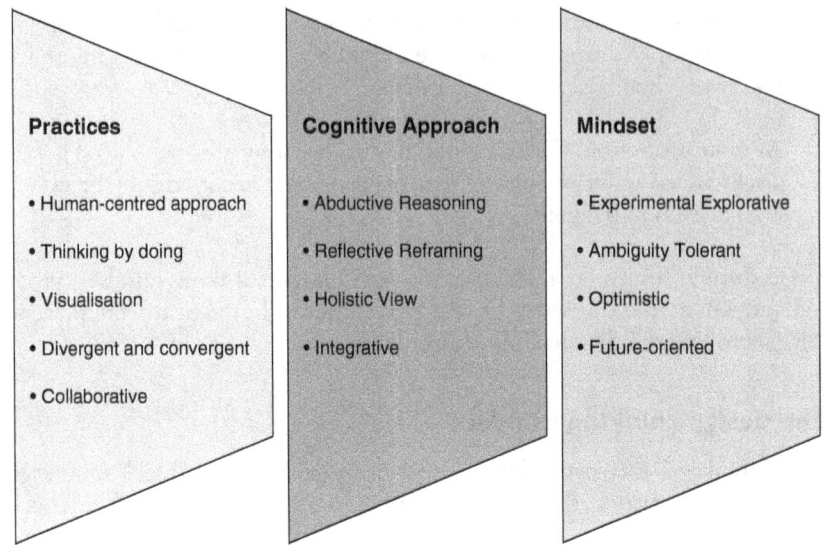

Figure 3.3 Mindset of a design thinker.

Source: Adapted from Hassi & Laakso, 2011 by Chambers, 2018

process including empathy, integrative thinking, optimism, experimentalism and collaboration (Brown, 2008). This is underpinned by a growth mindset (Dweck, 2006) wherein the design thinker perceives his ability not as fixed but flexible, and as something that can be developed through effort. This disposition allows the design thinker to 'infer possible new worlds' (Martin, 2009, p. 65) or opportunities. The attributes of a design thinker's mindset (Hassi and Laakso, 2011) are captured in Figure 3.3.

Fundamentally, the design thinker is curious, creative and courageous. Windahl (2017, p. 280) describes the importance of these three characteristics when desirability, rather than feasibility or viability, is the locus of innovation activities. She asserts that curiosity ignites empathy and deep understanding of the human experience; (b) creativity awakens 'logical leaps' in understanding opportunities and (c) courage enflames learning through iterations, which reduces cognitive bias. Curiosity has four dimensions (Merck, 2018) (see Figure 3.4), these are: openness to people's ideas; joyous exploration; stress tolerance and deprivation sensitivity.

This rounded view of curiosity helps to explain how curious people react with open, non-defensive attitudes and effortful thinking. Such a disposition can be of benefit in an everchanging and unpredictable environment, as individuals are less likely to perceive change as stressful and more likely to adapt effectively. When partnered with creativity and courage, it becomes even more potent as it unleashes the design for impact. For designers, the space in which this happens is really important. In fact, design is seen as an embodied practice in space.

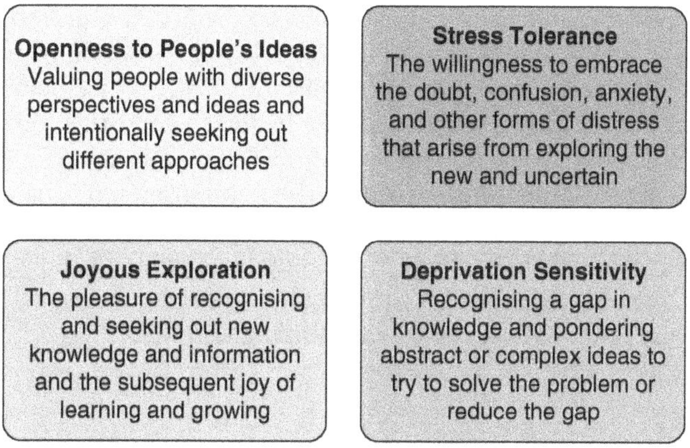

| **Openness to People's Ideas** Valuing people with diverse perspectives and ideas and intentionally seeking out different approaches | **Stress Tolerance** The willingness to embrace the doubt, confusion, anxiety, and other forms of distress that arise from exploring the new and uncertain |
| **Joyous Exploration** The pleasure of recognising and seeking out new knowledge and information and the subsequent joy of learning and growing | **Deprivation Sensitivity** Recognising a gap in knowledge and pondering abstract or complex ideas to try to solve the problem or reduce the gap |

Figure 3.4 Dimensions of curiosity

Source: Merck, 2018

The design thinking space

The physical environment that we construct is as much a social phenomenon as it is a physical one (Proshansky, 1970). In fact, when generating ideas, it becomes really important to be very fluid and have the ability to move in and out of different concepts and different people's voices as an idea is coming to fruition. So, creating a space that allows movement and allows an active posture really allows collaboration to move more smoothly, and can push creativity by allowing people to participate when they want, step out when they don't and allow leadership to move throughout the group (Doorley & Witthoft, 2011). It affords designer autonomy as ideas bounce off people and the space in which they work. For this to happen, Lawson (2001, p. 8), asserts that we often need to tell space how to behave, so that *it* serves *our* purpose. Norman (2002) describes how we do this by outlining space typologies – A *space type* being a dedicated space for a particular activity at a specific time. He outlines how space has an inherent affordance, in other words it is an enabler for the particular activity taking place in that space. Every time the configuration changes, so, too, does the space type. The more flexible the space – the easier the transition. According to Thoring et al. (2018), there are five types of creative spaces:

> (a) The **personal space**, for working and learning alone; (b) the **collaboration space** for working or learning together with co-workers, classmates or teachers; (c) the **presentation space**, for giving presentations, consuming lectures and displaying or examining creative work examples; and (d) the **making space** in which people are able to experiment, try things out, build stuff and make noise and (e) the **intermission space** for transition and recreation. The latter includes spaces not intended for creative design work but connect other space types: hallways, cafeterias, the outdoors – and provide spaces for breaks (my emphasis, p. 64)

Thoring and colleagues have also added another qualitative aspect to this typology and that is 'space quality.' This is linked to Norman's notion of *affordance* – and is more nuanced. It measures the ability of a space to facilitate a specific purpose, independent from the space type. In their words, they highlight five qualities of a creative space: (a) space as a knowledge processor; (b) space as an indicator of culture; (c) space as a process enabler; (d) space as a social dimension and (e) space as a source of stimulation.

In the next section of the chapter, we use a case study to showcase design thinking (design ethics, mindset, process, use of space and pedagogy). This case study centres on an international design thinking workshop.

Case study

On 25th February 2020, the Association Internationale des Écoles Superièure d'Éducation Physique[1] (AIESEP) hosted a Specialist Symposium. Those who attended had answered the following AIESEP call:

> Clearly, physical literacy is a broad concept. Whilst the original term had strong philosophical orientations towards the concepts of phenomenology and existentialism, recent developments of the concept have largely focused on a more pragmatic interpretation. From our vast experience educating professionals in the area of physical literacy in physical education, physical activity and sport, it appears that the application of the concept of physical literacy has led to a focus on more rudimentary skills which has moved physical literacy away from its original and more holistic focus intended by Whitehead (2007; 2013).
>
> AIESEP now wonder if it might be timely to pause and reflect on the nature and purpose of current interpretations of physical literacy and to examine how other newer and related ideas might provide an understanding of the complex interplay between the individual and his/her ecological environment in the physical education, sport and physical activity contexts.
>
> This AIESEP design thinking workshop is an opportunity to engage in a 'design sprint' to innovate and iterate new pedagogies to promote physical literacy in the 21st century PE, sport and physical activity contexts. We invite all those who have a vested interest in promoting physical literacy amongst children and young people to join us in this unique workshop setting.
>
> This symposium follows on from our Physical Literacy roundtable in AIESEP 2019 (Adelphi)…giving us the opportunity to continue this important conversation (Chambers, Aldous & Bryant, 2020).

The design challenge was 'to redesign pedagogies of physical literacy' – an educational challenge which is intergenerational, multi-sectoral and multi-cultural. In this AIESEP symposium, the design thinking workshop format encouraged participants to work together through a number of phases to 'redesign the pedagogy of physical literacy.' The spirit of the workshop was one of the dynamism. It was

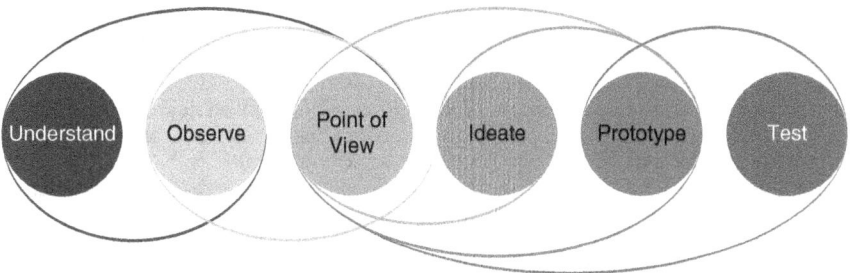

Figure 3.5 Six step design thinking process.

Source: Hasso-Plattner Institute, 2018

fast-paced and relied on participants embracing a growth mindset, interacting with the space and following the Hasso-Plattner Institute (2018) six-stage design thinking process (see Table 3.1 and Figure 3.5).

Participants

There were 92 participants who self-selected to participate the symposium. They comprised: curriculum developers, PE teachers, Physical Education Teacher Education faculty, academics, sports coaches, politicians, etc. They were drawn from 17 countries Belgium, Canada, China, The Netherlands, England, Finland, France, Germany, Ireland, Italy, Japan, Luxembourg, Northern Ireland, Poland, Switzerland, Taiwan and Wales. The participants had little to no experience of design thinking, but were experts in PE, PA and/or sport and in particular physical literacy. Participants were divided into Master-Teams A, B, C or D. These master-teams were then subdivided into four further sub-teams e.g. Master-Team A became sub-team A1, sub-team A2, sub-team A3 and sub-team A4. Each team had an English speaking leader. Master-Team and sub-team lists were on the walls outside the room. Participants were greeted by one facilitator to ensure that all located their sub-team space quickly.

Design ethics

When working on a design challenge, it is important to remember those who will be most impacted by the solution i.e. the end-user. The design thinking coach and/or facilitator must attend to design ethics as this is a human-centred innovation. As such, particularly in relation to service design, design thinking is able to humanise and visualise complex systems through research and scenarios. It can create new relations and interactions between the main actors and can lead to new knowledge. In order to facilitate this, the design thinking coach and/or facilitator must behave in an ethical manner by: being authentic; bringing awareness; knowledgeable about the subject matter; makes no assumptions, values every collaborator as an expert of their own lives, presents a willingness to learn and be respectful; and to be mindful

Table 3.2   Design principles and pedagogy of design thinking

Design principle	Pedagogy of design thinking
Design for transition	The creation of multi-stakeholder teams
	Establishment of clear rules of engagement
Accessible mutable system	An agile workshop agenda
	All activities were chosen to allow for maximum engagement
	Timeboxing helped participants to stay on task
Mutual learning through exploration	Mixed stakeholder teams and an identified leader
Facilitated learning about oneself and others	Reflexive exercises
Multiple levels of intimacy	Group reflection at each stage
At your discretion	Participants were advised that sharing of personal information was at their own discretion.

Source: Adapted from Smirnow, 2017

of confidentiality of every conversation and how it informs the design proposal (adapted from Smirnow, 2017, p. 40). These are crystallised in Smirnow's (2017) six design principles. The workshop used these to inform the pedagogy of design thinking, which guided the process of innovation (see Table 3.2).

Use of space

Interestingly, the workshop space for the AIESEP design thinking workshop exhibited three creative space types: collaboration space; presentation space and making space. The workshop space, both collaboration and presentation space (Thoring, 2018) was a large bright room with movable furniture. Furthermore, it exhibited three of Norman's (2002) five qualities of a creative space – it enabled knowledge processing, it was a process enabler and the space had a social dimension. It was organised into four zones according to the master-teams (A, B, C, D) with four tables per zone for the sub-teams (A1-A4; B1-B4; C1-C4; D1-D4). Each table had an allocated wall or window space for their work. Every sub-team was allocated markers, sticky notes, blue tack and A2 sheets of paper. The intermission space (Thoring, 2018) was a bright room for drinks, snacks and lunch.

Design thinking process

In this seminar, we used a six-step design process (see Figure 3.4) which was developed by the Hasso-Plattner Institute. The steps fall into **Problem Space** (Compassion) and **Solution Space**. As stated earlier, it is important to spend as much time as possible in the problem space – 80% and then the remaining time in the solution space. The design thinking pedagogy enables this to happen. The process began with Compassion – namely, empathising with the case study (persona) and being inclined toward action (see Figure 3.3 for an example persona).

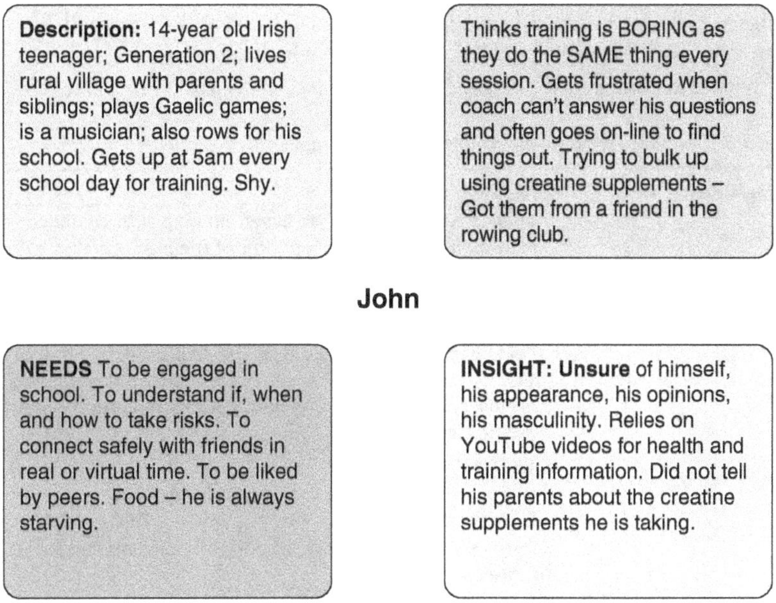

Description: 14-year old Irish teenager; Generation 2; lives rural village with parents and siblings; plays Gaelic games; is a musician; also rows for his school. Gets up at 5am every school day for training. Shy.

Thinks training is BORING as they do the SAME thing every session. Gets frustrated when coach can't answer his questions and often goes on-line to find things out. Trying to bulk up using creatine supplements – Got them from a friend in the rowing club.

John

NEEDS To be engaged in school. To understand if, when and how to take risks. To connect safely with friends in real or virtual time. To be liked by peers. Food – he is always starving.

INSIGHT: Unsure of himself, his appearance, his opinions, his masculinity. Relies on YouTube videos for health and training information. Did not tell his parents about the creatine supplements he is taking.

Figure 3.6 Example persona (John)

There are three sub-phases in the compassion space – understand, observe and point of view (synthesise) as outlined by Chambers (2018). Empathy is 'I understand how you feel,' whereas compassion is, *I understand how you feel and am driven to do something that has a positive impact on you.* This involves trying to really understand the case at hand and to settle on a point of view or synthesis of the issue at the heart of the case. For the purposes of starting to imbue compassion in participants, it begins with focusing on the end-user in PE and physical literacy – a composite case called John (see Figure 3.6). Participants are urged to think about John throughout the workshop and how what they will design will impact on how we support John on his physical literacy journey in the context of PE.

There were four design thinking challenges which were informed by the (a) problem statement and (b) the Megatrends in Education (Schleicher, 2019). Each design challenge was assigned to a Master-team:

Master-Team A: Redesign online and offline pedagogies for children in a world where there is limited funding.
Master-Team B: Redesign pedagogies for physical literacy for children in a world where sustainability is a core value.
Master-Team C: Redesign learning spaces and pedagogies to promote risky play in a world which is uber safety conscious.
Master-Team D: Redesign a factfulness approach to physical literacy in a world where pupils live in an echo chamber.

The agenda for the day was agile, with pedagogical tasks designed for each iterative phase of the design thinking process, which would encourage curiosity, creativity and courage (Windahl, 2017). The tasks are outlined in Table 3.3.

Table 3.3 The workshop design thinking process tasks

Problem Space 80% time	**UNDERSTAND** *Introduce Persona:* John was based on empirical evidence from own context. The function of the persona was to bring meaning to, evoke emotion from, participants i.e. John (aged 14) *Semantic exercise:* Sub-teams were asked to interrogate the meaning of the terminology in the challenge they had been set. *Stakeholder Map:* Sub-teams completed a stakeholder map for their challenge **OBSERVE** Prepare for and interview one stakeholder who is part of the sub-teams Sub-teams' members observe and note any interesting quotes **POINT OF VIEW (POV)** *Unpack:* They then unpacked what they had learned in 'in vivo' quotes *Synthesis:* They then synthesised this into a clear sentence, thus narrowing the design challenge
Solution Space 20% Implement + Evaluate	**IDEATE** *How might we?/how to?* Each member of sub-team formulates a 'How might we?' statement for the interviewee which addresses the POV Sub-team members share ideas *Power Dot:* Each sub-team member has two Power Dots. They are invited use these to choose the best two ideas for prototyping. **PROTOTYPE** a. *Idea napkin* Each sub-team produces an idea napkin for each of the two ideas b. *Synthesise* Sub-teams' group into Master-Team A, B, C and D e.g. A1, A2, A3, A4 group under Master-Team A Each sub-team presents their idea napkins to those in their master-team. Each master-team decides the best idea to put forward in the plenary. **TEST** This phase has not happened yet – The master-teams were invited to begin to scope their ideas We plan to have a follow-up design hackathon to implement and test the ideas put forward at AIESEP 2021 in Banff

Source: Adapted from Hassi and Laakso (2011)

Prototypes

In Table 3.4, the design challenge and the resultant prototype are shown for each of the four master-teams.

The participants reported that they were excited to learn the process of design thinking and believed it to be a very useful methodology when grappling with complex issues in multi-stakeholder groups. Group B's bicycle analogy was very useful in presenting the complexity of the pedagogy of physical literacy and the need for an interdisciplinary approach to the design, development and implementation of this important concept.

Table 3.4 Master-team design challenges and prototypes

Master-Team	Design Challenge	Prototype
A	Redesign online and offline pedagogies for children in a world where there is limited funding.	Creative journey – life-long and life-wide physical literacy: An ecological model with both a life-long and life-wide physical literacy model. This includes schools, employers etc.
B	Redesign pedagogies for physical literacy for children in a world where sustainability is a core value.	Interdisciplinary design teams for physical literacy: PL needs to be designed, implemented and evaluated by Interdisciplinary teams e.g. paediatricians, urban designers, PE teachers, employers, medical doctors, school staff, architects, politicians – bicycle metaphor (see Figure 3.7).
C	Redesign learning spaces and pedagogies to promote risky play in a world which is uber safety conscious.	Space as an enabler for physical literacy; Redesign school to promote risky play; Pedagogical scenarios/stories to help children to learn risky play and to translate it from PE class to playground to home.
D	Redesign a factfulness approach to physical literacy in a world where pupils live in an echo chamber.	Learning how physical literacy is informed by PE and by broader education goals – Gamification (Fortlife): There is a need for a clear physical literacy framework which can easily articulate its focus and how it links to PE; it is clear that PL fits with global goals of education; it is possible to capture children's attention by using gaming e.g. Fortlife – Are you ready to save your life?

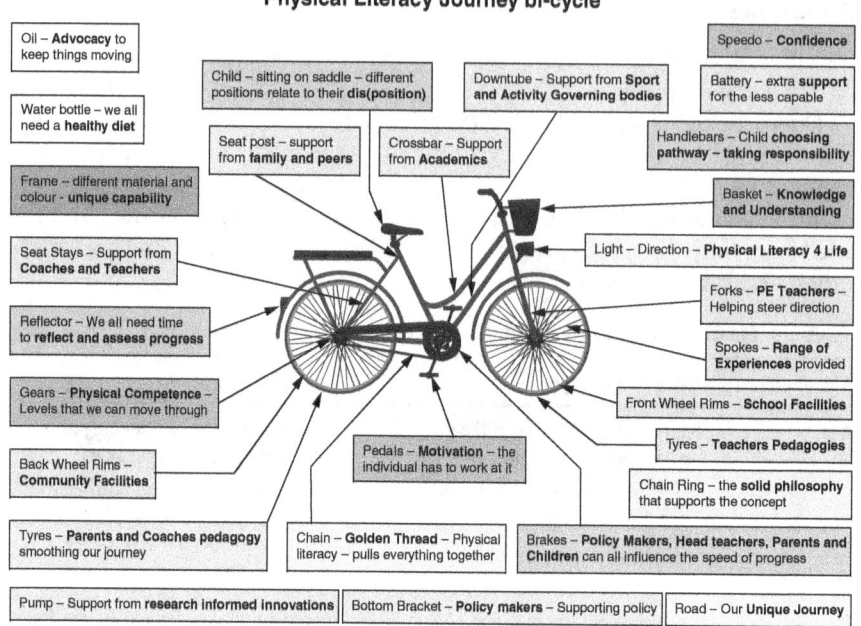

Figure 3.7 Physical literacy journey bi-cycle

Source: Green, 2020

Discussion on case study

The focus of the workshop was threefold: to bring stakeholders together from a range of cultures and standpoints, all of who have a vested interest in PE, PL and education more generally; to teach the process of design thinking to the participants and; to create a safe space for redesign of the pedagogies of physical literacy. When interrogating the prototypes developed during the workshop it is clear that this is a first step. Master-teams pointed to ecological issues i.e. the place of PL within PE and in broader education; the need to develop pedagogies which were more in step with Generation Z; the power of spaces to foster PL and finally the idea that PL was a lifelong and life wide endeavour. When all Master-teams had presented their ideas, Dr. Margaret Whitehead, the theorist who proposed physical literacy addressed the group, commenting that it was the first time she had witnessed and been part of a cross-cultural, cross discipline design workshop which focused on the pedagogy of physical literacy. She supported the notion of creating a professional learning community which could develop from this event and whom could develop pedagogies of PL which could be applied in contexts around the globe. It is clear from this workshop that the principles underpinning such a pedagogical approach are: life-long, life-wide, space as an enabler, gamification, the relationship between PL, PE and education. Participants have been invited to take part in the follow-on seminar in AIESEP 2021 in Banff, Canada.

Concluding remarks and lead into part II case studies

This chapter outlined the nuances of design thinking as a human-centred approach to innovation. The case study served to amplify the pedagogy of design thinking. In so doing, it highlighted the complexity of the crossdisciplinary inter-discipline of physical education and all of the actors who contribute to this field of study. It further captured the need for design thinking in grappling with complex problems in physical education. We will see a range of examples of design think-ing in action in Part II. In Part II, seven case studies are presented. Case studies had writing pods of academics and practitioners. They used a design thinking approach to tackle the following issue:

'Problem Statement:

Description: As a profession, we do not appear to have an agreed matrix of threshold concepts for PE.
Learning Need: PE teachers need to identify threshold concepts for PE so that they can plan implement and assess pupil learning in and through PE.
Insight: The absence of agreed threshold concepts in PE leads to ambiguity and a weakening of the perceived value of PE in the curriculum'.

The guidelines for development of their case studies were not prescriptive, but provided a handrail for consistency of approach. Each pod could choose a theme for their chapter, based on their expertise. Authors were encouraged to use any current research or ideas that might help to address the design challenge presented to them. They were asked to follow the Chambers Model of Design Thinking (2018) – moving through empathy, ideation and development toward a proposed solution. The author chapter guidelines were as follows for each section of each case study chapter.

Background

Step One: The two PE/PA/Sport academics meet for initial discussion. They identify a Practitioner (a PE teacher or sports coach) with whom they work and ask them to be involved – All three will be named co-authors of the chapter.
Step Two: Provide a short personal/professional background of each of the two academics. For the practitioner and proficient performer, this could include insight into the personal values, activity interests and professional training

(e.g. degrees, PETE). For the performer, this could also include the level at which they have performed and also any competitions in which they have participated.

Step Three: A joint discussion should take place between PE/PA/Sport Academics and Practitioner to identify a physical activity area in which they all have significant expertise (e.g. games, parkour, snorkelling, dance, gymnastics, etc.). *Please do not be limited in your choice to the PE curriculum.*

Step Four: The Practitioner identifies a proficient performer* in that physical activity with whom they have a professional rapport (e.g. current or former student). *It is important that the selected performer can clearly articulate knowledge of their bodily movement when performing that identified physical activity.*

Empathising with the performer

Step Five: From the perspective of the performer, the academics and practitioner seek a clear understanding of their experience being in 'flow' or 'in the zone' during a performance? Please provide a clear insight into the methods used to do this and the theoretical underpinnings of your approach?

Ideation

Step Six: The academics and practitioner jointly analyse the performers perspective on being 'in flow' and identify any key threshold concepts which emerge during this process.

Development

Step Seven: Synthesise these threshold concepts into a conceptual framework which could (b) be used by physical educators when teaching PE, and (b) which are also fundamental to the culture of PE/sport coaching more broadly.

In Part II, writing pods of seven case study chapters will walk readers through their design thinking process and present suggested concepts, threshold concepts and pedagogical approaches for the cross disciplinary interdiscipline of PE.

Acknowledgement

Thank you all participants of the AIESEP Seminar who used design thinking to unlock key pedagogical considerations for physical literacy.

Note

1 AIESEP is an international professional association which develops, disseminates and promotes high quality research and praxis in PE, physical activity and school sport.

References

Archer, B. (1979). Design as a discipline. *Design Studies, 1*(1), 17–20.

Blackman, T. et al. (2006). Performance assessment and wicked problems: The case of health inequalities. *Public Policy and Administration, 21*, 66–80.

Borja de Mozota, B. & Peinado, A. (2013). New Approaches to Theory and Research in Art & Design lead Educational Programs – Can "Design Thinking" spark new answers to old problems? *Annual Conference of the College of Art Association (CAA)*, New York.

Brown, T. (2008). Design thinking. *Harvard Business Review*, 86(6), 84–92.

Brown, T. (2016). Design Thinking: Thoughts by Tim Brown – Unlock your Organization's Creative Potential. Retrieved on April 8, 2017 from https://designthinking.ideo.com/blog/unlock-your-organizations-creative-potential

Buchanan, R. (1992). Wicked problems in design thinking. *Design Issues*, The MIT Press, 8(2), 5–21.

Chambers, F. C. (Ed.) (2018). *Learning to Mentor in Sports Coaching: A Design Thinking Approach.* Oxon, OX: Routledge.

Chambers, F. C. (2018) CREATEing Research with Children and Young People - Values, Voice and Ethics: Monitoring and Evaluation from a new perspective *CEREPS Lisbon 27–29 June.*

Chambers, F. C., Aldous, D., & Bryant, A. S. (2020). Design Thinking Workshop Pedagogies to promote Physical Literacy *AIESEP Specialist Seminar* 25th February 2020.

d.school (Producer). (2010). Empathy mapping. Retrieved December 29, 2017 from https://dschool.stanford.edu/ resources/

The Design Council. (2020). The Evolved Double Diamond. Retrieved August 18, 2020 from https://www.designcouncil.org.uk/news-opinion/what-framework-innovation-design-councils-evolved-double-diamond

Doorley, S., & Witthoft, S. (2011). *Make Space: How to Set the Stage for Creative Collaboration.* New York: Wiley.

Dweck, C. S. (2006). Mindset: The new psychology of success. Random House.

Goligorsky, D. (2012). Empathy and Innovation: The IDEO Approach, Lecture, Boston, MA: Harvard Business School.

Green, N. (2020). The Physical Literacy Journey Bi-cycle. At F.C. Chambers, D. Aldous, A.S. Bryant (2020) Design Thinking Workshop Pedagogies to promote Physical Literacy *AIESEP Specialist Seminar* 25th February 2020.

Hassi, L., & Laakso, M. (2011). Design Thinking in the Management Discourse: Defining the elements of the concept. *18th International Product Development Management Conference, Innovate through Design.* Delft, The Netherlands.

Hasso-Plattner Institute. (2018). HPI Academy. (Online) Available at: https://hpi.de/ (Accessed May 14, 2018).

IDEO (2009). *Human Centred Design Toolkit.* San Francisco: IDEO.

Lawson, B. (2001). *The Language of Space.* Oxford: Architectural Press.

Liedtka, J. (2015). Perspective: Linking design thinking with innovation outcomes through cognitive bias reduction. *Journal of Product Innovation Management, 32*(6), 925–938.

Lockwood, T. (2016). *Design Thinking.* Retrieved February 20, 2017, from Lockwoodresource.com/insight/design-thinking.

Longmuß, J., Höhne, B., Bräutigam, S., Oberländer, A., & Schindler, F. (2016). Agile Learning – Bridging the Gap between Industry and University. *Proceedings of the 44th SEFI Conference.* Tampere.

Luchs, M. G., Swan, S., & Griffin, A. (2016). *Design Thinking: New Product Development Essentials from the PDMA*, London: Wiley.

Martin, R. (2009). *The Design of Business*, Boston: Harvard Business School Publishing.

Merck. (2018). *The State of Curiosity Report*, Germany: Merck.

Peters, B. G. (2017). What is so wicked about wicked problems: A conceptual analysis and research program. *Policy and Society*, 36(3), 385–396.

Meyer, J. H. F., & Land, R. (Eds.) (2003). Threshold concepts and troublesome knowledge. *Linkages to Ways of Thinking and Practising' in Improving Student Learning – Ten Years On*, Oxford: OCSLD.

Norman, D. A. (2002). *The Design of Everyday Things*. Boston: MIT Press.

Proshansky, H. M. et al. (1970). *Environmental psychology: Man and his physical setting*, New York: Holt, Rinehart, and Winston.

Rittel, H. W. J., & Webber, M. M. (1973). Dilemmas in a general theory of planning. *Policy Sciences*, 4, 155–169.

Sammon, D. (2016). *Action Design Approach*. University College Cork: Cork University Business School.

Schleicher, A. (2019). 10 global megatrends facing education. Organisation for Economic Co-operation and Development. Retrieved on 1st October 2019 from: https://www.bbc.com/news/business-47030362

Shearer, A. W. (2015). Abduction to argument: A framework for DT. *Landscape Journal*, 34(2), 128–138.

Smirnow, C. (2017). *Pathways to Gender Identity: An Engagement Framework for Gender Inclusivity in Educational Institutions*, New York City: Parsons School of Design.

Thoring, K. et al. (2018). Creative environments for design education and practice: A typology of creative spaces. *Design Studies*, 56(C), 54–83.

Whitehead, M. (2007). Physical literacy: Philosophical considerations in relation to developing a sense of self, universality and propositional knowledge. *Sport Ethics Philosophy*, 1(3), 281–299.

Whitehead, M. (2013). The history and development of physical literacy. ICSSPE Bulletin Journal of Sport Science and Physical Education, 65, 21–27.

Windahl, C. (2017). Market sense-making in design practice: Exploring curiosity, creativity and courage. *Journal of Marketing Management*, 33(3-4), 280–291.

Womack, J.P., & Jones, D.T. (2003). *Lean Thinking: Banish Waste and Create Wealth in Your Corporation*. New York: Simon and Schuster.

Part II

Movement case studies: A design thinking approach

Teacher educators and preservice teachers as designers: Exploring Laban's framework within gymnastics settings – An approach in physical education teacher education

António Rodrigues and Joanne Moles

Context

Portugal

Physical education (PE) in Portugal is a *curriculum* subject in both primary and post-primary schools. The National *Curriculum* PE for post primary schools has three main development areas: physical activities (sports, rhythmic and expressive, nature and outdoor), health related fitness (functional and coordinative capacities) and knowledge area (reflection and integration about experiences of physical activities as social phenomena). Post-primary teachers are required to have a master's degree qualification. Primary school PE usually is taught by generalist teachers although in some schools could be taught jointly or less usual only by a specialist PE teacher.

Ireland

Physical education in Ireland is a curriculum subject in both primary and post-primary schools. The National Council for Curriculum and Assessment publish detailed and far-reaching curricula which often may be aspirational because of the shortage of curriculum space. Recent changes include the provision of a Leaving Certificate Examination in PE which is perceived as providing status for the subject. PE is central to a short course on Wellbeing in the Junior Cycle and a short course on Artistic performance includes Dance as a core aspect. Post-primary teachers are required to have a specialist degree qualification. Primary school PE is usually taught by generalist teachers.

Background
António Rodrigues

António Rodrigues has a PhD and a Master's degree in Educational Sciences from Technical University of Lisbon and a degree as Physical Education (PE) teacher from the same University; he has a complementary academic training in social sciences (Anthropology). He taught PE in all school levels for several years before he embraced the challenge as teacher educator (TE) at Faculty of Human Kinetics, University of Lisbon mainly preparing teachers of PE. As a PE teacher he worked in governmental departments and non-governmental organizations in programmes and projects related to youth at-risk, health promotion in schools and communities and continuing professional training for several health, education and social professionals. He is a Researcher at Faculty of Human Kinetics and UIDEF at University of Lisbon, has multiple research interests and worked in several projects, related with youth studies, school culture, physical education teacher education, children and youth use of digital and educational technology, science and nonformal education, teacher occupational socialization, among other subjects.

Joanne Moles

Joanne Moles has a PhD from Loughborough University, a Master's degree from the University of Limerick and an initial teaching qualification from Stranmillis College Belfast. She taught in post-primary schools and for most of her career was concerned with preparing teachers of PE both in Ireland and the UK. She coached the Irish Netball team and was for many years a Principal Tutor with the Irish and the UK Swimming Associations. She recently worked with post-graduate teachers facilitating critical inquiry. The space afforded by (almost) retiring has allowed Joanne to publish and to read – a true joy.

Introduction

In his short book, 'Thumbelina. The culture and technology of Millennials,' Michel Serres (2012), tell us the story of a little girl in both the present and future as someone who is not concerned with the old order of knowledge. The information on bookshelves, waiting for her to read every page sequentially, presented by the masters of any subject in form of lecture, or as in lesson form, has no value for her. Thumbelina is from the generation that is constantly circulating, gesticulating, and frolicking, a cognitive agility that is mimicked in the dance of her thumbs as they type out messages and manipulate digital images. She is constantly on the move. She embodies movement. For Michel Serres (2012) our contemporary institutions are no longer fit for purpose and await renegotiation by a new generation that is able to think critically according to a pluralist ontology. Formerly, in the classroom, youngsters found themselves in rows, eyes looking forward, transfixed, passive and inert. Now, those rigid spaces are exploding. Knowledge could be anywhere at the distance of little thumbs, they do not have to wait passively for the wisdom of the master to learn, to be someone. It is an emergence of a new cogito, a new human self. The 21st century competencies summarised in research studies (c.f. Voogt and Robin, 2012) present several dimensions such as, social-cultural, cognitive, metacognitive and technological, that go further than the ancient emphasis in *cogito ergo sum* paradigm of the western societies. Physical Education Teacher Education (PETE) is a privileged *place*[1] where *discourses* shape PE *practices* and vice-versa, where challenge to the Cartesian myth is facilitated by encouraging a holistic view of PE in which the body/mind continuum is seamless.

Let us start at the very beginning. We are two professionals who have never met, living in different countries (Portugal and Ireland). With several years working in PETE in our countries, we see ourselves as experienced teacher educators with some previous experience in teaching PE at schools. One of us had experience in competitive artistic gymnastic for nine years. One of us was a competitive springboard diver and an international netball coach. Our life experiences in physical activity and sport were diversified and developed in different contexts (formal, non-formal, clubs, schools and informal practice), and within different types of activities. (e.g. swimming, yoga, track and field, basketball and outdoor activities), some of them we continue to practise on a regular basis.

Although we had some experience in other approaches, using student-centred models of inquiry – e.g. inquiry-based learning, problem-based learning, project-based learning and action-research, neither of us had expertise in using design thinking approach. With this in mind, we explored the idea that we could discuss and do something together considering teaching gymnastic as part of the PE *curriculum*. We were aware of difficulties that we have seen in school PE practices when this *curriculum* subject is viewed beyond skilful and performative outcomes. In our initial discussions, we considered alternative ways of dealing with this problem; how to define and promote meaningful gymnastics experiences in PE classes? How to help prospective teachers in PETE to overcome the constraints associated with promoting gymnastic beyond a social and cultural model of teaching skill and sports in PE classes?

We used design thinking to stimulate reflection on the possibilities of Laban's framework as a way for prospective PE teachers to re-think and re-enact their practices beyond the pedagogical models they have experienced and those they have been trained to use. Recognising difficulties for beginning teachers in altering their mind-set regarding what it means to learn gymnastics, and by extension other *curriculum* subjects (e.g. sports and dance), beyond traditional ways, usually predominantly focused on skill performance and skills techniques. We draw on a Movement Analysis framework devised by Rudolf Laban (1971) to contextualise our thinking and to provide an outline for the research. We were concerned to move from concepts to exemplars rather than providing solutions to questions not yet asked. Laban's analysis of movement is easily accessed and the concepts are relevant to all human movement. This movement analysis could inform traditional pedagogies rather than necessarily replacing them. The teacher becomes knowledgeable through analysis of his or her practice rather than simply mechanically reproducing knowledge acquired elsewhere. We aver the importance of presenting an alternative (but not a substitute) framework where teachers and learners are made aware of concepts that they could use to respond to challenges they experience in PE classes in order to promote widely applicable physically embodied competencies. This chapter seeks to contribute to the above discussion in two different PETE contexts using design thinking with PE Preservice Teachers (PST). It presents the process in which we were involved as teacher educators with proposals and reflections of the PST enrolled in master courses in teaching PE in Ireland and Portugal invoking what we think represents a threshold concept based on Laban's Movement Analysis Framework to teach PE classes.

Physical education in 21st century. Critical thinking beyond the subject: The relevance of PETE

Recently, Lawson (2019) called for an appraisal of the recognition that 20th Century social institutions such as the two components of the 'physical education system' (PE & PETE) are not fit for purpose in the 21st Century.' Supported in his previous proposal (Lawson, 2012), he argues for a renewed 'physical education system' and for a new interdisciplinary agenda, where (re)design-oriented thinking and planning for young people's physical activity, sports, dance, and all other forms of play, is needed:

> Improved exercise, sport, and health outcomes for young people involve adaptive and wicked problems; and better outcomes are not likely to result systematically from today's fractured domains and splintered knowledge. And, while research is an invaluable resource in these new designs, they also require theoretically-sound, justifiable searches. The reminder here is that, when entirely new institutional designs are in order, the search always precedes the research. Where improved outcomes for young people are concerned, design-oriented searches carefully developed in school, community, neighbourhood, and policy settings are needed (Lawson, 2012, p. 83).

Teacher Education (TE) university-based programmes are commonly identified as important elements for prospective teachers and in some jurisdictions, for newcomers to the teaching profession (cf. Rossi et al., 2015). Reviewing twenty-five years of PETE research, McEvoy, MacPhail and Heikinaro-Johansson (2015), illustrate how some privileged *discourses* can impact the selective prioritisation of certain knowledge and practices neglecting or sidelining those which challenge the normative discourses of the institutions.

PETE should provide a *place* where students, teachers and PST acquire 'powerful knowledge' (cf. Young, 2014) in order to challenge the pedagogical status quo; knowledge is 'powerful' if it predicts, if it explains, if it enables you to envisage alternatives' (Young, 2014, p. 74). A timely recall from Dewey's work (1916, 1958), reminds us that one of the tools which we believe empower in all educational sites is the power of thinking reflectively. Moreover, reflection in practice is essential for considered teaching practices in TE (cf. Rovegno, 1992) that inform teachers' analyses of appropriate interventions in teaching and reflection-in-action learning (Schön, 1983). PETE should develop more moments of critical thinking regarding the selection and presentation of coursework in order to promote considered approaches to facilitate prospective teachers in sharing meaningful dialogue about ways in which they can positively relate to changing societies.

Teachers are challenged by the neo-liberal emphasis on education as a commodity which is primarily perceived as training a workforce to progress the economy (Biesta, 2013). This deflects from the role of a teacher as a fellow inquirer. The restrictions of pre-planned outcomes and the constraints to reproduce 'models of instruction' appear to us as unnecessary impediments to the development of teachers as informed and concerned educators. Bernstein (2000) warns of the problem of dislocating knowledge from the knower when knowledge becomes a commodity. Educating teachers as autonomous intellectuals with ethically informed practices appears to be a logical way in which to progress the rich potential of an educational encounter. Mooney Simmie and Moles (2019) make a case for teachers being facilitated as risk takers while accepting the Levinasian claim for ethics as the first philosophy. This plea argues for ethically based teachers who are perceived as responsible, autonomous professionals whose decision making about their students involves an understanding, not only of the subject content but of how it can facilitate the development of students whose thinking is informed and productive.

In physical activity (PA) across most pedagogical settings (e.g. school PE classes, sport sessions, sport coaching), demonstration, explanation and practice represent the dominant pedagogical form used by most teachers, coaches and instructors (Tinning, 2010). Information acquisition and regurgitation informs these predominant practices in PETE and, by extension, PE classes. In recent years, driven by constructivist ideas inter alia, there has been an evident interest in changing teaching practices from a teacher-centred approach to, as we mentioned previously, a more student-centred approach. These forms of pedagogy intend to deal with the lack of meaning outside school context, boredom and irrelevance that school PE has too frequently become for children and youngsters. PE in school needs to equate students' acquisition of competencies with satisfaction and enjoyment, in the sense that Mandigo and Couture (1996) defined fun and the inner love, intrinsic motivation for moving – i.e. balance between skills and challenge in tasks. Despite the declaration of Tinning (2010) 'there is no Holy Grail of PE pedagogies' (p. 65), *mutatis mutandis*, it is the opportunity to return to some progressive pedagogues from the beginning of the 20th century to deal with the challenges of the 21st century. Dewey (1958) inspires those pedagogues for whom sustained learning and living is part of the same experience of becoming, a process that cultivates the willingness to transform passive into active learning. In the *field* of movement studies, Laban incorporated Dewey's idea of learning as becoming. The Laban tradition emphasises looking at life itself through the lens of movement – the 'movement thinking' (Laban 1971, p. 17). From this perspective, everything in life is movement, and movement is change. Laban's movement framework, not only presented for dance, early years of childhood, or all other strands of PE *curriculum* but as something that has a potential to embody experiences in teaching and learning as lived experiences. With this in mind, the question that arose for us was whether is it possible to think about the action-in-the-present in PETE in order to reflect-on-the-future of long term-goals in PE?

Laban's analysis: An alternative focus for teaching and learning PE

By employing Laban's analysis of movement to progress students' understandings of concepts of movement as opposed to individual skills we thought that it provided not only a framework but the possibility of applying the analysis to various learning and training contexts and it has the additional benefit of allowing analyses in various forms – not only through movement. An added attraction of this form of pedagogy is the potential for dialogue between teacher and taught, sharing of concepts both in movement and in spoken language within shared perceptions and goals. This communication can progress critical analysis based on intrinsic awareness and not just scores and measures. Awareness of differences is seen as accommodation of and care for 'the other' as opposed to highlighting deficiencies (cf. Garrison, 2008)

Where the body moves:

Laban sees the body's movement occurring within a kinesphere which he describes as the space around the body within which movement can occur. This 'sphere' can be explored either in personal space – on the spot, or in general space – when the body, in its sphere, moves into new areas and this typically refers to direction, pathway and level. Moving in considered pathways – one's initials – can heighten understanding of changes of direction with smooth and angular pathways contrasted. The shape which the body is making can be considered – again extremes can be contrasted to encourage awareness.

When the body moves:

The movements can be quick or slow. They can be sudden or sustained. Movements can accelerate or decelerate and they can respond to complex rhythms. They can abruptly stop and start again either gradually or instantaneously.

In terms of Force:

People can move strongly or lightly. They can resist or yield to other forces. Contact with the ground can be firm and strong, or lightly moving over the top – playing with gravity.

Flow in movement:

In Laban's terms flow refers to whether the movements are simultaneous with everything moving together, like a cat springing, or successive with parts following after each other. Flow can be described as smooth (continuous) or broken.

Table 4.1 Concept relations of Laban's framework analysis

	Body	*Effort*	*Space*	*Relationships*
Locomotion	Feet, Hands and feet	Fast Slow Varied speeds	Directions Levels Pathway	Matching mirroring Negotiating obstacles
Weight transference	Moving on and over supporting parts. Adjacent and non-adjacent parts	Smooth or broken flow	Consuming space or restricted space	In contact or vaulting over Symmetry and asymmetry
Weight bearing	Points or patches	Number of supporting parts	Closed shape or extended shape	Supporting and assisting – with and against
Balance	Gaining maintaining and loosing balance	Static and dynamic balances	Extending or contracting	Counter balance and counter tension

Benefits of this process are that the language of Laban's analysis – Body, Effort, Space and Relationships, or Time, Weight and Flow (Table 4.1), can facilitate awareness and understanding around how movement is being perceived, both by an onlooker and by a performer. PETE students who were involved in using Laban's analysis frequently, in fact virtually exclusively indicated pedagogical problems as their primary concerns in teaching PE (cf. Sherborne, 2001). An ability to 'read' the movement of the class as a whole and of individuals within the class would help them to make informed meaningful interventions.

Design thinking as a possibility to re-orient, re-think, enact and (r)enact the practices of PETE

The perspective of using designer approaches with PE in schools can be found in some researches that highlight constructivist perspectives of learning (cf. Casey, et al. 2011; Phil, 2016; Hastie, 2010; O'Connor, Jeanes and Alfrey, 2016; Gray, Treacy and Hall, 2019). In PETE the perspective of educators as designers within continuing professional development focuses on critical thinking and reflection as practices to be developed in TE programmes (cf. Chen & Rovegno, 2000).

Design thinking involves creativity, process strategy, generation for alternatives, problem-solving design and reflexive practices, enhancing innovation in integrating multiple knowledge domains. Reinforcing those characteristics in PETE programmes allows us to embrace the challenges of educational processes in which they are involved. We used two of the five perspectives of design thinking categorised by Johansson-Sköldberg, Woodilla and Çetinkaya (2013), envisaging research as reflexive practice and as a problem-solving activity. The former, emphasises the role of reflection as the core of professional work and as a part of (teacher) practice (cf. Schön, 1983); the later, commonly associated with formulation of Rittel's and Buchanan's wicked problems (Buchanan, 1992). For the resolution of these problems, students need to participate in different kinds of thinking processes – e.g. empathy, integrative, creative and critical thinking – collect, edit, prototype and experiment ideas.

Reflecting on these assumptions, the idea of teaching gymnastics in mixed-ability classes presents as a subject beyond the sport education, game sense and inquiry-based learning that could go further than a practice for skilful children or youngsters – i.e. a possible 'wicked' problem for prospective teachers. Moreover, the idea of design thinking as a place where teachers (educators) reflect about their practices seemed to us an excellent opportunity to explore Laban's movement analysis framework as a threshold concept in PE system.

How can we? Developing creative ways of making a movement experience accessible to teach gymnastics in mixed ability groups of schoolchildren

We planned three sessions with prospective teachers (student teachers and PST) to be the *field* for reflection upon our case. We developed a context in which shared dialogue around the ways in which people move can promote interest and ensure reflective exploration. The possibility afforded us by having access to prospective teachers as part of our occupations offered us the opportunity to use and reflect upon a design thinking approach in PETE; moreover, PST are in an in-between position to reflect upon PE and PETE at the same time. The purpose was to explore the knowledge that they had about activities commonly grouped as 'gymnastics,' stimulate them to think critically and reflect about the possibilities of applying Laban's framework movement analysis to teach those activities in mixed ability classes and simultaneously to allow us to reflect about our own practices in PETE. This was our challenge.

Despite the physical distance between us, we collaborated, shared and questioned our intentions and purposes trying to get the best of our different perspectives and experiences. We tried to be empathetic, mostly with persons that face this kind of problems in their school days, looking for alternative solutions to explore and to present to Physical Educators. Laban's framework analysis appeared as an appropriate way to explore learning gymnastics as a process of becoming for prospective teachers and for students in schools, in acquiring 'powerful knowledge' applied to PETE&PE contexts.

Our sessions, one group in Ireland and two groups in Portugal, were developed adopting a problem-solving perspective – i.e. idealise and plan how to apply Laban's framework to teaching gymnastic for mixed abilities groups in elementary and secondary schools. With a slideshow presentation, we stimulated them to scaffold the problem we presented, with moments where they had to draw on their previous experiences and also create empathy with the needs of school students. They were encouraged to use Laban's movement analysis as a way of structuring ideas of teaching which was not reliant on prescribed outcomes. They recorded the ideas in stickers along with their thoughts; for constructing their 'prototypes' they used scenario paper. Finally, they discussed as a group their reflections about the feasibility of their 'prototype' and the relevance for their development and training in PETE programmes.

We believe that the design process undertaken by these students evokes their experiences, both positive and negative. In these processes, as previous athletes or as students, their state of '...flow arouses a regression to childhood when gymnastics seemed so easily undertaken' (sic). The concept of moving in a thoughtful, considered way was unfamiliar although the movement was free and natural. Students' responses on the 'stickies' showed very clear awareness of the limitations of the approaches they were adopting, reflecting their understanding that they need to follow the advocated pedagogic rules and generalised principles expounded and developed in their undergraduate courses.

The final phase involved application of their concerns and their movement understandings to create movement phrases. One of the students found this process very liberating and articulated how it will help her with some specific problems she was grappling – e.g. making gymnastics relevant to very different abilities. A group of students expressed that they had not even thought that this could be liberating; they tried to systematize Laban's ideas as something that overcame problems with presenting content to the less able in sport and games. Another student was enthusiastic because the process was so new. He attempted to answer the task but was apparently inhibited by the wide scope rather than a described learning outcome – he indicated that he would re-visit the process.

Design thinking helped them in the process of reflection about the proposed problem and allowed them to look 'outside the box' to get integrative thinking, or to reflect within Laban's framework when constructing the 'prototype' with alternative solutions.

At the end of these 'encounters' while we were experiencing this process of sharing ideas with our students we could say that we were also involving ourselves in a design based-learning process – i.e. becoming educators as designers and designers as educators.

Reflecting on Laban's movement analysis framework to inform a different approach in PETE & PE

In approaching this chapter we acknowledged difficulties that students have in teaching activities loosely grouped together as 'gymnastics.' Variations in understanding the concept often relate to the institution in which the PETE was undertaken, along with prevailing attitudes at the time a teacher took their course. Traditionally there were variations between traditional women's colleges in the UK and the men's colleges, with the former preferring a more child-centred movement-based approach, often informed by Laban's analysis (Webb, 1999). Men's colleges frequently favoured an approach which accepted criteria from the sport of Gymnastics with its focus on performing named skills which often are more achievable with high levels of strength, coordination and balance and undoubtedly not 'for all' activities. With the current commodification of education as the achievement of competencies, there is a requirement for measurable outcomes. A set of marking criteria makes grading and ranking a more accessible process and coincides with the preferred way of viewing education in the second millennium.

In an attempt to make this aspect of our subject less élitist and accessible to everyone, we like to think that our chapter will indicate a movement experience which is Safe, Appropriate, For all and Educational (SAFE). This experience challenges participants to 'use' their bodies efficiently to experience the exhilaration of moving in ways which are controlled and match a set of intentions without the aim of matching a prescribed form.

At the end of the sessions, our analyses indicated a strong sense of a prevailing dominant discourse, more linked to the use of prescribed teaching rules and strategies in students' reflections (e.g. progressions, pedagogical feedback, structuring tasks, academic-learning time, ...). Students are restricted in their practice by an acceptance of how things are 'supposed to be' and by applying design thinking they can move away from imposed practices and work form a wider perspective.

We opened this chapter, following Lawson's idea of contesting the ways the PE System (PETE & PE) needed to invoke (re)design oriented thinking and planning for young people's school PE and all other forms of PA. We highlight the relevance of PETE in that process of giving 'powerful knowledge' in order that prospective teachers reflect beyond the taken-for-granted assumptions about their educational encounters within schools (e.g. teaching and learning *curriculum* subjects). Drawing upon a design thinking approach, we sought to present Laban's movement framework as a threshold concept (Figure 4.1) to provide PSTs with the potential to explore other possibilities to be controllers of their own movements (as learners and teachers) and to overcome the traditional pedagogical models which inform their practices. It is argued that, despite the participants' open-mindedness to the possibilities of Laban's analysis in promoting physical

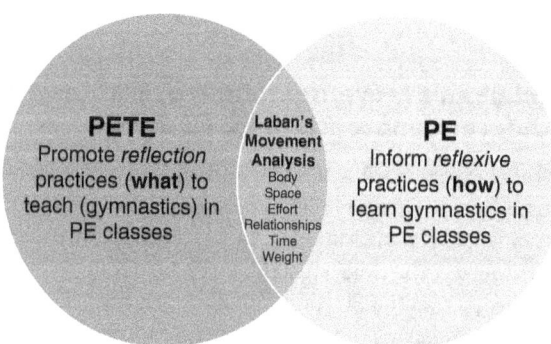

Figure 4.1 Laban's tramework as a threshold concept for PETE & PE

fluency, they seemed to perceive some *threats* to their security as teachers when they had to expand their planning with new perspectives rather than simply using their taken-for-granted actions. Moreover, despite the idea that they were not in a liminal phase of the appropriation of the concepts presented, we think the design processes can facilitate the experience of *flow* and involve us all in the PE System as designers. The potential to work together inspires dialogue and creativity which avoids the stagnation associated with pursuing known goals.

Note

1. Tim Cresswell (2004) refers to *place* as a way of "…seeing, knowing and understanding the world". (p.14)

References

Bernstein, B. (2000). *Pedagogy, Symbolic Control and Identity*, Oxford: Rowman and Butterfield.

Biesta, G. (2013). *The Beautiful Risk of Education*, Boulder: Paradigm.

Buchanan, R. (1992). Wicked Problems in Design Thinking, *Design Issues*, 8(2), 5–21.

Casey, A, Hastie, P., & Rovegno, I. (2011). Student learning during a unit of student-designed games, *Physical Education & Sport Pedagogy*, 16(4), 331–350.

Chen, & Rovegno (2000). Examination of expert and novice teachers' constructivist-oriented teaching practices using a movement approach to elementary physical education. *Research Quarterly for Exercise and Sport*, 71(4), 357–372.

Cresswell, T. (2004). *Place: A Short Introduction*. Oxford: Blackwell.

Dewey, J. (1916). Democracy and education. *An Introduction to The Philosophy of Education* (1966 ed.), New York: Free Press.

Dewey, J. (1958). *Experience and Education*. New York: The Macmillan Company.

Garrison, J. (2008). Ethical obligation in caring for the other, In D. Egéa-Kuehne (Ed.), *Levinas and Education: At the Intersection of Faith and Reason* (pp. 272–285), London: Routledge.

Gray, S., Treacy, J., & Hall, E. (2019). Re-engaging disengaged pupils in physical education: An appreciative inquiry perspective, *Sport, Education and Society*, 24(3), 241–255.

Hastie, P. (2010). *Student-designed Games: Strategies for Promoting Creativity, Cooperation, and Skill Development*. Champaign, IL: Human Kinetics.

Johansson-Sköldberg, U., Woodilla, J., & Çetinkaya, M. (2013). Design thinking: Past, present and possible futures, *Creativity and Innovation Management*, 22(2), 121–146.

Laban, R. (1971). *The Mastery of Movement*, London: Macdonald & Evans.

Lawson, H. (2019). The physical education system as a consequential social determinant, *Quest*, 72(1), 72–84 doi: 10.1080/00336297.2019.1627224

Lawson, H. (2012). Realizing the promise to young people: Kinesiology and New Institutional Designs for School and Community Programs, *Kinesiology Review*, 1, 76–90.

Mandigo, J.L. & Couture, R.T. (1996). An Overview of the Components of Fun in Physical Education, Organised Sport and Physical Activity Programs, *Avante* 2(3), 56–72.

McEvoy, E., MacPhail, A., and Heikinaro-Johansson, P. (2015). Physical education teacher educators: A 25-year scoping review of literature, *Teacher and Teacher Education*, 51, 162–181.

Mooney Simmie, G., & Moles, J. (2019). Teachers' changing subjectivities: Putting the soul to work for the principle of the market or for facilitating risk? *Studies in Philosophy and Education*, doi.org/10.1007/s11217-019-09686-9

O'Connor, J., Jeanes, R., & Alfrey, L. (2016). Authentic inquiry-based learning in health and physical education: a case study of 'r/evolutionary' practice, *Physical Education and Sport Pedagogy*, *21*(2), 201–216.

Pill, S. (2016). An appreciative inquiry exploring game sense teaching in physical education. *Sport, Education and Society*, *21*(2), 279–297.

Rossi, T., Hunter, L., Christensen, E.. & Macdonald, D. (2015). Workplace learning in Physical Education. *Emerging Teachers' Stories from the Staffroom and Beyond*, London: Routledge.

Rovegno, I. (1992). Learning to reflect on teaching: A case study of one preservice physical education teacher. *The Elementary School Journal*, *92*, 491–510.

Serres, M. (2012). *Thumbelina: The Culture and Technology of Millennials*, (trans. Daniel W. Smith), Lanham, MD: Rowman & Littlefield.

Sherborne, V. (2001) *Developmental Movement for Children*, Worth Publishing, Ltd.

Schön, D. (1983). *The Reflective Practitioner: How Professionals Think in Action*. London: Temple Smith.

Tinning, R. (2010). *Pedagogy and human movement: Theory, practice, research*. London: Routledge.

Voogt, J., & Roblin, N. (2012). A comparative analysis of international frameworks for 21st century competences: Implications for national curriculum policies, *Journal of Curriculum Studies*, *44*(3), 299–321.

Webb, I. (1999). *The Challenge of Change in Physical Education*, London: Falmer Press.

Young, M. (2014). Powerful knowledge as a curriculum principle. In. M. Young, D. Lambert, C. Roberts & M. Roberts (Eds.), *Knowledge and the future school. Curriculum and social justice* (pp. 65–88). London: Bloomsbury Academic.

Chapter 5

A ball of energy: The use of Laban movement analysis and imagery to develop a performer holistically in dance

Lowri Cerys Edwards, Jane Bellamy, Amy Rees and Gareth Stratton

Context

The following study took place in Wales, UK with a team of two higher education academic and one doctoral student.

Background
Dr Lowri Cerys Edwards

Lowri is a Lecturer in Sport, Physical Education and Health at Cardiff Metropolitan University. Lowri has a sporting background in artistic gymnastics, competing to a regional standard by her teens. She enjoyed Physical Education (PE) in school, and represented her school in gymnastics, athletics and cross country. In 2013, she gained a first class honours degree in BSc (Hons) Sport and PE at Cardiff Metropolitan University and began her doctoral studies. Lowri's PhD explored the effects of a PE professional development programme with primary school teachers on pupils' physical literacy. Her research interests include physical literacy and holistic physical development.

Jane Bellamy

Jane is Senior Lecturer in Dance on the Sport, PE and Health programme at Cardiff Metropolitan University. She has wealth of experience working within the Welsh Dance Industry as a performer, choreographer and teacher. She has worked within dance and arts organisations in both community and educational settings, collaborating with dance and arts practitioners from theatre, music and the visual arts. Jane's other interests focus on the healthy dancer and healthy dance practice in line with current research in Dance Science. She is currently exploring the role of yoga as a somatic practice within the study of dance in higher education and its wider application in education.

Amy Rees

Amy is a PhD student studying at Cardiff Metropolitan University. She began recreational gymnastics at the age of four, where she loved the creative aspects of gymnastics, which led her to start theatre and jazz dance. She soon began to explore different genres of dance including ballet, street, tap and contemporary. As a teen, Amy transitioned from the role of performer to coach in gymnastics, swimming and performing arts. In 2018, Amy completed a BSc (Hons) Sport and PE degree at Cardiff Metropolitan University and started a PGCE in primary education where she loved teaching PE lessons. Currently, Amy is enrolled as a full-time PhD student, exploring a collaborative approach in physical literacy between community and education in Wales.

Professor Gareth Stratton

Professor Stratton is Deputy Pro-Vice Chancellor, and Director of Strategy and Insight in the College of Engineering and School of Sport and Exercise Sciences, Swansea University. Professor Stratton whose academic interest is driven by his time as physical education teacher, has two main areas of research: children maturation and physical activity, and physical fitness and health. Professor Stratton has designed a significant number of physical activity interventions in clinical and healthy populations that aim to change children's behaviour, and promote positive wellbeing, and thriving and flourishing aspects of child development.

Introduction: Dance as a holistic activity

This case study proposes effective threshold concepts in dance using Laban Movement Analysis and *Imagery*. Dance was selected, as the practitioner within the team has an extensive experience teaching dance and applying Laban's principles in the context of dance. By definition, dance is considered a unique form of art, as performers express messages through bodily movements (Martin, 1989). As an activity, dance embraces the notion of embodied cognition, whereby the motor system influences our cognition, just as the mind influences bodily actions (Thompson, 2016). Adopting an enactive approach contributes towards embodied cognition, given that enaction views the 'lived body as a system that encompasses the interaction between body and mind, body and environment, and environment and mind, and focuses on embodied social interaction as mutual participatory sensemaking' (Anttila, 2016, p. 2). This enactive and holistic approach towards dance is consistent with a monist philosophical view, whereby an educator would acknowledge that the performer's mind and body are equally important and are inextricably connected for development to occur (Whitehead, 2007; 2013). Indeed, consistent with the messages from the physical literacy literature, dance embraces a more holistic approach to development in that it allows performers to experience and develop a sense of self and establish interactions with others and their environment (Whitehead, 2007; Thompson, 2016). Consequently, the authors believe that dance as a holistic activity makes a contribution to the PE pedagogy literature, in terms of its alternative pedagogical approaches used to develop performers.

Three of the authors have significant expertise in creative activities (LE, JB and AR). Lowri Edwards has an expertise in gymnastics, where dance and artistry feature in her favourite apparatus; floor and beam. Jane Bellamy has a wealth of experience in dance, having studied BA Dance at the Laban Centre for Movement and Dance in London and currently leads on the dance pathway for the undergraduate programmes at Cardiff Metropolitan University. Amy Rees has a background in dance, gymnastics and performing arts. These backgrounds shaped the authors approaches and philosophies towards teaching and dance practice.

Analytical concepts

Laban movement analysis

In dance, Laban Movement Analysis (LMA) is a multidisciplinary tool that practitioners adopt to describe, visualise, interpret and document performance and human movement (Laban/Bartenieff Institute of Movement Studies, 2020). LMA is a 'tool that can be used to refine awareness of movement, to describe actions objectively, and to encourage conscious reflection on the meaning of this dynamic dimension of human behavior' hence is widely applied in the field of dance (Moore, 2009, p. 35). The observation of LMA is considered an 'embodied practice,' as observing 'internal physical perceptions' are key foci for the observer (Laban/Bartenieff Institute of Movement Studies, 2020, p. 2). In order to achieve this embodied practice, LMA categorises movement elements into four main categories, namely: *Body, Effort, Space* and *Shape* (Tsachor & Shafir, 2017):

- *Body* refers to the 'what' of movement and describes parts of the body in relation to movement and how different body parts connect while moving.
- *Effort* relates to the 'how' of movement, that is – the mover's attitude, purpose and energy while completing the movement(s). *Effort* can be further classified into four factors: Weight (strong/light), Time (quick/sustained), Space (direct/indirect), and Flow (bound/free) (Laban & Lawrence, 1974).
- *Space* conveys the 'where' of movement, with consideration to directions, pathways and spatial tensions. *Space* also relates to a mover's 'kinesphere' as the reaching possibilities (far-, mid-, and near-reaching) of the limbs in relation to the space around the body.
- Finally, *Shape* expresses the 'why' of movement, and describes the variations in the body's form. *Shape* identifies how movements interact and respond to the environment and relationships with others.

Teachers can apply the LMA movement elements to their dance practice to maximise the learner's performance and movement capabilities. Furthermore, Tsachor and Shafir (2017) refer to the somatic benefits of utilising LMA as a means of exploring sensory awareness. According to Baston and Swartz (2007, p. 48), somatic approaches depend on 'augmented sensory processes while moving, and the re-distribution of movement efforts in order to facilitate a more psychophysical state of embodiment conducive to coordinated action.' In this sense, a somatic approach adopts the belief that the becoming (i.e. senses) are more important that the doing (i.e. physical practice) as a means of 'promoting embodied self-organisation (internal authority)' (Baston & Swartz, 2007, p. 48). Key to supporting internal authority, is to increase the teacher's awareness of the learner's internal sensory feedback/forward processes (Baston & Swartz, 2007). *Imagery* is a pedagogical tool frequently used in dance to develop internal authority feedback/forward (Mainwaring & Krasnow, 2010).

Imagery

Imagery is used in dance to improve 'concentration, dance technique, expressivity... motivation... and physical awareness' (Franklin, 2013, p. 24). Franklin (2013) proposes that a skilled dance teacher can use *Imagery* to promote embodiment, which is crucial for developing dance technique and to encourage greater bodily awareness. The skilled dance teacher would implement *Imagery* interventions for accomplishing technical progress, such as, (i) trial and error with a variety of different images and to collectively identify which image was most effective; and (ii) talk directly to a specific area of the body (e.g. arm) and request for the body part to provide the teacher with an image that would elicit a technical response (e.g. move softer). There are several types of *Imagery* that can be adopted to improve technique in dance, for example, *Direct, Anatomical, Spontaneous, Biological, Metaphorical* and *Sensory Imagery* (Franklin, 2013). For the purpose of this case study, the authors focused on *Biological* and *Metaphorical Imagery* as they frequently coincide. *Biological Imagery* refers to focusing on specific bodily areas, such as joints, and to place emphasis on how the body area influences your overall movement. *Metaphorical Imagery* is later used to focus on the specific body area to stimulate the desired movement technique. In short, *Metaphorical Imagery* uses an image or concept to encourage the learner to generate feelings and sensations of the imagined context (Samaritter, 2009). For example, the metaphor of a learner's 'body floating on water' is intended to create an image of elegant, flowing and soft movements. *Metaphorical Imagery* is often easier for the learner to achieve compared to *Biological Imagery* because of its interpretive nature (Franklin, 2013). However, caution is required with *Metaphorical Imagery*, as its interpretive nature may also promote undesirable changes to technique, namely, 'floating on water' for a learner that fears of water would look very different to the aforementioned.

Flow and dance

Jeong (2012) suggested that the use of *Imagery* in dance develops key antecedents of flow. Flow (otherwise known as 'being in the zone') is a concept that was formulated by Csikszentmihalyi (1990) and 'describes a complex psychological state that has important consequences for human life. Any measure of flow we create will only be a partial reflection of this reality' (p. 183). Indeed, flow occurs in dance when one performs to the best of their capabilities, resulting in complete concentration and immersion of the task, and often losing awareness of time and surroundings (Panebianco-Warrens, 2014). In developing flow theory, Csikszentmihalyi (1990) presented nine dimensions of flow. Three of the nine dimensions are conditions in which the experience takes place (Nakamura & Csikszentmihalyi, 2002), specifically, clear goals (i.e. the performer understands fully what they aim to achieve); challenge-skills balance (e.g. the balance between skills and the environmental demands placed on achieving the skill); and unambiguous feedback (i.e. continuous feedback to regulate the performer's responses to the demands). The remaining six dimensions describe qualities related to what the performance feels like in flow (Nakamura & Csikszentmihalyi, 2002), namely, sense of control (i.e. as if the performer can achieve anything); concentration on the task at hand (e.g. performer focuses completely on the performance); loss of self-consciousness (e.g. performer is wholly immersed in the performance); action-awareness merging (i.e. deep involvement with the task that leads to spontaneity and freedom); autotelic experience (the performance is an intrinsically rewarding experience); and, transformation of time (i.e. the sense of time is distorted, either slows down or speeds up in the moment). It is suggested that these nine dimensions of flow closely link with the four movement elements of LMA (Tsachor & Shafir, 2017). For example, Csikszentmihalyi (1990) discovered that dancers who had more experiences of flow felt more in control of the dance, thus influenced their energy while performing, and thereby connects with the *Effort* movement element of LMA (Tsachor & Shafir, 2017). Further, performers with deeper flow states felt less self-conscious (*Body*) and felt more in tune with the environment (*Space* and *Shape*) compared to performers with less intense flow states (Csikszentmihalyi, 1990; Tsachor & Shafir, 2017).

Using design thinking to explore a design challenge: Identifying the threshold concepts in dance

Participants

To identify threshold concepts in dance, Lowri Edwards (researcher-academic) invited an expert in teaching and practising dance, Jane Bellamy to be a co-author. Jane's professional background in teaching dance in higher education alongside her expertise in LMA, resulted in her playing a dual role as both the practitioner and the academic in this project (practitioner-academic). Dance was mutually agreed, based on the expertise of the practitioner-academic and to complement the gymnastics background of the researcher-academic. During the initial discussion, they both agreed on two concepts/pedagogical tools that are essential for dance educators to allow performers to reach a 'state of flow'; these were LMA and *Imagery*. Additionally, an appropriate performer was identified whereby the practitioner had a professional rapport (former university student) and that the performer was able to clearly articulate knowledge of their bodily movement when performing dance. The roles and responsibilities of the researcher-academic, practitioner-academic and dance performer are summarised below.

Roles and responsibilities of the researcher-academic, practitioner-academic and dance performer

> *Researcher-academic (LE):* Observe interactions between the practitioner and performer during a dance session, collect, transcribe and analyse informal interview data.
>
> *Practitioner-academic (JB):* Create a dance sequence, offer guidance, feedback and support to the performer, use *Imagery* strategies to develop performers dance performance and principles of L MA.
>
> *Dance performer (AR):* Perform the dance as requested by the practitioner, co-construct aspects of the dance sequence.

Procedures and methods

The dance session lasted approximately three hours and was divided into three sections. The first section lasted thirty minutes and concentrated on sensory awareness, namely breathing, stretching and postural alignment exercises. The second section was a warm-up dance and consisted of dynamic stretching, aerobic exercises and such as running in curved and straight pathways and lasted approximately thirty minutes. The third and final section involved devising, practising and performing the dance sequence, and lasted approximately ninety minutes. Throughout this process, the researcher-academic noted observations of the interactions between the practitioner-academic and the performer. Observations were structured loosely around the context, use of *Imagery* examples and teaching strategies employed by the practitioner-academic and responses from the performer. Every *Imagery intervention* was followed up by a discussion between the practitioner-academic and the performer. These informal discussions gauged the performer's thoughts, feelings and emotions about the type of *Imagery* example used. Following the three-hour dance session, a thirty-minute formal interview between the practitioner-academic and performer was conducted to encourage the performer to reflect on what interventions worked best for them. Using a co-constructed approach, the session comprised the design thinking steps of inspiration, ideation and implementation to develop the performer holistically (Brown & Wyatt, 2010).

Data analysis

Inductive thematic analysis combined with interpretative phenomenological analysis were employed to analyse the observations and informal discussions in this case study. Thematic analysis is defined as 'a method for identifying, analysing and reporting patterns within data' (Braun & Clarke, 2006, p. 79). An inductive approach of thematic analysis was adopted to identify codes/themes that naturally emerged from the data that were not predetermined by pre-existing theoretical framework (Elo & Kyngas, 2007). Interpretative phenomenological analysis was employed to analyse the audio recordings of the discussions between the practitioner-academic and performer to explore their lived experiences of the dance (Reid, Flowers & Larkin, 2005). Interpretative phenomenological analysis 'attempts to explore personal experience and is concerned with an individual's personal perception' (Smith & Osborn, 2008, p. 53). This form of analysis has previously been adopted by Panebianco-Warrens (2014) who explored the dimensions of flow and the role of music in professional ballet dancers, and therefore relevant for the present case study.

Discussion: Outlining the generation of threshold concepts in dance

By the end of the three-hour dance session, the performer had experienced a sense of being in the zone:

> It just really felt, kind of like I was in the zone. When you just get it, and it takes over your body, almost like a feeling of 'I'm not consciously making this move, my body is doing it' and it felt good to do it in that way. And, then I forgot about that you guys were watching. My body just took over (Formal interview, performer).

This discussion aims to critically explore the threshold concepts that enabled the performer to reach the above state of feeling and being 'in the zone.'

Sensory awareness

The first part of the session aimed to heighten the performer's sensory awareness and interactions with her body and environment. Here, examples of *Metaphorical and Biological Imagery* (Franklin, 2013) were introduced to the performer coupled with open questioning techniques targeted at getting the performer to think about her connectedness with her body. The first intervention concentrated on breathing techniques whereby the performer was asked to concentrate on an 'energy flow to breathe up the front of the body and down the back, down to the pubic bone and repeat in a circular motion of breath in a soft manner' (Observation, researcher). This is an example that connects the *Body* and *Effort* movement elements of LMA (Tsachor & Shafir, 2017).

Other examples to develop the performer's sensory awareness included images to improve the performer's posture (Ekarin, 2016). For example, the practitioner asked the performer to imagine her 'pelvis was "like a bowl of water" that does not tip too far forward nor too far backwards, but in a neutral position' and that there was 'an "orange under her chin" to lengthen the neck' (Observations, researcher).

Both *Biological and Metaphorical Imagery* techniques employed by the practitioner were deemed effective to develop the performer:

> The 'orange underneath my chin' gave me the right position for my head, I felt. And then that kind of linked into my posture, where I was going backwards before, the orange image helped me keep it all in there. And the 'bowl,' with my pelvis, keeping that tucked in, not spilling forward, not spilling backwards like it was before (Formal interview, performer).

Indeed, this somatic approach adopted by the practitioner of concentrating on the senses (becoming) over physical practice (doing) supported the performer to develop performance (Baston & Swartz, 2007).

Co-construction and continuous reflection

As part of the dance sequence, the practitioner continually asked open-ended questions to gauge how the performer felt after each *Imagery* intervention. Such questions provoked a co-constructed environment that encouraged both practitioner and performer to reflect on and explore the most appropriate images to develop the performer further. Three influential and effective *Imagery* examples were 'a ball of energy,' 'water' and 'roots.'

To develop on the *Body* movement element during the main dance sequence, "*a ball of energy*" was introduced to place emphasis on specific parts of the body, that is, arms, legs and hips. Further, this *Imagery* example explored how different body parts connected while moving (Tsachor & Shafir, 2017). To achieve this, reflective questions were asked by the practitioner, such as, 'where is the ball of energy taking you?' and 'where does the ball of energy want to go…what body part?' (Observation, researcher). The performer's responses consequently shaped how the dance sequence evolved. Hence, having an open-mind to change and work together to co-construct the evolution of the dance were key for success. According to the performer:

> The 'ball of energy' gave me direction on where that move was going. And then it gave me the ability to do the whole movement fully, without feeling as if it was half a move. The ball of energy, it was in my hands, so it really went 'out' stretched (Formal interview, performer).

The 'ball of energy' was 'frequently revisited throughout the dance' (Observation, researcher), particularly when the performer found a specific movement challenging. This was an effective tool to take the performer back a step and concentrate on one area of the *Body*.

To develop the performer's movement dynamics, *Imagery* of 'meandering water' was presented. The idea for the meandering water was for movements to be '*nice and smooth, it never ends and it keeps going*' (Formal interview, practitioner). This example referred to the *Effort* and *Shape* movement elements of LMA, as there was a focus placed on light energy and how this influenced the performers interactions with the environment (Tsachor & Shafir, 2017). During the reflections, the performer offered an honest and critical view on how the 'meandering water' influenced her performance:

> I found that the (meandering) water changed the way I was moving, and it changed my memory of how I was supposed to move…I did like it, for the bits that were more flowy, so the movement on the floor where I was dragging my hands and my feet and it gave my head a lot more lightness. So, I was able to extend my eyes and my chin to look at my hands. I felt a lot more light. But that didn't help with parts of the movement that didn't need to be light (Formal interview, performer).

Indeed, this open dialogue between the practitioner and performer was crucial to achieve the desired co-constructed approach, and during the aspects of the dance where movement dynamics needed to be sharper and more powerful, the *Imagery* of 'shooting water like a geyser' (Observation, researcher) was presented:

> I liked the shooting water because it made me pick up the pace in some parts and give me the energy back that the previous water image didn't. Then, it did make me lose control in the parts where I had a bit too much energy, so I lost a little bit of control. So, I needed the shooting water in some parts and then the light water in other parts (Formal interview, performer).

This highlighted the importance of including *Imagery* examples that offer a mixture of lighter and darker dynamics in relation to the performer's attitude, purpose and energy while completing movements (i.e. *Effort*; Laban & Lawrence, 1974).

Another key intervention was using the 'roots' *Imagery* to help with the performer's grounding, balance and to make the performer more aware of her physical *Space*. Advice from the practitioner included: 'rooting feet into the ground' and 'rooting limbs into space, thinking about extending the roots' (Observations, researcher). The performance was much improved after this intervention in terms of the performer's direction of gestures, pathways of extending limbs and altered the spatial tensions (Tsachor & Shafir, 2017):

> So, when I was doing it (dancing with roots), I felt more extended. My body felt a lot more extended. And that, it wasn't just me dancing. It didn't feel like it was just me in that little bubble dancing. I was getting pulled out and around and moving, it's hard to explain it, so I was doing the movements and traveling outwards, more so than before (Formal interview, performer).

Through co-constructed reflection, the practitioner and performer were able to work identify the reaching possibilities of the performer's 'kinesphere'; which in turn, positively developed the overall performance (Tsachor & Shafir, 2017).

Independent experimentation with music

The final aspect to develop the performer was experimenting with different types of music independently. During the independent experimentation, the practitioner trialled two different types of music, the first being soft classical and the second was upbeat. The performer did not respond to the classical music in the first attempt. However, in the second attempt, the performer stated that she 'felt more connected, especially in the more softer movements' (Informal discussion, performer) and she 'looked really focused, every move was completed to the highest standard and at the right time, facial expression and eye contact was not fixed' (Observation, researcher). This suggests that the music helped her reach the state of flow to be in the zone, supported by her view:

> It (the classical music) helped me, because it helped me feel a lot more balanced in a way because it pushed me. With the leg swings, sometimes I didn't feel like I was so controlled, but with the music as the tempo was higher, I felt, right this is when it happens. It gave me a cue to, let me know that's when it (the move) needs to finish and when start the next (Informal discussion, performer).

That said, it is important to acknowledge that not all interventions worked, for example, the performer did not respond at all to the upbeat music and said: 'I had a lack of focus, none of the moves felt finished' (Informal discussion, performer). Thus, being broad-minded while experimenting with different ideas is key.

The independent practice also gave the performer an opportunity to synthesise different *Imagery* interventions and select her preferred ideas. Specifically, the practitioner asked: 'I gave you some time to put some of these strategies together. How did you find this exercise?' (Informal interview, practitioner), and the performer responded:

> I kind of just let my body…I didn't think too much about which part I wanted to be which image…I just let my body do it and then, thought 'yeah, now I'm the light water'… 'this feels like the shooting water' … 'this feels like the roots'… and it kind of all came together without me having to think, 'ok now I'm the root,' it just came more natural, more of a flow (Informal interview, performer).

This illustrates that the somatic approaches employed by the practitioner allowed the performer to develop an amplified sensory process while moving (Baston & Swartz, 2007). That is, the performer adopted a 'state of embodiment conducive to coordinated action' (p. 48), which in turn, allowed the performer to feel and be 'in the zone.'

Conclusion: Generating threshold concepts in dance

Following a discussion between the researcher-academic and practitioner-academic, the following threshold concepts for dance are proposed:

1   Develop a sensory awareness in order to maximise the dance performance, beyond the just the physical;
2   Consider meaningful *Imagery* examples that resonate with the performer and complement the movement dynamics;
3   Have an open mind and open dialogue between the practitioner and performer to co-construct the dance sequence;
4   Continually reflect on performance in relation to the 'what', 'how', 'where' and 'why' of movement (i.e. *Body*, *Effort*, *Space* and *Shape*);
5   Consider the influence of music to alter the dynamics of the performance;
6   Allow time for experimentation and adopt a 'trial and error' approach with different *Imagery* examples and types of music.

Based on the findings of the case study, an important point to highlight is that often the four movement elements of LMA (*Body*, *Effort*, *Space* and *Shape*) are commented on separately (Tsachor & Shafir, 2017). However, through adopting somatic approaches and pedagogical tools such as *Imagery*, it should be acknowledged that the four movement elements naturally interact to develop the performer holistically.

References

Anttila, E. (2016). The potential of dance as embodied learning [Conference session]. *Proceedings of A Body of Knowledge: Embodied Cognition and the Arts conference*, California. December 8–10, 2016.

Batson, G., & Schwartz R. E. (2007). Revisiting the value of Somatic Education in Dance Training through an inquiry into practice schedules. Journal of Dance Education, 7(2), 47–56.

Braun, V., &Clarke, V. (2006). Using thematic analysis in psychology. *Qualitative Research in Psychology*, 3(2), 77–101.

Brown, T., & Wyatt, J. (2010). Design thinking for social innovation. *Development Outreach*, 12(1), 29–43.

Csikszentmihalyi, M. (1990). *Flow: The Psychology of Optimal Experience*. New York: Harper Collins.

Ekarin, J. (2016). Re-contextualizing dance skills: Overcoming impediments to motor learning and expressivity in ballet dancers. *Frontiers in Psychology*, 7, 431. doi: doi.org/10.3389/fpsyg.2016.00431

Elo, S., &Kyngas, H. (2007). The qualitative content analysis process. *Journal of Advanced Nursing*, 62, 107–115.

Franklin, E. N. (2013). *Dance Imagery for Technique and Performance* (2nd ed.). Leeds, UK: Human Kinetics.

Jeong, E.-H. (2012). The application of imagery to enhance "flow state" in dancers (Doctoral dissertation). Available from https://core.ac.uk/download/pdf/10836166.pdf.

Laban, R.V., & Lawrence, F. C. (1974). *Effort, Economy of Human Movement*. London: Macdonald Evans.

Laban/Bartenieff Institute of Movement Studies. (2020). Laban Movement Analysis. Available from https://labaninstitute.org/about/laban-movement-analysis/.

Mainwaring, L. M., & Krasnow, D. H. (2010). Teaching the dance class: Strategies to enhance skill acquisition, mastery and positive self-image. *Journal of Dance Education*, *10*(1), 14–21.

Martin, J. (1989). *The Modern Dance*. Pennington: Princeton Book Company.

Meyer, E., & Land, R. (2003). Threshold Concepts and Troublesome Knowledge: Linkages to Ways of Thinking and Practising within the Disciplines. Enhancing Teaching-Learning Environments in Undergraduate Courses Project, Higher and Community Education. Universities of Edinburgh, Coventry and Durham, TLRP ESRI. Occasional Report 4.

Moore, C. (2009). *The Harmonic Structure of Movement, Music, and Dance According to Rudolf Laban: An Examination of His Unpublished Writings and Drawings*. Lewiston, N.Y: Edwin Mellen Press.

Nakamura, J., &Csikszentmihalyi, M. (2002). The concept of flow. In C. R. Snyder, & S. J. Lopez (Eds.) *Handbook of positive psychology* (pp. 89–105). New York: Oxford University Press.

Panebianco-Warrens, C. (2014). Exploring the dimensions of flow and the role of music in professional ballet dancers, *Muziki*, *11*(2), 58–78.

Reid, K., Flowers, P., &Larkin, M. (2005). Exploring the lived experience. *The Psychologist, 18*, 20–33.

Samaritter, R. (2009). The use of metaphors in dance movement therapy. *Body, Movement and Dance in Psychotherapy*, *4*(1), 33–43.

Smith, J. A., & Osborn, M. (2008). Interpretative phenomenological analysis. In J. A. Smith (Ed.), *Qualitative Psychology: A Practical Guide to Research Methods* (pp. 53–80). London, UK: Sage.

Tsachor, R.P., & Shafir, T. (2017). A somatic movement approach to fostering emotional resiliency through Laban movement analysis. Frontiers in Human Neuroscience, 11, Article 410. https://doi.org/10.3389/fnhum.2017.00410

Thompson, E. (2016). Introduction to the revised edition. In F. Varela, E. Thompson, & E. Rosch (Eds.), *The embodied mind: Cognitive science and human experience* (Revised ed.). (xvii–xxxiv). Cambridge, MA: MIT Press

Whitehead M. (2007). Physical literacy: Philosophical considerations in relation to developing a sense of self, universality and propositional knowledge. *Sport Ethics Philosophy*, *1*(3), 281–299.

Whitehead M. (2013). The history and development of physical literacy. *ICSSPE Bulletin Journal of Sport Science and Physical Education*, 65, 21–7.

Chapter 6

Towards the identification of the threshold concepts in parkour: A case study

Rosalie Coolkens, Nicolas Vanhole and Cloes Marc

Context

Belgium is a federal state consisting of three communities and three regions. The three communities are the Flemish community, the French community and the German community. The three regions are Flanders, Wallonia and Brussels-Capital. The Flemish, French and German speaking communities each have their own educational government. Education (i.e. physical education) is compulsory between the ages of 6 and 18 or until one graduates from secondary school. Pre-primary education is available for children from 2.5 to 6 years and although it is not mandatory, almost all children are enrolled. University colleges provide teacher education through a three-year professional bachelor (i.e. undergraduate) programme. Teachers holding their professional bachelor's degree in physical education (PE) can teach this subject in primary school (i.e. ages 2.5–12) and in all first two stages of secondary school (i.e. ages 12–16). They can also teach in the third stage of secondary school (i.e. ages 16–18), but only in vocational education. In Flanders, there are 13 universities offering a Physical Education Teacher Education (PETE) programme. Their curriculum consists of 180 ECTS and with PE, students choose another school subject (e.g. history, biology and French) or a component called 'recreational movement.' This component prepares students in sports and physical activity in non-school settings. PETE educators at universities are not expected to hold a PhD. All three Flemish universities offer Educational Masters (i.e. graduate) programme. Educational Masters programmes in PE prepare students for teaching in the third stage of secondary education and at university colleges. However, it is also possible to teach PE in primary schools and in stages 1 and 2 of secondary education. More information can be found in other publications (see De Knop, Theeboom, Huts, De Martelaer, & Cloes, 2005; De Martelaer, Seghers, Cardon, Haerens, De Boever, & Cloes, 2014; Iserbyt & Coolkens, 2019).

Introduction: Parkour as physical activity area within Belgium

The following case study illustrates sets of threshold concepts within the context of parkour. We selected parkour because of its characteristics and the growing interest in the 'fun culture' described in 1995 by the French sport sociologist, Alain Loret (Loret, 1995). He demonstrated that, during the Eighties, the traditional sports were confronted with the development of new sporting motivations, which established new relationships with the body and nature (Loret, 1995). Far from the stadiums, those who want to be or claim to be sporting strive for the right to surpass themselves, to exceed, but also, more simply, to play, have pleasure, and feel convivial. Sport practice evolved in two cultures. On one hand, the practices inscribed in a 'digital culture' take place in domesticated and standardised sites characterised by norms, which make possible to establish hierarchical distinctions between competitors. On the other hand, so-called 'analogic' practices occupy the natural or urban ecosystem, without respecting the regulations. These subscribe to the 'fun culture.'

Parkour is an individual activity in which a person tries to overcome various obstacles by means of swings, jumping, climbing and running (Coolkens, Ward, Seghers & Iserbyt, 2018). Someone who practices such activity is a 'traceur' (French origin). More PE teachers in Belgium prefer parkour above gymnastics when developing motor competencies. In both Flanders and Wallonia, the government define standards to develop motor competencies as, a healthy and safe lifestyle, social skills as well as positive self-concept (Council for Qualifications and Curriculum, 2009). The government does not prescribe content domains in PE. The PE teacher could choose to use parkour, gymnastics or other content domains to reach the standards. In general, the purpose of PE is to develop basic movement skills, which enables children to successfully function within the society and to prepare children for active participation in the movement culture. Whilst parkour has become a popular sport in Belgium, it is still a relative new activity within the PE curriculum. Another general purpose of the PE curriculum is to develop basic movement skills which enables children to successfully function within the society and to prepare children for active participation in the movement culture. As in primary schools, the secondary school PE curriculum aims at facilitating the adoption of a physically active lifestyle (Council for Qualifications and Curriculum, 2009). The time allocation for PE is 100 minutes per week and lessons are delivered by PE specialists. However, through our collective experiences, we believe because parkour is a lifestyle sport accessible for both sexes and matches people's leisure-sport tastes (Green, 2016), it has a positive contribution to play within PE and nurturing young people to lifelong physical activity.

All three authors have a certain expertise in parkour. Rosalie Coolkens used parkour as a physical activity area during all her research (Coolkens, Ward, Seghers & Iserbyt, 2018). She completed an initiator course parkour run by GymFed, the Flemish Gymnastic Federation in 2014 where she met Nicolas Vanhole, expert in teaching and practicing parkour. Together with Nicolas Vanhole she developed a book Parkour Primitives (Coolkens, Van Oost, Vanhole & Iserbyt, 2018). This book provides a practical guide for teaching parkour at school and/or leisure context. On a regular basis, she gives workshops focusing on parkour for elementary and secondary, pre- and in-service teachers. Nicolas Vanhole is one of the first practitioners of parkour in Belgium. He was a gymnast and discovered parkour by watching the movie 'Yamakasi' together with clips from David Belle, the founder of parkour. In 2006, he started imitating parkour moves with some friends in his neighborhood. He described this situation, as 'the moment when it all started, the beginning of a nice parkour story.' Until now, he is one of the best parkour practitioners and teachers in Belgium. Marc Cloes never practiced parkour itself, but he considers that if parkour would have existed when he was an adolescent, it would have been his sport. In fact, in the seventies, he had been drawn to the Natural Method (Hébert, 1974) and some forms of the 'parcours du combattant' proposed in PE lessons. During his free time, he engaged with the outdoors; climbing regularly on natural obstacles and jumping from one to another one. This gave him an ability to practice gymnastics during his PE studies. During the first decade of the 21st century, he enjoyed discovering the upsurge of groups training in parkour; a new discpline. The gradual introduction of the latter in initial and in-service PETE has been a source of pleasure for him and he has favoured it in the courses for which he was responsible at the University of Liege. He is deeply convinced that the practice of parkour is accessible to all and allows young people to experience extraordinary sensations by allowing them to 'play' with their limits and enrich their motor skills in a natural way.

All authors have biographies that shaped our beliefs and thoughts on Parkour. For Rosalie, parkour is an ideal content domain in PE, since everyone can move on their own ability level. It allows for differentiation, there is nothing like wrong or right, it has a great opportunity for a transfer of physical activity outside the PE class and the sport exists of fundamental motor skills (i.e. locomotor activities such as jumping, running and climbing) necessary to adopt a physically active lifestyle. For Nicolas, parkour is a way of life. It is not only a sport that he discovers, it is his profession and it is his leisure activity. For Nicolas, parkour represents memories of adolescence when he spent hours playing in nature with friends, climbing in trees, jumping from one branch to another one or experiencing obstacle races during PE lessons. These personal experiences influenced certainly his professional vision of the importance of the discovery of the natural environment for children's motor development.

In the remainder of this chapter, we will discuss (1) the identification of the socialisation elements that contributed to the career of the expert, practitioner and teacher; (2) the analysis of the variables that are considered as key elements for effective practice in parkour; (3) the description of the teaching principles and their relationships with learners' involvement and (4) the identification of threshold concepts and implications for praxis within the context of Parkour.

Analytical concepts

Our understanding of the threshold concepts within parkour has been informed through our engagement with the socio-ecological approach (Cloes & Roy, 2010). This approach is often used in health behaviour research suggesting that human behaviour results from an interaction between environmental, individual and interpersonal factors. A socio-ecological model emphasies the importance for interventions to target several levels of influence simultaneously to change an individual's behaviour. In drawing upon these principles, we consider that 'being in the zone or teaching to get in the zone' always take place in the context of a complex culture (Sallis et al., 2006). It is the combination of individual, environmental and policy influences to achieve changes in certain behaviour. As a 'new sport,' opinions that people have about Parkour are influenced by their own engagement with that specific activity with less normative influence from the society than traditional sports.

Using Design Thinking

To explore threshold concepts in parkour, Rosalie Coolkens and Marc Cloes began by identifying an expert involved in the practice and teaching of the activity. Based on her professional background, Rosalie proposed Nicolas Vanhole. As illustrated by his biography, Nicolas has been involved in several projects that both of them implemented during the last 10 years and he matched the profile needed.

After receiving Nicolas' agreement to be interviewed, the two academics discussed possible core concepts necessary 'to be in the zone' (practitioner perspective) or 'to bring someone in the zone' (teacher perspective) during parkour. The two sport pedagogy specialists prepared a semi structured interview guide, identifying a list of topics to be covered. Two main parts were planned: (1) Questions for expert teacher in parkour (background information; information about teaching parkour); (2) Questions for parkour practitioner (Background information; Information about doing parkour). This information seemed necessary to understand the students' learning needs when practicing parkour. Even if the expert's history began by practicing parkour before becoming a specialist teacher, we opted for beginning the interview with questions focusing on the teaching expertise. Such choice was based on the assumption that one should avoid influencing the teacher's representations on the notion of flow and focus his attention on the sensations perceived during practice.

The interview lasted 1.5 hours and was recorded and transcribed verbatim with a digital dictaphone. Both academics intervened freely, according to the responses of Nicolas. The sport pedagogy specialists separately selected key concepts within the practitioner responses and shared their analysis to begin identifying some threshold concepts. In the next section of the paper, we will develop four main topics: (1) The identification of the socialisation elements that contributed to the career of the expert as practitioner than teacher; (2) The analysis of the variables that are considered as key elements for an effective practice in parkour; (3) The description of the teaching principles and their relationships with learners' involvement; (4) The development of threshold concepts and implications for praxis.

Discussion: Outlining the generation of threshold concepts in parkour

Socialization elements that contributed to the career of the expert

During the interview, we explored some components from all layers of to the socio-ecological model (Sallis et al., 2006) that influenced his choice at the age of 16 to start with parkour. These included media (movie and online clips), neighbours, possibility to choose the hours when he wanted to train on a voluntary basis, activity looking cool, support of his parents etc. Nicolas seemed to have a natural predisposition for acrobatic activities. When he was a child, he practiced judo and was always trying to do 'some flips' in different locations. His mother insisted that he begin gymnastics. Nicolas started to practice parkour when doing gymnastics over many years. It was during a week internship for gymnastic training organised in another club: '... we saw a movie, a French movie: "Yamakasi." I think a lot of people discovered parkour through Yamakasi. So, I saw the movie and I was like, oh it's really cool. It's like gymnastics but even cooler.' (Interview – 0:10:51). This illustrates the impact of media, parents, sports club coupled with Nicolas' natural predisposition for acrobatic activities.

Interestingly, Nicolas did not begin parkour immediately but after watching online video clips of David Belle: 'I think I saw the movie when I was eleven and I saw the clips when I was fifteen ... It was on a Sunday afternoon after gymnastics training ... I persuaded my friends, ... We saw clips online and we try to imitate all those moves in a small playground.' (Interview – 0:11:31). One interesting thing is that that experience experienced with close friends: 'Just my really good friends of school ... a lot of people who I still see weekly...' (Interview – 0:13:46). Moreover, proximity of an appropriate place played a role: 'We were only living a minute by bike from my place, so it takes a kilometer and let's go jump on the streets.' (Interview – 0:14:02). Another factor to consider is the contact with few other groups who were training in parkour, and particularly one group formed in the same town. The practice was organised on a free basis: 'It's really free. It's like ... parkour. Like you text your friends and then some of them might be doing homework and some of them would {answer} I'll be joining ...' (Interview – 0:18:39). This part emphasise the importance of enjoyment and friendship, which are, according to Nicolas, central to the parkour culture. After one year, Nicolas' group established contacts with more skilled practitioners: '... we started talking to international people who gave us some advice on how to train and how to warmup.' (Interview – 0:19:39). In addition, they attended to international events where it was possible to receive cues to learn new approaches.

After three years of parallel practice, when entering into Higher Education, Nicolas decided to continue only parkour: 'I end up in gymnastics because it was like always at the same hours every week, so it was quite difficult to keep training and study. And, with parkour, I could just choose the hours when I wanted to train' (Interview – 0:09:29). This illustrates the transfer possibilities of parkour as an activity, as you don't need a gymnasium or coach. At the same time, with his friends, he started to teach twice a week in a sport facility. The activity continued but remained amateur until the group was invited to teach at the local circus school. The classes were immediately, full and there were some promotional events to sustain interest. It is noteworthy that he did not want to compete: 'I used to do competitions as a gymnast, which were really stressful. I hated it.' (Interview – 0:31:15). After graduation (Bachelor in PE), Nicolas and his friend worked in the circus school: 'I think we started with two classes 6–9 and two 9–12, then we did beginners, advanced, and adult classes … From that moment, every year we were making more classes.' (Interview – 0:29:52).

As underlined in the retrospective study of Nicolas' story, we believe that one of the conditions to perform parkour is the availability of fundamental motor skills, with a specific emphasis on acrobatic skills. As already mentioned, when he was a child, he practiced judo and was always trying to do some flips everywhere. '…Then my mum was like: "I really want you to stop trying those things on the grass or on the concrete. I want you to go to the gymnastics club." I start doing gymnastics and then I start doing parkour which is the same thing as gymnastics…' (Interview – 0:20:13). His mother insisted on him starting gymnastics. Gymnastics is an ideal content to develop the fundamental motor skills such as climbing, rolling, jumping, gliding and swinging. Such basis and experience allows the learner to feel competent and to progress in parkour in a safe way. Support of others (friends, parents, other practitioners …), availability of models (video clips, organisation of events …), and opportunities to develop structures (circus school) were other determining factors in this case. For current beginners, we consider that the professional development of teaching staff should contribute to the growing of the discipline. The latter has several advantages: a philosophy focused more on personal progression than on competition, a tradition of friendly support between participants, the reputation of being a cool activity, the low requirement of infrastructures. Alongside immersion in different environments, another key element of learning to move in parkour, is learning to practice safely.

Key elements of an effective/safe practice of Parkour

At the beginning, Nicolas and his friends were imitating all online video clips that they could find without respecting safety requirements: '… we were copying all those clips, but we didn't really know what we were doing. I think it was the most damaging year for the body until now …' (Interview – 0:14:02). Parkour is often seen as a dangerous activity but there are always different ways to do something, so safety can remain a priority. Moreover, Nicolas pointed out that the key factor is to show that the learner is competent: '*What I think is really important in parkour is success.*' (Interview – 1:03:49). Competence will grow with practice. Our expert has parkour sessions twice a week and weekly conditioning activities.

Among the necessary competences that someone doing parkour needs, the number one is to be able to determine ones' capability: '*... I can see it {the move to do} and judge myself, check if I'm able to do it and I can make a good judgement to know if I can try it in a safe way.*' (Interview – 1:11:47). A second determining competence is to try any movement in a controlled way, knowing exactly what to do if it does not work as expected: '*I can feel the jump, but I know exactly what to do if I don't make the jump ...*' (Interview – 1:12:30). A *traceur* should also be able to find a solution when facing an obstacle by using what has been learnt and by imagining new way of doing a movement: '*If they start thinking for themselves, they can see a jump, know how this is maybe too difficult, and {} do it in that {their} way.*' (Interview – 1:16:26).

Feeling is important in parkour: '*You do the warmup, you start jumping and there's always a moment you never know what it is, but there's always that moment when you feel warm and ready to do things you wanted to do.*' (Interview – 0:48:55). At the beginning of a session, the *traceur* tries small challenges then, little by little, increases the level of difficulty. In parallel, his level of readiness grows as well as his inner happiness: '*... your mind starts to get more and more into parkour. The body gets more and more into parkour.*' (Interview – 0:50:10). These feelings tell that one is ready to do a specific movement:'*. you are like "OK, I feel ready, I can do big jumps, I can do more challenging stuff"*' (Interview – 0:51:52).

It does not happen during each session. Sometimes, one feels ready to conquer one big jump as if the body and mind were under full control. Keeping calm is a priority: '*... people think that we do things because we can feel adrenaline. That's not the case, we wait until the adrenaline slows down because adrenaline doesn't give you a lot of control ...*' (Interview – 0:56:50). Taking a break, breathing-in and -out are necessary. It helps to be highly focused and to know exactly what to do. One can feel the movement to be done; the confidence is at a maximum: '*You feel completely ready to do certain jump and that's the best moment in parkour.*' (Interview – 0:57:13). Such feelings can be also possible in beginners: '*I think as soon as you know how to take decisions, as soon as you know how capable you are, I think you can feel the zone.*' (Interview – 1:21:30). Getting in the zone could be linked to the challenges the *traceur* is facing: '*When you have a challenge and it's hard enough and you have to work for.*' (Interview – 1:23:57). It means that the zone is linked to the personal characteristics and that teachers should encourage their learners to find it. As parkour offers easy individual adaptations, any practitioner should find a way to enter into his/her zone. That could explain why parkour is more valued than many other sports, given levels of mastery required before experiencing a sense of competence. If the learner decides alone which challenge he/she has to achieve, the intensity of the feeling will increase: '*I think getting into the zone will be more intense if you created, if you found that challenge yourself.*' (Interview – 1:24:00). And when one has achieved one challenge, it will be needed to practice again, but training is the only way to realise a dream.

Teaching the vision of parkour

The vision of the parkour teaching is based on an open non-competitive approach. Aiming for individual progression instead of competing against someone else: '*It's important to grow as a person … (there is) any competition so the whole atmosphere of the class is completely different . It is not about winning or losing what creates a different atmosphere.*' (Interview – 0:25:08).

Within parkour, the learner needs a training team that encourages and helps him/her to find and try out different tricks in different environments. Each teammate has another *vision of the environment*. All those visions and ideas together makes it a lot more interesting. Most parkour events exists of training together or workshops where someone is teaching certain parkour moves. There are some events with three kinds of competitions: a style, a speed and a skill competition. In the style competition, the learner shows the jury in predefined space what he/she can do. The speed competition is like a race while the skill competition where the '*traceur*' has to complete challenges. More recently, a new parkour activity appeared: the chase tag. It is a pursuit race with obstacles in the play area.

For Nicolas, it is important to avoid the comparison with others. In fact, when someone achieve a movement (vault, jump …), it is expected that teammates praise the performance. Such philosophy encourages people to interact and train: '*That's the reason why so many people train, just like encouraging each other and then try together.*' (Interview – 0:37:40). And reinforces teamwork: '*So that makes it like so much more interesting to train together because you have so much more things that you can try because everybody has different parkour vision.*' (Interview – 0:38:40). It is like the DNA of the activity: '*I think as soon as you're coming to a class, you can feel it and can see the way people train, give positive feedback to each other, and encourage each other.*' (Interview – 0:40:53).

Parkour sessions start with warming up and running. However, there are always entertaining and fun tasks to avoid boredom. Fun is a key element in the development of learners' experience of parkour. Another principle is mobility, para training, and conditioning but always connected to parkour tasks. Teaching parkour respects most of the conditions suggested to develop motivation (Viau, 2000). In addition, grouping of the learners in small groups lead by one teacher focusing on specific tasks corresponds to one of the TARGET framework dimensions (Ames, 1992). What teachers say and do is what creates a more task-involved or ego-involved climate. There are six factors that teachers have control over when they teach: (a) the task they ask their students to perform (T), (b) the amount of authority they allow their students to have (A), (c) the way rewards are given to students (R), (d) the way students are grouped (G), (e) how students are evaluated (E), and (f) the amount of time they allow students to complete a task (T). The acronym for each of these components is TARGET (Ames, 1992). The TARGET principles guide the approach in creating motivational climates being task-involving or ego-involving. In the interview, Nicolas strives for a task-involving climate during teaching i.e. different tasks are given to the students; the latter can choose the task they want to practice; they have equal opportunities to receive rewards; they work in small groups; evaluation is self-referenced; and time to practice is flexible. As a part of each lesson allows participants choice, autonomy is also promoted, for example, where and how to train: *'It's a big value because you can see how responsible, even a 6 year-old, can train. That's really cool to see.'* (Interview – 0:43:55). Open tasks where learners have to find their own solutions are also proposed systematically.

In summary, the whole teaching approach towards parkour applies all principles contributing to the development of a task involving climate and includes the following additional principles which link to parkour:

a.   During the cool down/stretching, the teachers show an inspiring video creating motivation. Using new technologies can also increase motivation. In the same vein, when trying new movements, taking and sharing video can be helpful to other people, as it can break a mental barrier by demonstrating that it is possible.
b.   Another teaching principle is to adapt the tasks to the level of each learner to maintain them in the area of 'délicieuse incertitude' (Brunelle, Drouin, Godbout, & Toussignant, 1988): *'Everybody has a way to do it.'* (Interview – 1:04:40). In that way, Nicolas considers that nothing is wrong for the learner as long as it is safe and that it respects the property. It means also that when learners find their own way to achieve a challenge, the teacher has to encourage them. This is not a priority for children: *'The main goal is to show to people what [they] are capable [to do] with the body in a certain situation.'* (Interview – 1:25:40).
c.   A final teaching approach important in parkour is for the teacher should go outside as often as possible as the diversity of the environment is more important: *'I think training outside is so important because … [in] a parkour gym, we can't recreate what is outside, how the structures are in a really strange shape.'* (Interview – 1:30:33).

Conclusion: Generating threshold concepts in and for parkour

The discussion between an expert in parkour and two specialists in sport pedagogy has been an interesting experience, as all had to engage in reflective practice aiming to better understand what is happening in the teaching-learning process in a new activity. Based on the experiences and the information collected through Nicolas' interview, we propose a series of threshold concepts that are crucial to the teaching *but also* experiencing parkour,

1.   Agree to try a movement and perceive it as a possible challenge;
2.   Learn to control his/her movement to guarantee is/her safety (maintaining a low level of excitement, imagining the movement to be realised, identifying the possible risks);

3. Demonstrate supportive behaviours to his/her classmates;
4. Be able to show persistence;
5. Show autonomy and creativity to find way to overcome barriers;
6. Listen to his/her body.
7. Develop a goal orientation for task mastery.

We pointed out that its success in parkour can be explained by characteristics specific to the fun culture, environmental influences but also by a series of pedagogical principles that are applied by the teachers to implement a task-involving climate. Parkour seems a nice activity to develop physical literacy in youth. A possible next step is to find ways in which these threshold concepts could now be nurtured within Physical Education more broadly.

References

Ames, C. (1992). Classrooms: goals, structures and student motivation. *Journal of Educational Psychology, 84*, 261–271.

Brunelle, J., Drouin, D., Godbout, P., & Tousignant, M. (1988). *La supervision de l'intervention en activité physique*, Montréal, Canada: Gaëtan Morin Editeur.

Cloes, M., & Roy, M. (2010). Le cheminement de l'approche écologique: du paradigme processus-produit au modèle heuristique du processus enseignement-apprentissage. In M. Musard, M. Loquet, & G. Carlier (Eds.), *Sciences de l'intervention en EPS et en sport: résultats de recherches et fondements théoriques* (pp. 13–33). Paris, France: Editions Revue EP.S. Retrieved from http://hdl.handle.net/2268/35774

Coolkens, R., Ward, P., Seghers, J., & Iserbyt, P. (2018). Effects of generalization of engagement in parkour from physical education to recess on physical activity. *Research Quarterly for Exercise and Sport, 89*(4), 429–439. doi: 10.1080/02701367.2018.1521912

Coolkens, R., Van Oost, J., Vanhole, N., & Iserbyt, P. (2018). Parkour primitives. *Praktijkboek.* Oud-Turnhout, Belgium: Gompel & Svacina.

Council for Qualifications and Curriculum. (2009). Decree of 30 April 2009 to ratify the final and developmental objectives in elementary and secondary education. *Department of Education and Training of the Flemish Government.* Accessed through https://www.kwalificatiesencurriculum.be/

De Martelaer, K., Seghers, J., Cardon, G., Haerens, L., De Boever, E., & Cloes, M. (2014). Physical education stimulating a healthy lifestyle and critical sports consumption in Belgium. In M.-K. Chin & C.R. Edginton (Eds.), *Physical Education and Health Global Perspectives and Best Practice* (pp. 43–56). Urbana, IL: Sagamore.

De Knop, P., Theeboom, M., Huts, K., De Martelaer, K., & Cloes, M. (2005). The state of school physical education in Belgium. In U. Pühse &M. Gerber (Eds.), *International comparison of Physical Education. Concepts. Problems. Prospects* (pp. 104–131). Oxford: Meyer & Meyer Sport.

Green, K. (2016, April). Can physical education be effective and, if so, how? *Paper Presented at the Consensus Conference Children, Youth and Physical Activity*, Copenhagen, Denmark.

Hébert, G. (1974). La méthode naturelle. *Education physique virile et morale. Tome 1 – Doctrine et enseignements pratiques* (7ème édition). Paris, France: Vuibert.

Iserbyt, P., & Coolkens, R. (2019). Physical education teacher education in Flanders (Belgium). In A. MacPhail, D. Tannehill, &Z. Avsar (Eds.), *European Physical Education Teacher Educaion Practices: Initial, Induction, and Professional Development* (pp. 25–26). Maidenhead, United Kingdom: Meyer & Meyer Sports.

Loret, A. (1995). *Génération Glisse. Dans l'eau, l'air, la neige…la révolution du sport des "années fun"*. Paris, France: Autrement.

Sallis, J., Cervero, R., Ascher, W., Henderson, K., Kraft, M., & Kerr, J. (2006). An ecological approach to creating active living communities. *Annual Review of Public Health*, *27*, 297–322.

Viau, R. (2000). Des conditions à respecter pour susciter la motivation des élèves. *Correspondance*. 5(3), 2–4.

Chapter 7

Unravelling threshold concepts in outdoor education

Christophe Schnitzler, Håkon Engstu and Mathilde Wassner

Context

In this chapter, we put forward the cultural phenomenon called *friluftsliv*, which is how outdoor education may be understood in Norway. Friluftsliv translates literally as 'open-air-life.' A more in-depth definition shows that it is a way '*...to stay and be physically active in open air in the leisure time with the aim of environmental change and nature experience*' (Klima- og Miljødepartementet, 2016). For Norwegians, friluftsliv is a way of living, thinking as well as a cultural practice. It encompasses a broad range of activities such as walking, hiking, biking, skiing, sunbathing, canoeing, fishing and hunting. Friluftsliv is also historically, culturally and politically supported, as in Norway, there is a 'right of access' to land, enacted in the *Outdoor Recreation Act* of 1957. It gives all individuals, regardless of citizenship, a right to pass through, and a right to rest and remain outdoors, regardless of land ownership (Hofmann, 2018). In that, friluftsliv is not equivalent to outdoor education, but this section aims to show how friluftsliv can contribute to threshold concepts in outdoor education. In this chapter, we will see how Friluftsliv is taught at the University of South-Eastern Norway, campus Notodden, in an international program in English.

Introduction: Threshold concepts in outdoor education – A proposal

School systems across the world have the duty not only to help the youth population to be part of the world but also to take up tomorrow's challenges. Safety, health, economic productivity, and wealth production are among the dominant challenges facing our society. In developed countries, these views based on the growth of the economy have links to a triple heritage of Greek, Judeo Christian, and Cartesian Rationalism, based on naturalistic and analogic ontologies. Naturalistic ontology postulates that there is a dichotomy between nature and humanity; analogic ontologies claim that there is a clear hierarchy among living creatures, a fundamental distinction in occidental societies (Descola, 2005). This anthropocentric vision focuses on the needs of people and views nature in light of these needs (Hoffman &

Sandelands, 2005). This has led the path to the development of pragmatist environmental pedagogical approaches in Outdoor Education (OE) in PE, based on ethics that postulates that the intrinsic values have little practical value (Light, 1996).

The examination of different articles and curriculum across developed countries (Smith, 1987; French programs in PE, Norwegian program for outdoor education) show that these approaches have led to the systematic promotion of three threshold concepts of OE: (1) safety education, (2) health promotion, (3) competence development. However, ecological concerns are growing worldwide and seem to call into question the appropriateness of anthropocentric views of nature (Kopnina, 2017), and invite an investigation of other ontologies in which the frontier between human and non-human world is blurred. Descola (2005) highlighted the existence of two other ontologies on which different civilisations on identified with to manage the relationship between humans and their environment: animism (in which things only differ by their appearances) and totemism (a totem being the link between human and non-human). These ontologies have led to a more eco-centric approach of the relationship between humans and nature, based on monist philosophy leading the path for two additional threshold concepts of OE: (4) cultural transmission and (5) sustainable development literacy.

The objective of this chapter is to unfold these threshold concepts and highlight the potential pedagogical benefits of each of them. Our point is to show that to achieve rich learning outcomes, a curriculum in outdoor education should be able to address all five of these threshold concepts. In the second part, we will present an outdoor education curriculum based on the Nordic concept of friluftsliv, which simultaneously promotes those five threshold concepts.

First threshold concept: Outdoor education for safety education

In most OE curriculum, there is a clear concern about ensuring security in outdoor education (Inspection Générale de l'Éducation Nationale IGEN, 2016). But an epidemiological approach to risk should not solely be taken into account when teaching OE. Delignières (1993) distinguishes three different types of risks: objective, subjective, preferential. Concerning objective risk, Dickson, Chapman, & Hurrell (2000) showed a rate of injury of about 1.3% in outdoor sports, and that the activity considered as high risk had, in fact, the lowest number of injuries as compared to other sports like basketball. This illustrates the finding that the public's perception of risk is different from that of experts (Dickson et al., 2000), and is, therefore, an opportunity to promote safety education through OE. This perception of the risk is called perceived risk (Delignières, 1993). For example, a slingshot top-rope climbing lowering in rock climbing might have a very low level of objective risk but be perceived by the pupil subjectively as very risky. During the learning process, he/she might comprehend that the situation is not objectively dangerous and decide to take the risk to engage in the situation. In that case, the learning process consists of matching objective risk and its subjective perception. The role of the educator is here to help the learner to perceive the opportunities for actions (called affordances) within the environment (Seifert et al., 2014). Outdoor education also offers the opportunity to change what Delignières (1993) calls the preferential risk. This risk is, to the participant, the most cost-effective level of risk he/she tolerates. For example, in rock climbing, to get a good grade, a pupil might present a climb route difficulty just below his/her level to be sure to complete it, otherwise, in order not to lose everything when falling. Outdoor activities therefore provide plenty of opportunities to help students adjust their preferential risk level with teachers helping them to perceive the affordances, and therefore contribute to safety education.

Second threshold concept: Outdoor education for social and motor competence development

A competence-based approach attempts to certify student progress based on demonstrated performance in some or all the aspects of a putative role in society (Grant, 2018). In a world where technology and complexity become more predominant every day, competence development is a key threshold concept to be promoted in school settings, being presented as a passport to youth's autonomy. Ewert (2012) describe a series of seven processes to explain the impact of outdoor and adventure programs on participants that lead to the development of competences (Figure 7.1).

The OE may improve social competence, that is, the capacity to be effective in social interaction (Rose-Krasnor, 1997). Smith (1987) wrote that OE helped,

> to promote the personal and social development of pupils by increasing their knowledge and understanding of themselves as individuals and as members of groups. This includes helping them to: -grow in awareness of their own physical capabilities; -learn to work independently and co-operatively; -communicate their experiences to others; -respond expressively and creatively to stimuli; -gain confidence, self-reliance, and perseverance (p. 213)

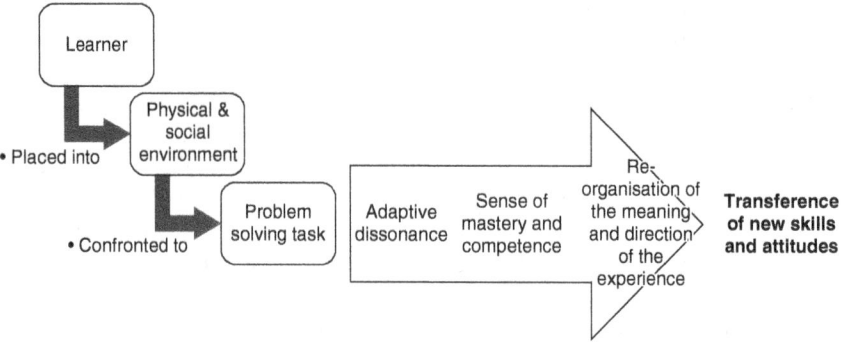

Figure 7.1 Potential processes to explain the impact of outdoor and adventure programs on competence development among learners.

Source: Adapted from Ewert 2012.

Different academic work has backed this claim with children (White, 2012), teenagers and young adults (Breunig, O'conell, Todd, Anderson, & Anderson, 2017), at-risk children (Ungar, Dumond, & Mcdonald, 2005).

A motor competent person in OE is able to confront versatile environments and environmental conditions one can find in, orienteering, rock climbing, and so on (Walsh and Golins, 1976). Seifert et al. (2014) showed that to become competent, a performer should actively interact with his/her environment to perceive the affordance it provides. This exploration might result in the emergence of different coordination patterns. By taking up different challenges in changing and versatile environments, and with the expert help provided by the teacher, pupils are in a configuration where they learn to face higher levels of complexity, thus fully contributing to motor competence development.

Third threshold concept: Outdoor education health promotion

In a meta-analysis, Mygind et al. (2019) showed that 60% of the studies indicated benefits for mental, physical, and social outcomes for children and teenagers. They noted a predominance of psychosocial benefits (self-esteem, cognitive indicators). Children, particularly boys, have a 1.37 odd of an epoch to be in moderate-vigorous PA levels in green spaces as compared to non-green urban environments (Wheeler et al., 2010). Viewing green spaces increases the autonomic control of the heart. Walking in green spaces improves self-esteem to a greater extent compared to attending social club activities. People who walked on farmland tended to perceive less stress and negative affect compared with walking in an urban environment (Barton, Griffin, & Pretty, 2012). State anxiety reduction has been reported following green exercise experiences (Marselle, Irvine, & Warber, 2013) and correlations between active involvement in environmental groups and positive health, wellbeing, and social connectedness established (Mackay & Neill, 2010). A meta-analysis revealed that a walk/run in a natural environment (e.g. public parks) provides psycho-emotional benefits, such as revitalisation and feelings of tranquillity (Li et al., 2011). To Yeh et al. (2016), the affordances provided by green environments might have this health-enhancing effect, as 'the ever-changing variety of information [within green environments] enables individuals to select locations that hold their fascination and attention and contribute to feelings of respite.' (p. 948)

The definition and scope of health broadened further recently. In the 1984 version, the WHO defines health as 'the extent to which an individual or group is able to realise aspirations and satisfy needs and to change or cope with the environment' (p. 4).

It, therefore, becomes a resource subject of teaching (Potdevin, Porrovecchio, Dieu, Racodon, & Schnitzler, 2017). Baldwin, Persing, & Magnuson (2004) outlined that outdoor and adventure education programs often seven common characteristics:

1 Planned and purposive use of adventure-based activities with specific goals.
2 Real-life learning contexts.
3 Participant becomes an agent of change.
4 Goal-directed challenges necessitating the use of individual or group generated solutions.
5 Outdoor or natural environment setting.
6 Small group (usually ten or less) context.
7 Structured facilitation.

Using these, PE should envision outdoor education as a way to both enhance bio-physical health through green exercise, but also to help learner enhancing their health literacy by promoting outdoor and/or adventure curriculum

Eco-centered threshold concepts

Promoting safety education, competence development, and health often requires impacting the environment in which OE takes place, which might explain the exponential development of outdoor facilities in the last decades (ski stations, golf, kayak and rock climbing). These facilities are good examples of unsustainable development practices in a world with limited resources. Often, the question of societal sustainability is set aside in OE, even though it has become a vital question. Barnosky et al. (2012) consider that the overuse of the planet's resources might lead to a global collapse that could jeopardise the existence of the human race (Barnosky et al., 2012). In 2017, the United Nations adopted the 2030 Agenda for Sustainable Development. Among the 17 goals, the sustainable development goal n°4 highlights the need to *'ensure that all learners acquire the knowledge and skills needed to promote sustainable development, including, among others, through education for sustainable development and sustainable lifestyle'* (United Nation, 2017, p. 21).

Dale and Newman (2005) advocate that sustainable development education and literacy is essential and should incorporate an interdisciplinary approach that should focus on the interaction between social and ecological systems. However, sustainable development education still seems to be characterised by stakeholders' disagreement, unclear goals, poor understanding and data uncertainty, making it a 'wicked problem' (Blackman et al., 2006). In the following section, we examine how sustainable development literacy and cultural transmission can be threshold concepts of OE complementary to those presented above in this article.

Fourth threshold concept: Outdoor education as a vector of sustainable development literacy

Achieving sustainability literacy through OE need a more eco-centered approach to the relation of human with its environment. It requires a change of perspective that positions humanity not aside but belonging within the environment thus promoting more contemplative practices, which allow the participants to 'be absorbed' in their environment (Gurholt, 2008). Schultz, (2000) showed experimental evidence for three different types of environmental concerns, that is, egoistic (me, my lifestyle, my future and my health), altruistic (all people, children and my community), and biospheric (animals, plants, marine life and birds). Promoting sustainable development literacy requires the promotion of biospheric concerns to learners, therefore, helping the learner to establish a comprehensive existential perspective that originates from aesthetic and emotional relations with nature through a direct and frequent encounter with nature (Sandell & Ohman, 2010). In Scandinavian countries, friluftsliv is included in OE as part of the curriculum moments of real encounter and contemplation with nature. Afterward, the learner is asked to reflect on these moments, to examine if and how they established a connection with nature.

Fifth threshold concept: Outdoor education as a vector of cultural transmission

There seems to be a contradiction in considering that OE is a place for cultural transmission. In naturalistic views, nature is, by definition, non-human, so how can it be a place for cultural transmission? A change of the underlying ontologies and philosophies is therefore necessary (Descola, 2005). If the natural environment is part of our culture, we are also part of nature and co-evolve. In that view, the opposition between nature and culture becomes irrelevant (Descola, 2005). The learner is thus invited to learn how people develop a harmonious relationship with their surroundings and preserve the balance within the ecosystem. They learn the history of their environment and how it has evolved in relation to human implantation, traditional buildings, or sheltering skills, the traditional use of natural resources for survival with minimum impact. How to use the local wood for heating purposes, how to use local plants for medical and nutritional purposes, what the local animals are, and how to fish and hunt them becomes part of this teaching.

In this first part of our chapter, we emphasised that five threshold concepts could be promoted to achieve rich learning outcomes (Dennehy & Chambers, 2019) in outdoor education: security, competence development, health literacy, sustainable development literacy and cultural transmission. Most of the outdoor and adventure education curricula throughout the world promote the first three threshold concepts, probably because they are compatible with the goal of competence development. But as sustainability becomes a major challenge in the 21st century and onwards, it is very likely that the latter two questions will soon be a major issue in education. The sum requires curriculum planners to include not only anthropocentric competence-based approaches but also promote eco-centric approaches that necessitate contemplative and emotional encounters with nature. The second part of this chapter display an example of a 1-year outdoor education program which seeks to promote these 5 threshold concepts simultaneously.

Promoting these five threshold concepts simultaneously: An example from the international outdoor education program at University of South-Eastern Norway

Friluftsliv pedagogies

The main goal for teaching friluftsliv in Norwegian school is to develop pupils' competences and skills needed to perform friluftsliv on their own. '*In the Norwegian tradition, friluftsliv is not regarded as a special form of education. It reflects on the educational opportunities that may be sought and taken advantage of, in and through friluftsliv*' (Haslestad, 2002). Friluftsliv is, first of all, *friluftsliv* – a tradition and a way of living (Tordsson, 2006), influenced by institutionalised pedagogical practices (Hofmann, 2018). To Bjørn Tordsson (2006), these pedagogies rely on two alternatives. First – the methods we use in teaching skills like reading a map or paddling a canoe can be seen as didactical and pedagogical approaches *in* friluftsliv. Second is the perspective of friluftsliv *as* pedagogics: the simple life in nature, where we participate as whole human beings with our thoughts, bodies and feelings, is in itself a way to develop human qualities (Tordsson, 2006).

Friluftsliv in physical education program, sport, and outdoor learning

The core of the learning process within the study program in Physical Education, Sport and Outdoor Learning (PESOL) at the University of South-Eastern Norway consists of trips and visits to local schools, which promotes the acquisition of threshold concepts such as knowledge, skills and competences. The didactics rely upon the discovery learning principles (Gurholt, 2008), experiential learning (Hofmann, 2018), and friluftsliv guidance (*friluftslivsveiledning*) (Hofmann, 2018). The teacher is a supervisor during the classes and the different trips organised during the program. Here, the term supervision is used here to describe the educational work of the teacher and leader of groups in nature, incorporating ideas of modern education (Hofmann, 2018, p. 71). '*The nature guide's task is to teach people about nature. The friluftsliv guide's task is to teach people to enjoy being in nature*' (Ulstrup, 2007).

Friluftsliv and safety education

We focus on competencies and skills needed to perform friluftsliv safely as part of both school and everyday life, in different natural environments, and at different times of the year. Students learn to aid and rescue their partners but also how to skilfully handle different types of equipment (Utdannings- og forskningsdepartementet, 2003). By the end of the semester, students should be able to: '*Plan, carry out and evaluate trips and outdoor activities in different landscapes and surroundings*' and '*Be equipped for outdoor life activities in different landscapes and surroundings'* (University of South-Eastern Norway, 2019). A fundamental notion promoted is summarised by the Norwegian expression *'tur etter evne' (trip according to one's abilities)*, meaning planning trips in which everyone will be able to participate (Hofmann, 2018). Students are gradually given more responsibility within the organisation of the trips. For each trip, teachers or students draft three plans A, B and C. Plan C is a safety plan, taking into account critical situations such as an accident or other predicaments (Hofmann, 2018, p. 100). Teachers also teach safety during the trips, through instructions of first aid or rescue exercises in snow or on water.

Friluftsliv and social and motor competence development

In our program, students are expected to *'use outdoor life as a pedagogical method and a didactical tool in schools or with other target groups'* (University of South-Eastern Norway, 2019). They have to gather in small and bigger groups (from 2 to 30) to achieve different goals such as planning the trip, cooking dinner, write a report and so on. The teacher's role here is to help them in achieving the social potential in the group. Frilufstliv does not include the idea of motor competence development (Tordsson, 2010), but develops the idea of using the natural landscape as an arena for learning. Friluftsliv is therefore considered a facilitator to motoric development (Fjørtoft, 2010), so it is also assessed during the semester at USN – in addition to friluftsliv.

Friluftsliv and health promotion

The core goal of PE in Norway is to develop and stimulate lifelong physical activity, following friluftsliv objectives. *'Physical education as a general study subject shall inspire physical activity in all aspects of life and inspire lifelong enjoyment of being physically active.'* (Kunnskapsdepartementet, 2006). In this program, students learn how to *'use nature and outdoor landscapes as arenas for learning and activity, in school or as part of people's everyday lives'* (University of South-Eastern Norway, 2019). Friluftsliv, therefore, lays the path the condition for an active lifestyle.

Friluftsliv as a vector of sustainable development literacy

Friluftsliv contributes to the promotion of a holistic view of the relationship between man and nature. *'Outdoor life touches us in body, mind and soul. Education must corroborate the connection between understanding nature and experiencing nature.'* (Kunnskapsdepartementet, 2006. p. 38) In our program, students are thus encouraged to adopt an eco-centric perspective during their trips. Also, a key element in the program is the strong focus on carrying out the trips without *'leaving any trace behind.'* How clean the place is when a student leaves is part of the assessment: removing the remains from a fireplace, burning the toilet paper, taking the waste back from the trip, all this is part of the assessment.

Friluftsliv as a vector of cultural transmission

Frilufstliv represents a specific marker of Norwegian culture (Gåsdal, 2007), thus offering opportunities for intercultural education, as students should, at the end of the program, be able to: '*Reflect on intercultural questions regarding outdoor life and nature in different cultures and educational systems*' (University of South-Eastern Norway, 2019). Trips are key to immerse the students in Norwegian culture. They are meant to show local examples of practice as well as seeing these as national activities, in order to help the students understand the concept of friluftsliv as a cultural practice, with its own intrinsic value.

Friluftsliv is different from a mere sport in nature. For example, we do not present cross country skiing only as a sport, but also as an important part of Norwegian culture as it was a mean of transportation adapted to the local environment. In our program, we seek to teach students not only how to ski but also to help them reflect on the question of why they are skiing. In the next section, we will present some personal experiences and learning outcomes from one of these students who participated in this program.

Section 3: My Friluftsliv experience: A foreign learner's view on the curriculum

Interview of Mathilde W., a 21 years-old French student in the Friluftsliv education program in Notodden – September 2018 to June 2019.

Did you enjoy this year in Norway? Why?
I loved it, although initially I planned to go to Australia. I was positively surprised by what I experienced there in the nine months and the strength of the ties we built among students. It is probably the way the program was designed. Notodden is a small town in Norway. We were coming from 10 different countries, still we had something in common when we arrived: we were all lost at first in an unknown culture, living in the same place and discovering life in Norway together. The local students were used to this way of life, not us, so they probably did not feel this year with the same intensity as we did, even though we were in the same class during practice. These locals and international mixed classes helped to also create some bounds with the local students, but the links were just not as strong as among Erasmus students.
How many outdoor activities did you practice there, with how many teachers?
About 6: orienteering, children's outdoor playing, cross country skiing, ice skating, canoeing and hiking. We also had six different trips with an overnight stay. There were four teachers in total to support the entire program
What is an outdoor activity for you?
It is an activity that one can practice in a natural environment or outside urban life, in a natural setting.

What is a natural setting, then?

It is a space untouched by humans, but the definition is not so clear to me.

What is different when you compare outdoor activities in France and outdoor life/ Friluftsliv program in Norway?

In Norway, we sought to be more connected to nature. We slept in tents there, whereas in France it was always concrete structures. Also, the content was richer: in France, it was all about technique. In Norway, we spent time in nature; we were encouraged to appreciate it for what it was. There were technical contents also, but this was far from being the main goal of the teaching. There was also time to learn to read the natural environment: what are the different types of snow, of avalanches, which trees, plants or animals populated these places, what was the history of the place. In other words, there was more to learn than just being the fastest person to go from A to B. In Norway, we established a real connection with the place. I also learned to appreciate nature, developed a 'leave no trace' ethic, that is, respect the environment and leave it in the same state. I have learned different skills (how to kayak, ski and ice skate), but also how to use nature (what type of tree to cut to make fire, how to build a shelter, an igloo, or a sauna out of branches and stones) and finally to appreciate nature itself, from an experiential point of view by listening to birds, watching animals or its traces, or walking on an iced lake. The fact that we had to work in groups helped to develop my social skills, that is, learning how to 'let go' and trust other people work together to make things easier. For example, we had to cook for a large group in sometimes very uncomfortable settings (wood fire, challenging weather conditions). The group was a real resource and made things much easier to complete the task.

In France, there is no such emphasis for team building. Your friend will encourage you, but your grade, your performance, are individual. You don't need the group to be a good performer in outdoor education in France.

From your experience, how does French and Norwegian program compare in outdoor education?

I think by experiencing Friluftsliv in this Norwegian outdoor education program, I learned to appreciate nature for itself and realise how fragile it is, thanks to informal knowledge gathered through conversation with my teachers and peers during our trips. This preoccupation was not put forward in France. There was some information about nature reserves and endangered wildlife, but no knowledge was attached to it, and we were not encouraged to stay in nature to contemplate: we had to do something with it. In France, the end of the internship consisted of a timed circuit that provided us with a grade.

How important are outdoor activities to you now that you have been through this extensive outdoor education program in Norway?

I would say that before, it was just a matter of playing sports in nature. Now it is a way of appreciating nature through the effort, in a green environment

You plan to become a PE teacher. As a future professional, what is the importance you grant to outdoor activities within PE?

To me, this is a critically important activity. It is essential to exercise in the outdoors, but this is not the only reason. We should use natural settings and parks to teach children what nature is, how beneficial it is for them and their health.

Have you ever experienced the state of 'flow' in one of your outdoor activities?

One time on a trip, we did off-track cross-country skiing. It was very uncomfortable and hard, but I knew I was capable of doing it, and the landscape was wonderful, which created a unique feeling of satisfaction. I guess this was as close as I can be from this state of flow, as I felt at the same time safe, connected to my environment, competent and healthy.

Conclusion

In this chapter, we sought to highlight the different threshold concepts that could be promoted within outdoor education. From the literature, at least five have emerged: (1) safety education, (2) health promotion, (3) competence development, (4) sustainable development literacy and (5) cultural transmission. We also linked these threshold concepts to the promotion of different views of the relationships between humans and nature. Also, concept 1–3 requires an anthropo-centered approach, concept 4 and 5 requires a more eco-centric approach to our relationship with nature. In the second part of the chapter, we argued that the Norwegian approach of Friluftsliv indeed implicitly integrated the challenge of promoting these five threshold concepts simultaneously and provided examples for each of them. Finally, the interview in the last part of the chapter gave us an insight into the effectiveness of the program concerning these threshold concepts, and how experiencing the Friluftsliv approach might differ from more traditional outdoor education programs provided in other countries like in France. It might not be possible to transpose Friluftsliv as it is in different countries, as it being so culturally situated. However, we think that these practices should be adapted to the specificities of each culture to make them relevant, bearing in mind that quality education in outdoor activity should provide rich learning outcomes, and this, based on at least the five threshold concept we highlighted.

Acknowledgement

We wish to thank Gilian Cante for helping us proofreading the document.

References

Baldwin, C., Persing, J., & Magnuson, D. (2004). The role of theory, research, and evaluation in adventure education. *Journal of Experiential Education, 26*(3), 167–183.

Barnosky, A. D., Hadly, E. A., Bascompte, J., Berlow, E. L., Brown, J. H., Fortelius, M., … Smith, A. B. (2012). Approaching a state shift in Earth's biosphere. [Review]. *Nature, 486*(7401), 52–58. doi: 10.1038/nature11018

Barton, J., Griffin, M., & Pretty, J. (2012). Exercise-, nature- and socially interactive-based initiatives improve mood and self-esteem in the clinical population. [Clinical Trial]. *Perspect Public Health*, *132*(2), 89–96. doi: 10.1177/1757913910393862

Blackman, T., Greene, A., Hunter, D., McKee, L., Eliott, E., Harringon, B., ... Williams, G. (2006). Performance Assessment and Wicked Problems: The Case of Health Inequalities. *Public Policy and Administration*, *21*(2), 66–80.

Breunig, M., O'conell, T., Todd, S., Anderson, L., & Anderson, Y. (2017). *The Impact of Outdoor Pursuits on College Students' Perceived Sense of Community*. 551–572. Retrieved from https://doi.org/10.1080/00222216.2010.11950218

Dale, A., & Newman, L. (2005). Sustainable development, education and literacy. *International Journal of Sustainability in Higher Education*, *6*(4), 351–362. https://doi.org/10.1108/14676370510623847

Delignières, D. (1993). Risque préférentiel, risque perçu et prise de risque. In J. Famose (Ed.), *Cognition et performance* (pp. 79–102). Paris: INSEP.

Dennehy, N. & Chambers, F. C. (2019). *Connected Curriculum: Principles of Assessment*. University College Cork: 10.

Descola. (2005). *Par-delà nature et culture*. Paris: Gallimard.

Dickson, T., Chapman, J., & Hurrell, M. (2000). Risk in outdoor activities: The perception, the appeal, the reality. *Journal of Outdoor and Environmental Education*, *4*(2), 10–17. doi: 10.1007/bf03400717

Ewert, A. (2012). The role of adventure education in enhancing health-related variables. The international journal of health, wellness, and society, *2*(1) 75–87.

Fjørtoft, I. (2010). Promoting motor skills in young children: learning through landscapes. In K. Thomson, & A. Watt (Eds.), *Connecting paradigms of motor behaviour to sport and physical education* (pp. 118–130). Tallin: TLU Press.

Gåsdal, O. (2007). Norwegians and friluftsliv; are we unique? In B. Henderson, & N. Vikander (Eds.), *Nature First: Outdoor Life the Friluftsliv Way* (pp. book). Toronto: Natural Heritage Books.

Grant, G. (2018). On competence: A critical analysis of competence-based reforms in higher education European council (2018): Council recommendation of 22 may 2018 on key competences for lifelong learning. *Official Journal of the European Union*.

Gurholt, K. P. (2008). Norwegian Friluftsliv as Bildung – a Critical Review. In P. Becker & J. Schirp (Eds.), *Other ways of learning*. Marburg.

Haslestad, K.-A. (2002). På leting etter friluftsliv i grunnskolens læreplaner: ser vi en utvikling fra vage anbefalinger til klare føringer? *Norsk pedagogisk tidsskrift (trykt utg.)*. 86(2002)nr. 4, 251–262.

Hoffman, A., & Sandelands, L. (2005). Getting Right with Nature. *Organization & Environment*, *18*(2), 141–162. doi: 10.1177/1086026605276197

Hofmann, A. R. (2018). *Norwegian friluftsliv: A way of living and learning in nature*. Münster: Waxmann.

Inspection Générale de l'Education nationale IGEN. (2016). l'exigence de la sécurité dans les activités physiques de pleine nature.

Klima- og Miljødepartementet. (2016). *Meld. St. 18 Friluftsliv*. Oslo. Retrieved from https://www.regjeringen.no/contentassets/9147361515a74ec8822c8dac5f43a95a/no/pdfs/stm-201520160018000dddpdfs.pdf.

Kopnina, H. (2017). Testing ecocentric and anthropocentric attitudes toward the sustainable development (EAATSD) scale with bachelor students. *REBRAE*, *10*(3), 457. doi: 10.7213/rebrae.10.003.ao08

Kunnskapsdepartementet. (2006). *Læreplanverket for Kunnskapsløftet.* (82-486-0397-0). [Oslo]: Kunnskapsdepartementet; Utdanningsdirektoratet.

Li, Q., Otsuka, T., Kobayashi, M., Wakayama, Y., Inagaki, H., Katsumata, M., ... Kagawa, T. (2011). Acute effects of walking in forest environments on cardiovascular and metabolic parameters. [Controlled Clinical Trial Research Support, Non-U.S. Gov't]. *Eur J Appl Physiol, 111*(11), 2845–2853. doi: 10.1007/s00421-011-1918-z

Light. (1996). compatibilism in political ecology. In A. a. K. Light, E. (Ed.), *Environmental Pragmatism* (pp. 161–184). New york: Routledge.

Mackay, G., & Neill, J. (2010). The effect of "green exercise" on state anxiety and the role of exercise duration, intensity, and greenness: a quasi-experiment study. *Psychol of Sport & Exerci, 11*(3), 238–245.

Marselle, M., Irvine, K., & Warber, S. (2013). Walking for well-being: Are group walks in certain types of natural environments better for well-being than group walks in urban environments? *Int J of Envir Health Res and Public Health, 10*(11), 5603–5628.

Mygind, L., Kjeldsted, E., Hartmeyer, R., Mygind, E., Bolling, M., & Bentsen, P. (2019). Mental, physical and social health benefits of immersive nature-experience for children and adolescents: A systematic review and quality assessment of the evidence [Review]. *Health Place, 58,* 102136. doi: 10.1016/j.healthplace.2019.05.014

Potdevin, F., Porrovecchio, A., Dieu, O., Racodon, M., & Schnitzler, C. (2017). Eduquer à la santé par l'activité physique. En quoi les modèles de l'évolution du concept de santé influencent-ils les stratégies d'éducation à la santé chez les enseignants d'Education Physique et Sportive? *Revue Education, Sport et Santé.*

Rose-Krasnor, L. (1997). *The nature of social competence: A theoretical review.* Social Development, 6(1), 111–135. doi: 10.1111/j.1467-9507.1997.tb00097.x

Sandell, K., & Ohman, J. (2010). Educational potentials of encounters with nature: reflections from a Swedish outdoor perspective. *Environmental education research, 16*(1), 113–132. doi: https://doi.org/10.1080/13504620903504065

Schultz, P. W. (2000). New Environmental Theories: Empathizing With Nature: The Effects ofPerspective Taking on Concern for Environmental Issues. *Journal of Social Issues, 56*(3), 391–406. doi: 10.1111/0022-4537.00174

Seifert, L., Wattebled, L., Herault, R., Poizat, G., Ade, D., Gal-Petitfaux, N., & Davids, K. (2014). Neurobiological degeneracy and affordance perception support functional intra-individual variability of inter-limb coordination during ice climbing. [Comparative Study Research Support, Non-U.S. Gov't]. *PLoS One, 9*(2), e89865. doi: 10.1371/journal.pone.0089865

Smith, P. (1987). Outdoor education and its educational objectives. *Geography, 72*(3), 209–216.

Tordsson, B. (2006). *Perspektiv på friluftslivets pædagogik.* Haderslev: CVU Sønderjylland, University College.

Tordsson, B. (2010). *Friluftsliv, kultur og samfunn.* Kristiansand: Høyskoleforl.

Ulstrup, S. (2007). Nature Guidance and Guidance in Friluftsliv. In B. Hendrson &N. Vikander (Eds.), *Nature First – Outdoor Life The Friluftsliv Way.* Toronto: Natural Heritage Books.

Ungar, M., Dumond, C., & Mcdonald, W. (2005). Risk, resilience and outdoor programmes for at-risk children. *Journal of Social Work, 5*(3), 319–338. doi: 10.1177/1468017305058938

United Nation (2017). Transforming our world: The 2030 agenda for sustainable development.

University of South-Eastern Norway. (2019). Study plan for Physical Education, Sport and Outdoor Learning, 2019, from https://www.usn.no/english/academics/study-and-courseplans/#/studieplan/932_2019_H%C3%98ST

Utdannings- og forskningsdepartementet. (2003). *Rammeplan for Faglærerutdanning i kroppsøving og idrettsfag*. Oslo: Utdannings- og forskningsdepartementet Retrieved from http://www. regjeringen.no/upload/kilde/kd/pla/2006/0002/ddd/pdfv/175791-2rammeplan_2003_faglaererutd_kroppsovingidrettsfag.pdf.

Walsh, V., & Golins, G. L. (1976). *The Exploration of the Outward Bound Process*. Denver, CO: Colorado Outward Bound School.

Wheeler, B. W., Cooper A. R., Page, A., Jago, R. (2010). Greenspace and children's physical activity: A GPS/GIS analysis of the PEACH-project. *Preventive Medicine, 51*(2), 148–52. doi: 10.1016/j.ypmed.2010.06.001

White, R. (2012). A sociocultural investigation of the efficacy of outdoor education to improve learner engagement. *Emotional and Behavioural Difficulties, 17*(1), 13–23. doi: 10.1080/13632752.2012.652422

Yeh, H. P., Stone, J. A., Churchill, S. M., Wheat, J. S., Brymer, E., & Davids, K. (2016). Physical, psychological and emotional benefits of green physical activity: An ecological dynamics perspective. *Sports Med, 46*(7), 947–953. doi: 10.1007/s40279-015-0374-z

Cultivating values through *Budo*: Instilling *Reigi* (Respect) in Japanese Junior High School *Kendo*

Yoshinori Okade, Kazuhiro Shibata and George Jennings

Context

Japan has one Curriculum of Study (CoS in education) at each school level, elementary school (6-12 years old), junior high school (13-15 years old) and senior high school (16-18 years old). This document is legally mandated by the Japanese Government (MEXTb). Time allocation, objectives, content and treatment of each subject content are thereby described in this document. School curricula must be implemented based on this document, which is revised every ten years according to education policy. In order to maintain curriculum flexibility, descriptive detail in the CoS is currently not so precise. Therefore, to provide more exact information to deepen understanding on the subject content among teachers, the Guideline for the CoS is developed based on the efforts of Working Group members.

The first two authors are working group members for developing the current Guideline for the CoS in junior high PE (MEXT, 2008). The second author (Kazuhiro Shibata, Ryutsu Keiza University) is a member of the working group for developing a newly revised Guideline for the CoS in PE in junior high school for pupils aged 13–15 years-old (MEXT, 2017b). He has worked as a PE teacher in junior high school and teaches Kendo as a specialist in teaching *Budo* in junior high school. The first author (Yoshinori Okade) was responsible for developing the current Guideline for the CoS in teaching games in junior high school and the chair of the working group for the newly revised Guideline for the CoS in elementary school (MEXT, 2017b).

Further contextual information for this chapter is provided around the concept of *Budo*. *Budo* is an umbrella term for traditionalist Japanese martial arts, and it is one of the compulsory elements in junior high PE for all students. Students must learn one of the *Budo* arts from the three options of *Judo*, *Kendo* or *Sumo*. However, *Budo* is difficult to teach because of the safety requirements, the necessary interpersonal skills and the time restrictions to teach it. Consequently, students cannot acquire enough skill to enjoy arts like *Kendo* in an authentic context. Meanwhile, *Kendo* experts experience difficulty in transforming the art's traditional pedagogy for school children. Therefore, Kazuhiro has tried to find developmentally appropriate content to teach *Kendo* based on the Course of Study (CoS), developed unit plan and lesson plan and checked their effectiveness for revising the CoS.

Introduction to the flexible Japanese PE curriculum

In this chapter, we wish to introduce how subject content was modified in PE from formal sport disciplines – namely the case of a *Kendo* unit in junior high school in Japan. Most of the documentation we use in this chapter was derived from the text supported by the MEXT for the research on *Budo* in PE (Tokyo Women's College of Physical Education, 2019). The second author developed the unit plan (including objectives of the unit, time allocation, flow of the unit and activities) and lesson plan (including objectives, assessment criteria and plan, teacher behaviour, set of the equipment for the lessons), cooperated with two PE teachers in junior high schools and implemented the lesson plan (Tokyo Women's College of Physical Education, 2019). In what follows, the rest of the chapter will focus on: 1) The place of *Budo* and *Kendo* in Japanese PE, 2) the specific mixed-methods intervention in the case study school and 3) findings from the qualitative element of this study. We then close with some implications for physical educators in other countries who might benefit from instilling the value of respect within their learning communities and countries.

Budo and Kendo in the Japanese CoS of PE

Budo, quite literally, means 'path/way of the warrior,' and is now used as an umbrella term for the Japanese martial arts such as Aikido, Judo and Iaido. Despite the technical differences between these armed and unarmed arts (and combat sports), they all promote self-discipline and express elements of traditional Japanese culture within a curriculum otherwise dominated by Western sporting and athletic traditions. After the Second World War, the name of *Budo* was newly introduced in the CoS in 1989. Instead of *Budo*, *Kakugi* was used as the name of this content area; it was the compulsory content area for boys from the CoS in 1958 in junior high school and 1960 in senior high school. From the CoS in 1969 in junior high school and that of in 1970 in senior high school, it was a compulsory content area for boys, although girls could also elect it. From the CoS in 1989, either *Budo* or dance must be elected by both boys and girls. *Kendo* is one of the *Budo* styles used in PE teaching. Within Japanese junior high schools, students have to select and learn one form of *Budo* from *Judo, Kendo* or *Sumo* in the first two years of study. *Budo* has been a compulsory content area in junior high PE since the current CoS (MEXT, 2008) fully implemented from 2012. This policy is accepted also in the newly revised CoS (MEXT, 2017a).

As a form of self-cultivation, *Budo* traditionally emphasizes both mental and physical education and therefore promotes the training of body-mind discipline and the development of human character and values (Yuasa, 1987). According to Tokyo Women's College of Physical Education (2019), the educational values of *Budo* are explained from the following three perspectives:

1. *Budo* is different from Western sport disciplines because it aims to develop holistic human education.
2. In *Budo*, manners (showing respect to others) are highly valued. Valuing respect to the teacher and fellow students in a specified manner makes one possible to control oneself and show one's respect to others. Such self-control would be one of the important elements to educate the whole person.
3. In games of *Budo*, the focus is not placed on victory as the result of competition, but on cooperation, in which pupils are focused on learning the 'Do' – (way of living) together. Based on this concept, one has to be careful in designing PE lessons that are not only shaped around the focus on victory.

In the Guideline for implementing the CoS, the key characteristics of Budo are explained in the following manner:

> *Budo* is the traditional Japanese original culture developed from *Bugi* or Bujutsu. *Budo* is the physical activity which makes it possible to enjoy the fun and pleasure to compete against each other and improve each other's performance. *Budo* is game-based, Through engaging in *Budo* actively, it would be emphasized to understand the traditional way of thinking and make possible that students respect their opponent in practice and competition in each other (MEXT, 2017a, p. 143).

Japanese traditional values entail perspectives such as developing humanity, mutual respect of others and self-control and recognising others as partners to learn cooperatively. These are traditional values and also the expected way of behaviour in Japan (MEXT, 2019). So emphasising *Budo*, a traditional Japanese movement culture, as the content of PE would be meaningful to value Japanese culture and traditions and would also contribute to educate Japanese youngsters who live in the world of an increasingly internationalised society (MEXT, 2010).

On the other hand, the decision to include the principles of *Budo* within the course of study has also received a number of critiques. This particularly relates to the introduction of *Judo*, for example, one critique suggests it would be dangerous to teach for educators who have no *Judo* experience (Uchida, 2011). Also, from the historical background in the Second World War, in which the sharp *katana* (blade or 'Samurai sword') was used for Japanese military executions and atrocities against civilians, concerns were raised about martial art techniques originally developed to kill others, even though modern teachers were emphasizing more traditional and peaceful Japanese values.

In response to these critiques and challenges, the MEXT programme has developed the 'Guidelines for teaching Budo in PE.' The focus of these guidelines is orientated to PE teachers who have little experience in teaching *Budo* in PE settings (MEXT, 2008). In addition to the guidelines the first two authors have helped to develop, several martial art federations, such as the Japanese

Kendo Federation, have developed similar documents for PE teachers. An out-line of the key principles to teach Kendo in junior high PE (MEXT, 2010) are illustrated below,

- The level of each skill to be taught is considered from two perspectives. One is the operation of the sword and another is the movement of the body. In using these two perspectives, skills were classified and distributed among 1st and 2nd grader or 3rd graders (aged 13–15 year old).
- These distributions should be treated as being flexible as based on objectives in a PE lesson.
- The content of *Kendo* is divided into three areas of: 1) skill, 2) attitude and 3) knowledge, thinking and decision making.
- Skills are divided into: 1) basic skills and 2) interpersonal skills. These two skills should be taught in relation to each other.
- In terms of attitude, keeping the traditional way of thinking, such as *Reigi*, respecting each other, upholding rules, being fair, upkeeping health and safety should be recognised as the most important content in *Kendo*.
- Enjoyment and fun should also feature in *Kendo*.
- In terms of knowledge, thinking and decision making, to learn how to make decisions for selecting the appropriate activity and adjusting game rules based on individual skills. Especially, in the *Kendo* sparring-based game, one has to simultaneously attack and defend in an interpersonal manner, to find out one's own favourite skills appropriate to their own ability, devising activity based on promised practice and free practice to hit the opponent effectively in finding good timing and fainting.
- Aspects of knowledge include the history of *Kendo*, the traditional way of Japanese thinking, terminology and modes of practice, methods for improv-ing fitness, rules of the game and judgement criteria.

The above illustrates, how MEXT (2012) has a clear request to uphold safety in *Judo* lessons from different aspects such as teacher, unit plan, facility and emer-gency response. Also, MEXT (2010) has requested teachers to implement *Kendo* lessons systematically and appropriately. It should focus on basic practice and intro-duce practice based on a developmental level of their skills. As a consequence, it means that specialists in teaching *Budo* in and out of school have tried to develop an appropriate and easy-to-use document for teaching Budo in school. The similar process has informed the development of *Kendo* within the context of Japanese PE.

From the PE curriculum to Kendo classes

Some Japanese PE teachers are noticeably flexible in developing more appropriate activities within the learned content of PE based on the revised CoS. For example, Honda (2015, 2018), Kikuchi et al. (2014) and Tateno and Honda (2016) all introduced the Teaching Games for Understanding (TGFU) model in order to teach *Budo*. In this model, developed for team sports like football (Mitchell, Oslin & Griffin, 2013), games should be centered to teach tactics and skills including decision making, on-the-ball-skills and off-the-ball-movement. Tactical complexity and developmental appropriateness should be considered to modify the full game. In the case of *Kendo*, game rules and equipment were modified in order to exaggerate tasks and to adjust students' developmental stage and learning experience. Also in *Kendo* units, one uses questioning to find tasks to be achieved and give times for improving their game performance in an authentic context. The principle of introducing *Budo* to PE is not new. That said, there was little supporting evidence on the effect of such an instructional model in teaching in *Budo*. In this sense, taking *Budo* as a compulsory content area, rather than informing other practices such as TGFU, gave a rich opportunity to teachers to rethink appropriate content and instructional model in PE for teaching *Kendo* based on using 'assessment for learning' strategies for keeping an alignment between the content, instructional models and assessment (Leirhaug & Annerstedt, 2016; Tannehill et al., 2015). For example, through adopting peer assessment strategies, students can get important feedback from their fellow pupils and also from teachers to improve their game performance, social skills, attitude of respect for peers and their understanding how to find their tasks and value of *Kendo* as a Japanese traditional martial art. In summary, as these examples illustrate, there is real potential for the principles of *Budo* and *Kendo* to influence the practice of PE.

In what follows, we outline how the principles of *Kendo* have been introduced within PE and how these can be assimilated within the ideas found within assessment for learning principles. First, we outline the scope of the project and then some reflections on the experiences of the co-authors in developing the *Kendo* unit.

The mixed-methods collaborative project

Based on the description in the CoS, Prof. Shibata developed assessment standards for each grade across three years in junior high school. Aligned with such assessment criteria, he also developed modified games, and lesson plans for each unit plan for giving equal opportunity to learn for all students. He gave all these documents to the teachers who implemented the unit (Table 8.1). Based on the assessment items, Shibita used the assessment tool to measure students' self-assessment on outcomes of each domains in the units such as the questionnaire he developed and the standardised formative assessment on PE (Takahashi, 2003). Quantitative data was analysed by the second author and compared between each grade. Professor Shibita conducted qualitative interviews with the teachers at four stages of the intervention, beginning with a 90-minute interview per teacher and then three 10-minute discussions. These were transcribed verbatim and then thematically categorised based on distinct yet interrelated units of meaning (Sparkes & Smith, 2014). The first author, Yoshinori Okade, conducted an interview with the second author to check the intention and result of the research. This interview was recorded and used as additional information

Table 8.1 Teacher characteristics

Teacher	Time to have implemented the Kendo unit and the number of students	Teaching experience
Teacher A (male)	5.10.2017-8.11.2017 76 male students (15 years old)	5 years' teaching experience as a PE teacher in a junior high school Non-specialist in teaching Kendo
Teacher B (female)	15.11.2017-13.12.2017 63 female students (15 years old)	7 years' teaching experience as a PE teacher in a junior high school Specialist in teaching Kendo

for interpretation of both data sets. Furthermore, at the end of the intervention and the unit, students were asked to describe their impressions (both positive and negative) of the unit in writing. Results of the three qualitative data sets were interpreted based on the intended curriculum.

The third author, George Jennings, is a native English speaker and martial arts researcher. Towards the end of the project as a relative outsider and former student of *Kendo* in Britain, he became involved in helping to edit and to write the final report in the English language, and to assist in interpreting the overall message from the findings in terms of self-cultivation and *Budo* philosophy. George's role also entails the position of a critical friend offering alternative perspectives on the data and the earlier interpretation. For reasons of space, we have chosen to select the qualitative data for analysis and representation in this chapter. The key overlapping theme that emerged from our analysis was the concept of respect, which connected strongly with the other important findings of manners and risk and safety. Sociological considerations on the influence of culture and gender on the difficulties of ensuring total respect are also considered in the following sections.

Discussion: The challenge of cultivating respect through PE

The value of respect has been a broad yet fairly universal construct in various societies and civilisations around the world. Within an increasingly intercultural and globalised society, it has been identified as one possible construct for all of humanity to cherish regardless of their specific culture (Haydon, 2006) although respect is rarely part of any overt or even hidden school curricula or research about them (for an exception, see Sari & Doğanay, 2009). The principle of respect might therefore be considered as a new threshold concept for PE, especially as it now operates within an international and multicultural context.

Within the context of Japan, the martial arts, with their origins in military warfare and civilian protection, and their subsequent appropriations in the fields of education, leisure and sport, have different approaches to culturally-specific principles of respect. Nevertheless, respect for the art, the institution, the teacher and fellow students are paramount in nearly all styles. In *Kendo* and other *Budo* arts, respect to the teacher (*Sensei* –'person who has gone before') and school (*dojo* – 'place of the Way') is displayed through the ritual bowing at the start of class and between partners prior to sparring (*randori*). A certain level of control is also required to show respect for the welfare of fellow students.

Although the above ideals are enacted within regular dojos, the situation is not so straightforward for a nine-week course taught once an academic year. After three years teaching the *Kendo* unit, the teachers described their experience through quotations exemplified through the following extracts:

> In the first half [of the unit], students could check their skills they learnt one year before. They could improve and widen their skills hitting while moving backwards after having enough time to learn hitting while moving forwards. Learning in a group to check each other's performance was effective in improving their skills. They could be also familiar with Kendo in using different step-by-step modified games. Having experienced guest teachers in every lesson was so good. On the other hand, I have felt that using smaller spaces to teach Kendo was a little bit dangerous, but too much space would be difficult to observe students. This problem should be considered in the future. (Teacher A)

The quotation from Teacher A shows the collaborative nature of the course within limited physical confines in which the students can thrive with their newly found skills. However, Teacher B raised concerns in terms of students' difficulty of uniting mind and body and finding their favourite movements, which are normally found through a longer process of self-cultivation, as illustrated below:

> It was hard to introduce exercise including elements of the exercise for releasing the body and mind in every lesson. In the 3rd year, students have shown higher motivation in activities in free practice for improving their skills than assessment game. This makes students find tasks and their solution by themselves, select their favourite skills. Even though they should have much time to engage in basic practice to be mature in acquiring skills and be able to use them in a game, they would be so impressed if they could achieve it. (Teacher B)

Taken together, these extracts highlight how, even though they have different teaching backgrounds, the teachers were satisfied with implementing the Kendo unit designed by the second author. They have recognized students' skill improvement and motivation to engage in the Kendo unit. They have also recognised cognitive domains outcomes in relating with skill improvement. This result shows the effectiveness of the unit plan to achieve goals described in the unit because they could achieve the similar outcomes even though they had quite different backgrounds in teaching Kendo in junior high school PE.

In addition to the focus around the cognitive domains, gender has also been a crucial factor in the spread and delivery of martial arts within Japan. Up to the present day, martial arts have been male-dominated activities focusing on physical and symbolic power enacted through close-quarters combat using a variety of sensuous experiences such as prolonged and painful touch (Channon & Jennings, 2013). Respect for the teacher is not always reciprocated with respect for the student. Illustrative of this context and the balanced attention to both positive and negative impressions of the intervention, this study shows some of males had negative experience in *Kendo* lesson because they were hit violently so many times. Such negative experiences were reported after the unit:

> *I have experienced some negative experiences such as smell and pain. But I have experienced much more from this Kendo Unit. I couldn't enjoy the Unit because I have felt that hitting other people with the Shinai (bamboo sword) would be dangerous and also violent if we have hit the wrong part of the body. (Male pupil, 15 years old, t.68)*
>
> *In Kendo lessons, members in the Kendo club have hit me without any performance level adjustment. Teachers should add some caution to follow the rule to such students and make them engage in the proper activity. Last year, I had a headache. Kendo is a dangerous sport discipline. So the teacher should take care of it; the lesson gives a good opportunity to learn Reigi (showing respect to others). (Male pupil, 15 years old, t73)*

As the reason of this negative assessment, we should consider the different equipment in both schools alongside teacher education in terms of the levels of care and respect required from them. In this male unit, the teacher used a relatively heavy bamboo sword, but in the female unit, the teacher used the same equipment with 1st and 2nd graders. It would be a small difference for the male unit, but it could significantly influence the student's experience of the *Kendo* unit of assessment as suggested in the following sentence: A heavy sword might be difficult to use for low-skilled boys (Interview with 2nd author).

Conclusion

Through this chapter, we have sought to provide an overview of the philosophical principles of *Budo* and the role of *Budo* in the Japanese junior high school PE CoS. We have also offered an insight on the three-year research project through in-depth qualitative interviews with the pioneering teacher-researcher, the facilitating PE teachers and some of the pupils involved. Inductive analysis revealed the key theme of *reigi* (respect) overlapping technical development with issues of safety, risk and enjoyment. We argue that the principle of respect, so important in the martial arts, might act as a threshold concept for PE both in Japan and beyond. This is because the ideal of respect for others, for seniors, for institutions and traditions is fundamental for the education of young people and proper functioning of a society or nation-state. As PE (and contact sports in particular) has special features of risk, intimacy, pain and interaction between students and teachers (Gard & Meyenn, 2000), mutual respect might be best taught within this element of the curriculum.

Further work will share findings from the extensive quantitative analysis of questionnaires in terms of how the value of respect aligned with different cognitive and affective domains from a more psychological perspective. Moreover, an extensive reflection will be drawn up on the intervention in order to enhance the exiting programme as a form on ongoing action research. Finally, the authors also aim to examine how the principles from the *Kendo* unit (such as respect) might transfer to other elements of the PE curriculum, as found with some of the lesser skilled boys suddenly developing in basketball and soccer.

References

Channon, A., & Jennings, G. (2013). The rules of engagement: Negotiating painful and intimate touch in mixed-sex martial arts. *Sociology of Sport Journal*, *30*, 487–503.

Gard, M., & Meyenn, R. (2000). Boys, bodies, pleasure and pain: Interrogating contact sports in physical education. *Sport, Education & Society*, *5*(1), 19–34.

Haydon, G. (2006). Respect for persons and for culture as a basis for national and global citizenship. *Journal of Moral Education*, *35*(4), 457–471.

Honda, S. (2015). A study on tactical learning in Kendo that encourages students to engage in cooperative learning. *Bulletin of Fukuoka University of Education*. Part VI, Research for teaching practice, *64*, 1–8, (in Japanese).

Honda, S. (2018). A study of the teaching of kendo to beginners by applying rhythmic movements: A focus on basic striking actions. *Research Journal of Budo*, *51*(1), 45–54, (in Japanese).

Kikuchi, K., Yoshino, S., Shibata, K., Sato, Ui, S., & Saito, T. (2014). The effect of teaching game approach on kendo skill acquisition. *Japan Journal of Physical Education, Health and Sport Sciences*, *59*, 789–803, (in Japanese).

Leirhaug, P.E., & Annerstedt, C. (2016). Assessing with new eyes? Assessment for learning in Norwegian physical education. *Physical Education and Sport Pedagogy*, *21*(6), 616–631, http://dx.doi.org/10.1080/17408989.2015.1095871

Meyer, J., & Land, R. (2005) Threshold concepts and troublesome knowledge (2): Epistemological considerations and a conceptual framework for teaching and learning, *Higher Education*, 49, 373–388.

MEXT Notification of Budo and Dance as compulsory content (in Japanese). www.mext.go.jp/sports/b_menu/sports/mcatetop04/list/1371915.htm, retrieved October 13, 2019.

MEXT. (2008). The Course of Study Section 7 Health and Physical Education in junior high schools. http://www.mext.go.jp/component/a_menu/education/micro_detail/__icsFiles/afieldfile/2011/04/11/1298356_8.pdf, October 13, 2019.

MEXT (2010) Toward Implementing Kendo Teaching based on the new Course of Study (School physical education document to teach practice No.1 The guideline for teaching Kendo, (in Japanese) (http://www.mext.go.jp/a_menu/sports/jyujitsu/1306064.htm) (2019.10.14).

MEXT (2012) Request: keeping safety in Judo lesson in physical education in according with making Budo compulsory content in physical education. (http://www.mext.go.jp/b_menu/hakusho/nc/1318538.htm), (in Japanese).

MEXT (2017a) The Guideline for Health and Physical Education in junior high school, (in Japanese)(http://www.mext.go.jp/component/a_menu/education/micro_detail/__icsFiles/afieldfile/2019/03/18/1387018_008.pdf) (2019.10.20)

MEXT (2017b) The Guideline for Physical Education in elementary school, (in Japanese) (http://www.mext.go.jp/component/a_menu/education/micro_detail/__icsFiles/afieldfile/2019/03/18/1387017_010.pdf)(2019.10.20)

MEXTb. The Course of Study. https://www.mext.go.jp/a_menu/shotou/new-cs/idea/index.htm, March 18, 2020.

Mitchell, S .A., Oslin, J. L., & Griffin, L.L. (2013). *Teaching sport concepts and skills*. Champaign, IL: Human Kinetics.

Sari, M., & Doğanay, A. (2009). Hidden curriculum on gaining the value of respect for human dignity: A qualitative study in two elementary schools in Adana. *Education Sciences: Theory & Practice*, 9(2), 925–940.

Sparkes, A. C., & Smith, B. (2014). *Qualitative Research Methods in Sport, Exercise and Health: From Process to Product*. London: Routledge.

Takahashi, T. (2003). *Observing and Assessing Physical Education*. Meiwa publisher, (in Japanese).

Tannehill, D., van der Mars, & MacPhail, A. (2015). *Building Effective Physical Education Programs*. Jones & Bartlett Learning.

Tateno, R., & Honda, S. (2016). A study on kendo lessons that effectively combine task-oriented games with skill-up drills and games. *Research Journal of Budo*, 2, 71–82. https://www.jstage.jst.go.jp/article/budo/49/2/49_71/_pdf/-char/ja, September 29, 2019.

Tokyo Women's College of Physical Education. (2019). 3rd Commissioned Project Report on Improving Budo Teaching and Enhancing Teaching Ability, (in Japanese).

Uchida, R. (2011). Judo accident and head injury: Feedback from 110 deaths in the school. *The Journal of the Organization for the Creating and Development of Education*, 1, 97–103.

Yuasa, Y. (1987). *The body: Towards an Eastern mind-body theory*. Albany, NY: SUNY Press.

Chapter 9

Gaelic games case study conversation: In flow and in the zone

*Wesley O'Brien, Nathan Hall,
Lisa M. Barnett and Orlagh Farmer*

Background

As part of the methodology employed within this case study chapter, two PE academics (WOB and NH) collected qualitative interview data with a high-performing Ladies Gaelic Football female athlete (OF), by specifically investigating how the female athlete experiences being 'in the zone' within competition. The interview seeks to critically examine the well-established elements of physical literacy through a recent high-performance episode, from the perspective of the female athlete. An additional author (LB), with specific expertise in motor competence and physical literacy served as a critical layer within the content for chapter development (see step eight). The methodological process within this case study followed a number of sequential steps, as illustrated in the chapter to follow:

> **Step One:** Biography Physical Education Academics and Female Athlete
> **Step Two:** Context of the Case Study Conversation
> **Step Three:** Critical Incidents from the Case Study
> **Step Four:** Empathy Mapping (Design Thinking)
> **Step Five:** Define the Problem Statement
> **Step Six:** Unpacking the Case
> **Step Seven:** Take-Home Messages
> **Step Eight:** Case Study Critique and Commentary

Step one: Biography physical education academics and athlete

Biography physical education academic one

Dr Wesley O'Brien, is the current Programme Director of the B.Ed Sports Studies and Physical Education Degree, in the School of Education, at University College Cork (UCC). Wesley, a Lecturer in PE and Coaching Science, is an expert in childhood movement and physical activity promotion. He is currently supervising postgraduate research in the fields of PE, wellbeing, motor competence, childhood physical activity, physical literacy and sport participation. Wesley is a Principal Investigator on nationally funded longitudinal projects in Ireland, such as the National Consensus Statement for Physical Literacy, the Children's Sport Participation and Physical Activity (CSPPA) study, Project FLAME, Gaelic for Girls and State of Mind Ireland. Since the completion of his PhD in 2013, Wesley has been very research active, with the publication of 30+ peer-reviewed journal articles, 3 book chapters, 2 national reports, 2 television broadcasts, and contributed to over 90 national, and international conference presentations. In terms of coaching experience, Wesley has played Gaelic Games (Hurling, Gaelic Football) at both club and university level for 25+ years, and he has also extensively coached across the sports of Ladies Gaelic Football, Gaelic Football, Camogie and Hurling at club, university and national level.

Biography physical education academic two

Dr Nathan Hall is a university professor from Winnipeg, Canada. He has developed expertise in both the areas of sport psychology (Masters degree in Human Kinetics, specialising in sport psychology) and PE (Doctorate in Secondary Education specialising in physical education). For the past six years, he has dedicated considerable amounts of his time and efforts to conducting research in the areas of PE and physical literacy. He has experience teaching in the public and private school system, and presently teaches physical and health education pedagogy courses to pre-service teachers. Nathan is an advocate for the inclusion of non-traditional sports and alternative environment physical activities as part of a well-balanced and effective school-based PE program. In 2018, he was a visiting scholar at University College Cork where he conducted research on alternative environment physical activities, and sought out knowledge and understanding of Irish sports that are uncommon in Canadian schools (i.e. Gaelic Games) so that he could introduce these activities to teachers back in Canada. Nathan has presented over 100 professional development workshops, related to movement and PE, to local, national, and international teachers and coaches.

Biography physical education teacher and athlete

Ms Orlagh Farmer, is a qualified PE teacher at post-primary level in Ireland, and is also a final year PhD student (previously awarded the 2018/19 Irish Research Council [IRC] PhD Scholarship) in the Sports Studies and Physical Education Programme, within the School of Education at University College Cork. Orlagh is current member of the Cork Senior Ladies Gaelic Football team, and is a part-time lecturer in Dundalk Institute of Technology. In the current book chapter, Orlagh will serve as the athlete in 'flow' or 'in the zone,' from a recent Ladies Gaelic Football performance.

Step two: Context of the case study conversation

The context of the following chapter relates to a high-performing female athlete's perception of 'flow' during performance. To achieve this, the chapter revolves around a conversation between the two identified PE academics, who critically investigate the nominated athlete's knowledge and understanding of being in 'flow' or 'in the zone,' during a recent LGF performance. LGF is a national Irish field sport, under the umbrella of 'Gaelic Games' for female athletic participation. Founded in 1974, LGF is recognised as one of the fastest growing female sports in Europe; there are currently over 1000 clubs in Ireland, as the game seeks to reach women and girls across the island. One way in which LGF is also being introduced to females across Ireland is through school based PE programmes.

In the Republic of Ireland, PE is taught by non-specialist teachers (generalist cross subject expertise) at the Primary school level, and they are following the 1999 Primary School Education Curriculum for children aged 4 to 12 years of age. At the Secondary school level, specialist PE teachers deliver the curriculum. For Junior Cycle (12– 15 years of age), since 2017, teachers deliver PE content under the Wellbeing Area of Learning. For Senior Cycle (16–18 years of age), new curricular options were introduced in 2018: Option 1) an examinable Leaving Certificate subject known as Leaving Certificate Physical Education (LCPE); Option 2) a non-examinable subject framework, known as Senior Cycle Physical Education (SCPE).

From an analytical perspective, this chapter delves into the pillars of PE (as a curricular subject), and the external school focus of high-performance in sport. Both PE and sport are empirical threshold concepts within the literature, and from the perspective of this chapter, both disciplines synergistically link to physical literacy as an evolving concept for analysis. In this particular episode, the conversation (see transcript listed) focuses on the athlete's understanding of the well-established physical literacy elements (motivation, confidence, competence, knowledge, understanding and physical activity behaviour), and further examines how this physical literacy concept overlaps and/or interlinks with LGF elite adult performance in an 'All-Ireland' national sporting semi-final occasion.

> **Location:** Following the completion of this semi-final, this conversation is taking place via a Skype conversation meeting between the physical education academics (Ireland and Canada) and the elite performer (Ireland).
> **Timing:** The semi-final performance finished in the middle of August, 2019, and this conversation is taking place approximately four-weeks post athlete performance.
> **Space:** Round-table office discussion in Cork, Ireland, with Skype connectivity to Winnipeg, Canada.
> **Focus:** The aim of this face to face/electronic conversation between the physical education academics and the performer is to examine being in the 'zone'

within athletic performance, through the physical literacy lens of Irish Gaelic Games. Furthermore, the outcomes of this conversation attempt to unpack high-performance sport terminology, specifically being in the 'zone' and physical literacy, by interlinking accessible physical education comparative threshold concepts for children and youth.

Step three: *Critical incidents from the case study conversation*

Nathan: How motivated would you say you were personally to perform the physical skills required to be effective in that game?

Orlagh: I'd say I was really, really motivated to be honest coming up to the game. And so I put in a lot of extra work and skill based work and fitness work prior to the game, and particularly all season really.

Nathan: Could you give a little bit of an explanation as to why – this specific game and the specific opponent – influenced your personal motivation to perform?

Orlagh: Yeah, definitely with the opposition team that we were playing, Dublin, it's a little bit of a history in the past with Dublin. And they were going for three in a row, and they were kind of the team to beat per se.

Wesley: From your own personal perspective, how do you think you physically performed in Croke Park during that game?

Orlagh: I think on a personal level I thought I did well, and I thought I made use of the ball. I thought I did quite well, particularly in the first half of the game.

Wesley: Was there a particular period in the game that you might have felt that you were really in the zone?

Orlagh: Yeah, I think that reflecting on the game, again, I think particularly after the 5 minute mark, I think, up until half time. And I think, the fluency was there, but in that kind of game, I kind of can't remember. Like I can't remember making that pass, or I can't remember taking that ball in because I was so in the zone.

Nathan: Is there something about that initial point in the half or in the game that made you feel that way?

Orlagh: Well it's always the start of the game really your nerves are still going too, but I think always when you kind of touch the ball first, or make, you know, to make contact with the ball, I think that just settles me, you know.

And at half time, then I suppose kind of it was an opportunity to kind of reflect upon how I was doing as well.

Nathan: What understandings did you take away from this particular game with respect to the factors that influenced your ability to reach that level of flow.

Orlagh:	Actually, I suppose one thing that I remember from the game, and particularly in the second half, there was kind of a period where Dublin were up four points, and it remained that way for about 15 minutes in the game.
	I remember looking up at the clock with 11 minutes to go, and I felt – not only just me but I just felt in terms of the team environment as well, that we almost gave up.
Nathan:	You've played a lot of games in your life; how is this one different then as far as fatigue?
Orlagh:	I suppose I learned really that, although I thought I was fit, there's lots of room for improvement as well. There was periods where I thought I could have had, you know, maybe executed some of my skills better.
Wesley:	And a big part of being physically fluent or physically literate is your ability to move well. Do you think you were able to do the basics of LGF well during your performance?
Orlagh:	Yeah, I think so. I used the ball to the best of my ability.
Wesley:	Was there any moment in the game where you felt that there was quite a lot of skill requirements needed of Orlagh Farmer in the game?
Orlagh:	Yeah. At one point in the game I was up in the forwards, and I gave the pass away (to the opposition). But you know, there was a lot to take in in the sense that do I push off or don't I, and I decided not to. And I think they got a goal out of that error as well.
Nathan:	Did your actual self confidence to perform those movements fluctuate during the game?
Orlagh:	I think it remained quite consistent in the first half, in terms of executing skills and contributing to the team. As I had mentioned about the second half, I suppose the last 10 minutes in particular, when we were kind of making minor errors, I did maybe lose a small bit of confidence.
Wesley:	Physical literacy and the affective domain, was there any stage in the game that you felt you needed to show empathy or cooperation?
Orlagh:	Yeah. I think the goal chances that we missed, the two girls that missed the goal chances, I think I was kind of empathetic towards them.
Wesley:	How resilient do you think you were during this recent game in Croke Park?
Orlagh:	Low resilience in the second half, I wanted to do more attacking, I wanted to make that run, but I couldn't run.
	But then another time in the first half, I remember tracking back and making possession, and there was a score made out of that as well. So I think at that time in the first half, yes, I was highly resilient.
Nathan:	How did this game influence your confidence to perform at this level moving forward?

Orlagh: I actually gained a bit of confidence from the semi-finals, because, especially in the first half of the game, I can remember certain instances where I said to myself, 'I actually can do this, I need to do more of this in the next game or next year.'

Nathan: How did this actual game influence your personal motivation moving forward to continue training in this sport?

Orlagh: I do think that I can improve physically for next year. But I think maybe losing is giving me that desire as well to kind of put in that extra bit of time in the gym or, you know, practice the skills a bit more, to get that extra 1% or 2%.

Step four: Empathy mapping

The empathy map (Figure 9.1) is a succinct summary from step three's critical incidents within the case study, and is based on the principle of design thinking from the perspective of what the *athlete says, thinks, feels and does,*' as reported previously by O'Brien et al. (2018). This empathy map was compiled in joint discussion by the two PE academics (WOB & NH), following their critical review of the case study transcription (step three).

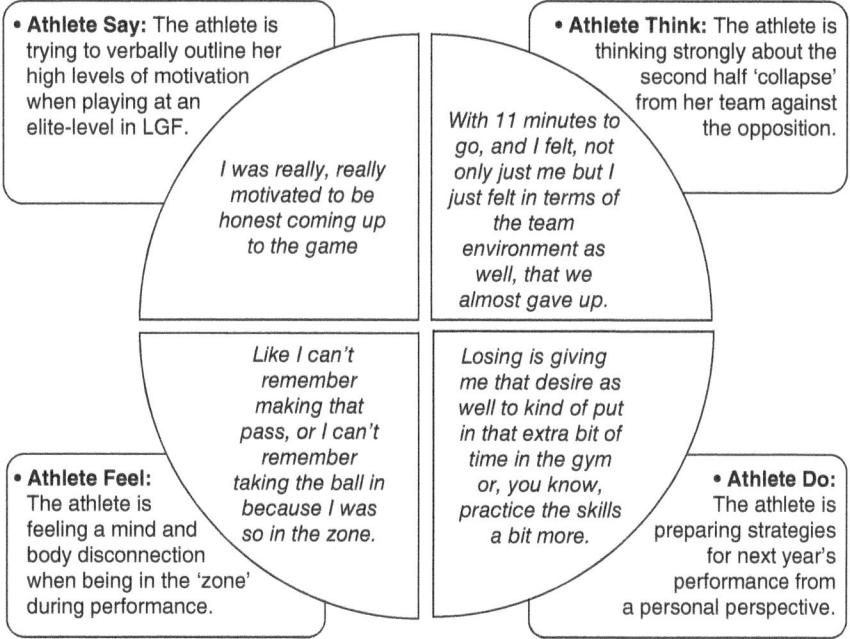

Figure 9.1 Empathy map for the LGF high-performing athlete

Step five: Define the problem statement for the female high-performing athlete

The problem statement (Figure 9.2) is a succinct summary from step four's empathy mapping exercise, and is again based on the principle of design thinking from the perspective of the athlete's attributes and learning, again as reported previously by O'Brien et al. (2018). This problem was compiled in joint discussion by the two PE academics (WOB & NH), following their empathy map presentation earlier (step four).

Step six: Unpacking the case

This case study of a LGF athlete, and her experience in competing at one of the highest levels in her sport provides interesting insight into how physical literacy (Edwards et al., 2017; 2018) is connected to both movement proficiency and a state of flow, that is sometimes achieved when participating in physical activity. When the case summary (pp. 7–9) and the developed LGF athlete empathy map is thoughtfully examined, explicitly accessing the voice (Aldous et al., 2016) of the participant, the applications for physical educators can start to be teased out and critically discussed. Specifically, links can be made to key PE threshold concepts

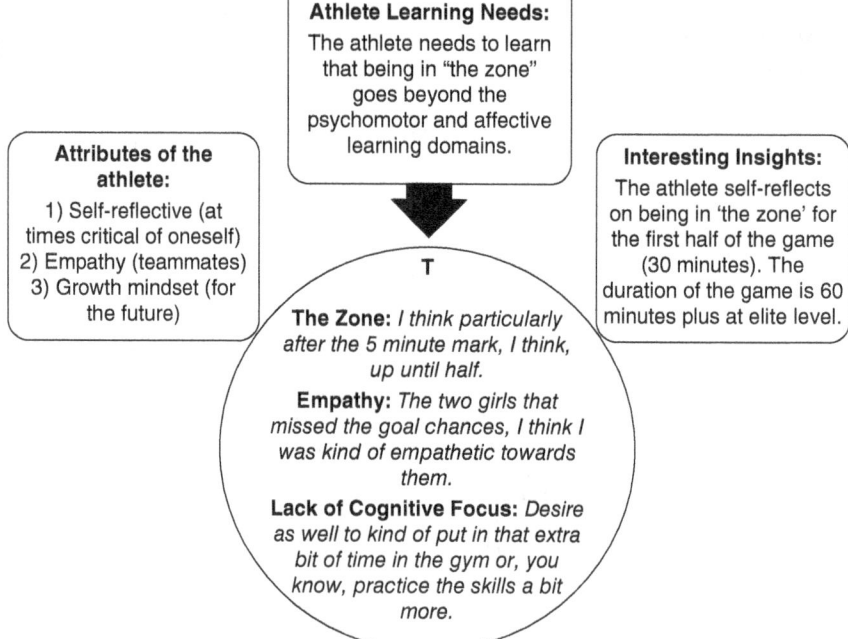

Figure 9.2 Problem statement for the female high-performing athlete

that should be covered with all students, as part of an effective PE programme, such as: dedicated consideration of cognition and knowledge attainment; value of being a reflective learner; importance of eveloping a sense of empathy for others when engaging in physical activity; need to understand the role of personal arousal level and motivation when it comes to engaging in physical activity; and the overall benefit of developing physical literacy when it comes to participation in physical activity.

The concept of physical literacy (Cairney et al., 2019; Lounsbery & McKenzie, 2015; Tremblay & Lloyd, 2010) is at the heart of this particular case. It has been argued that '*the hallmark of physically literate individuals is that they foster a love of physical learning, so they seek physical challenges, value physical effort, and persist in the face of physical obstacles*' (Dudley, 2015, p. 244). Most competitive athletes who are passionate about the sport they participate in would fit this profile, and based on the discussion provided in the current case study, the LGF athlete acknowledges many of the tenets associated with physical literacy (Edwards et al., 2017; 2018). Consequently, anyone who believes that physical literacy development is a fundamental part of quality PE, is therefore likely to see value in competition and sport – as long as it can be framed and delivered in an inclusive manner – as part of a PE program (Killingbeck et al., 2007; Longmuir & Tremblay, 2016; Lounsbery & McKenzie, 2015).

Cognition, knowledge attainment, and reflective learning

When you contemplate the summary and problem statement of the elite LGF athlete focused on herein, it is apparent that this individual has not given much consideration to cognitive learning during her athletic experience and more importantly, the possible cognitive improvements that could be made following her experience (post-game planning). A lack of focus on developing knowledge and cognition is also, unfortunately, sometimes an issue in PE. Far too often, PE programmes focus too much on the 'physical' and not enough on the 'education,' and yet knowledge attainment should play a key role (Nyberg & Larsson, 2014). Barnett et al. (2019), acknowledge some of the cognitive tenets of physical literacy in their 'Guidelines for the Selection of Physical Literacy Measures in Physical Education in Australia,' when outlining that '*the cognitive domain covers conscious and unconscious knowledge and understanding, including problem solving and decision making, awareness of rules and tactics*' appreciation of healthy and active lifestyles, and processing of feedback and reflection' (p. 121). Knowledge and understanding are also major cognitive components of physical literacy (International Physical Literacy Association, 2017), along with motivation and physical confidence (Barnett et al., 2019; Keegan et al., 2019). Thus, this current case study is a good reminder supporting Pickard and Maude's research (2014) which suggests that *physical literacy should not be viewed as an end product to be aspired to, but rather a state in which we live throughout our lives*' (p. 22). Aligning physical literacy to the educational pathway within PE (Killingbeck et al., 2007; Longmuir &

Tremblay, 2016; Lounsbery & McKenzie, 2015), the authors argue in this current case study that there is always some leverage to advance our physical literacy journey, and elite athletic experiences (as presented in the transcriptearlier) do not negate this fact.

That said, it is not as though the athlete in this case study did not consider the cognitive domain, she simply put less emphasis on it when compared to the physical or psychological domains. She did, however, acknowledge in the earlier conversation the need for and value of effective decision making during her performance. This is very applicable to physical educators, since it indicates that sports might be a good place to help teach the cognitive skill of decision making. Researchers have also supported this assertion (Mesquita, Farias, & Hastie, 2012). Additionally, the athlete noted that she engaged in at least some form of reflective practice during the half time break and following the game. Reflection, is also part of the cognitive domain of physical literacy (Barnett et al., 2019), and PE research (Romar, Haag, & Dyson, 2015). Thus, the case study examined in this chapter provides support for physical educators to encourage their students to be reflective learners in PE, no matter how skilled or knowledgeable they may be. Even those at the highest levels of elite sport participation still have areas that need improvement with regard to physical literacy (Jackson, 1996; Meggs et al., 2019), and cognition, in all forms, should not be overlooked.

Developing a sense of empathy

Building students' social skills through PE is a key aspect of school based learning, and developing a sense of empathy should be part of this educational focus. Though the concept of empathy was not the most deeply discussed concept by the LGF athlete in this case study, it is a concept that should be considered seriously by physical educators. Many emotions can be felt by athletes during a sporting competition, or for that matter, by any individual participating in physical activity. Thus, the PE environment can be an ideal place to develop students' empathy (García-López & Gutiérrez, 2015). It is not only important that physical educators learn to be empathetic towards all students, but also that they teach their students to do the same. The athlete in this case study described feeling empathetic towards other players on her team, specifically when they missed scoring opportunities. This is a great example of how sports inherently foster empathy, and also demonstrates that there is still room for an individual to consider how others around them are feeling.

Arousal and motivation

Motivation is another central component of physical literacy (Barnett et al., 2019; Keegan et al., 2019; Whitehead, 2010; IPLA, 2017). It has been posited that embodied physical literacy (Shearer et al., 2018) will only be present, if the individual is able to motivate themselves to participate in physical activity by means of regulating their own behaviour (Chen, 2015). This would be applicable to all individuals, including those who are being asked to partake in physical activity during a PE class, and elite level athletes that require the highest levels of physical activity prowess to achieve success in their chosen sport. The athlete discussed in this case study provided support for this, specifically when discussing how she employed both extrinsic and intrinsic forms of motivation to not only prepare for physical activity performance, but also for motor skill acquisition and/or improvement. It should also be noted that, that the self-reflective nature of the discussion for this case study even appeared to have a positive impact on the athlete's motivation. Specifically, the athlete demonstrated various emotions during the discussion, and explained how this reflection was making her want to train even harder, to become more proficient and subsequently allow her to be in 'the zone' (Jackson, 1996; Meggs et al., 2019) more consistently. Interestingly enough, research in PE has consistently endorsed a mastery oriented motivational climate as a means to improve student fostered self-determined situational motivation and physical activity (Parish & Treasure, 2003; Valentini, Rudisill, & Goodway, 1999). Thus, the important role of motivation, especially mastery oriented motivation, should not be overlooked when it comes to enhancing physical literacy.

The need to better comprehend optimal human functioning by examining themes, such as excellence in performance and positive subjective experiences has been stressed in positive psychology (Seligman & Csikszentmihalyi, 2000). In sport and physical activity, optimal human functioning is most commonly associated with the idea of being in 'the zone' (as referred to by the LGF athlete in this chapter's case) or what is commonly referred to as 'flow' in the physical activity performance literature (Jackson, 1996; Meggs et al., 2019; Swann et al., 2012). This is when an individual or group achieves a harmonious and intrinsically gratifying state characterised by deep focus and the elimination of extraneous emotions and thoughts. It is a feeling that everything is going seamlessly, even when faced with a considerable challenge or barrier (Csikszentmihalyi, 2002). Swann et al. (2012) summarised 10 factors (e.g. focus, preparation, motivation, arousal, confidence, thoughts and emotions, feedback, environmental and situational conditions, performance, team play and interaction) which in their positive form facilitated flow, and in their negative form inhibited flow. The LGF athlete who was the focus of this chapter's case indicated that she was in a state of flow during much of the first half of the game (all but the first five minutes), specifically when the score was close (teams were even at half time but the opponents dominated the second half). If we apply Swan and colleague's factors that facilitate or inhibit flow, it could be deduced that the reason the LGF athlete did not experience similar flow in the second half might be attributed to a drop in arousal level due to fatigue, as well as reduced confidence and positive team interaction, because of a growing score differential.

In sport and all forms of physical activity, including during PE, the psychological state of the athlete or student is directly connected to their participation levels and effort. This is very clearly demonstrated in the case of this LGF player. The authors acknowledge the athlete using terms like 'motivation' and 'desire,' and her discussion of feelings relating to dispiritedness, being in 'the zone' and a disconnection between body and mind. Similarly, individuals being tasked with participation in PE are also highly influenced by psychological factors such as motivation, self-efficacy, goals and personal values (Blankenship, 2017). Therefore, this case study provides a very strong support for the notion that improving participation in all physical activities for athletes (or students alike) necessitates attention to both the physical and the psychological factors, with potential intervening stakeholders comprising of physical and coach educators (O'Brien et al., 2018).

Step seven: Take home messages

These take-home messages are pillared on the model of physical literacy construction, as presented by Barnett et al. (2019). In this final section, the authors discuss the psychological, social and physical domains of physical literacy (Figure 9.3), and how they relate to flow in 1) the current athlete context, but also, 2) the future of curriculum-based PE.

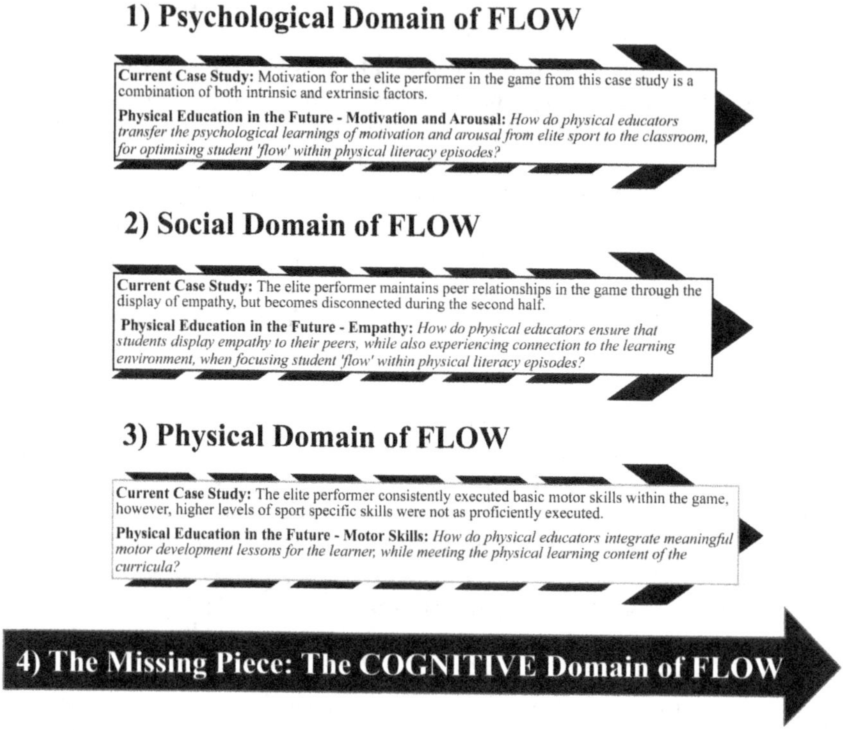

1) Psychological Domain of FLOW

Current Case Study: Motivation for the elite performer in the game from this case study is a combination of both intrinsic and extrinsic factors.

Physical Education in the Future - Motivation and Arousal: *How do physical educators transfer the psychological learnings of motivation and arousal from elite sport to the classroom, for optimising student 'flow' within physical literacy episodes?*

2) Social Domain of FLOW

Current Case Study: The elite performer maintains peer relationships in the game through the display of empathy, but becomes disconnected during the second half.

Physical Education in the Future - Empathy: *How do physical educators ensure that students display empathy to their peers, while also experiencing connection to the learning environment, when focusing student 'flow' within physical literacy episodes?*

3) Physical Domain of FLOW

Current Case Study: The elite performer consistently executed basic motor skills within the game, however, higher levels of sport specific skills were not as proficiently executed.

Physical Education in the Future - Motor Skills: *How do physical educators integrate meaningful motor development lessons for the learner, while meeting the physical learning content of the curricula?*

4) The Missing Piece: The COGNITIVE Domain of FLOW

Figure 9.3 The four domains of flow

Current case study

The athlete needs to learn that being in 'the zone' at the elite level is beyond psychological, psychomotor (physical) and affective (social) learning domains. Experiencing true physical literacy and flow in elite LGF for the athlete will need to seek strategies to increase levels of reflective practice, knowledge and understanding (cognitive) of tactical viewpoints, game strategies, rules and game knowledge.

Physical education in the future – reflective practice and cognition

How do physical educators address the often-neglected reflective practice and cognitive components of physical literacy, when seeking to achieve student experiences of flow?

Step eight: Case study critique and commentary (Lisa Barnett)

This chapter used the concept of physical literacy to analyse and understand the experiences of a female LGF athlete; described as being 'in flow.' Physical literacy is introduced in terms of elements such as motivation, confidence, competence, knowledge and physical activity behaviour. The International Physical Literacy Association (IPLA, 2017) definition does include the first four mentioned elements, but I would suggest physical activity behaviour is a desirable outcome of being physically literate rather than another element. Australia's definition and framework provides a comprehensive understanding of physical literacy, covering four domains (physical, psychological, social and cognitive) (Sport Australia, 2020). When authors analyse the case study, many of the elements that emerge, beyond the common descriptors for physical literacy (such as motivation and self-perception), are the less commonly defined aspects of physical literacy that feature in the Australian framework, such as tactics (when the athlete mentions '*do I push off or don't I.*') and collaboration ('*but I just felt in terms of the team environment as well, that we almost gave up*').

On another note, I am interested in the author statement that '*... anyone who believes that physical literacy development is a fundamental part of quality physical education, is therefore likely to see value in competition and sport – as long as it can be framed and delivered in an inclusive manner.*' Whilst there is certainly value in sport and competition, there are youth who will never seek to engage in these types of physical activity – even if they are set up as inclusive. In a qualitative study of adolescents, we found some interesting insights relevant to this point (Barnett, Cliff, Morgan, & van Beurden, 2013). One point of difference between young people who did organised activity and those who did not, was attitudes to 'competition.' Youth in the organised activity groups spoke of competition against others as being motivating and keeping them involved, whereas youth in the non-organised group suggested that having less emphasis on competition against others and focusing more on social aspects may help raise activity levels.

The discussion of flow is interesting and pertinent to physical literacy. Children experience flow in play, where they are self-directed in their chosen pursuit (Russ, 2009). Yet as children age, they are funnelled into more and more structured activity, with less time for play and seeking their own direction [although, it is important to note that there are examples of structured play that can assist flow in children (Neiva, 2016)]. So in fact, does our school system of PE and sport discourage youth away from states of flow that they may have experienced when younger? A recent systematic review (Sierra-Díaz, González-Víllora, Pastor-Vicedo, & López-Sánchez, 2019) reported that motivation in PE was related to flow state, and that traditional direct instructional approaches impact negatively on the more self-determined motivation forms. Authors in the current article also speak of the importance of mastery climates in PE when encouraging motivation. I wonder though if this approach is enough to encourage the state of flow in all youth, or can we do more?

Authors conclude with the statement 'improving participation in all physical activities for athletes (or students alike) necessitates attention to both the physical and the psychological factors....' Whilst I agree, I would add that students and athletes are not often synonymous, and to assist the typical young person (who may rarely have experienced pleasure in physical pursuits) to develop a state of flow in physical activities may also require understanding of how flow is achieved in a non-athlete.

References

Aldous, D., Sparkes, A. C., & Brown, D. H. K. (2016). Trajectories towards failure: Considerations regarding post-16 transitions within the United Kingdom Sport-Education sector. *Sport, Education and Society*, 21(2), 166–182. https://doi.org/10.1080/13573322.2014.890929

Barnett, L. M., Cliff, K., Morgan, P. J., & van Beurden, E. (2013). Adolescents' perception of the relationship between movement skills, physical activity and sport. *European Physical Education Review*, 19(2), 271–285. https://doi:10.1177/1356336x13486061

Barnett, L. M., Dudley, D. A., Telford, R. D., Lubans, D. R., Bryant, A. S., Roberts, W. M., ... Keegan, R. J. (2019). Guidelines for the selection of physical literacy measures in physical education in Australia. *Journal of Teaching in Physical Education*, 38(2), 119–125. https://doi.org/10.1123/jtpe.2018-0219

Blankenship, B. (2017). *The Psychology of Teaching Physical Education: From Theory to Practice*. New York, NY: Routledge.

Cairney, J., Dudley, D., Kwan, M., Bulten, R., & Kriellaars, D. (2019). Physical literacy, physical activity and health: Toward an evidence-informed conceptual model. *Sports Medicine*, 49(3), 371–383. https://doi.org/10.1007/s40279-019-01063-3

Chen, A. (2015). Operationalizing physical literacy for learners: Embodying the motivation to move. *Journal of Sport and Health Science*, 4(2), 125–131. https://doi.org/10.1016/j.jshs.2015.03.005

Csikszentmihalyi, M. (2002). *Flow: The psychology of optimal experience* (2nd ed.). New York, NY: Harper & Row.

Dudley, D. A. (2015). A conceptual model of observed physical literacy. *The Physical Educator*, 72(5), 236–260. https://doi.org/10.18666/TPE-2015-V72-I5-6020

Edwards, L. C., Bryant, A. S., Keegan, R. J., Morgan, K., Cooper, S. M., & Jones, A. M. (2018). 'Measuring' physical literacy and related constructs: A systematic review of empirical findings. *Sports Medicine*, 48(3), 659–682. https://doi.org/10.1007/s40279-017-0817-9

Edwards, L. C., Bryant, A. S., Keegan, R. J., Morgan, K., & Jones, A. M. (2017). Definitions, foundations and associations of physical literacy: A systematic review. *Sports Medicine*, 47(1), 113–126. https://doi.org/10.1007/s40279-016-0560-7

García-López, L. M., & Gutiérrez, D. (2015). The effects of a sport education season on empathy and assertiveness. *Physical Education and Sport Pedagogy*, 20(1), 1–16.

International Physical Literacy Association. (2017). IPLA. Retrieved from https://www.physical-literacy.org.uk/

Jackson, S. A. (1996). Toward a conceptual understanding of the flow experience in elite athletes. *Research Quarterly for Exercise and Sport*, 67(1), 76–90. https://doi.org/10.1080/02701367.1996.10607928

Keegan, R. J., Barnett, L. M., Dudley, D. A., Telford, R. D., Lubans, D. R., Bryant, A. S., ... Evans, J. R. (2019). Defining physical literacy for application in Australia: A modified delphi method. *Journal of Teaching in Physical Education*, 38(2), 105–118. https://doi.org/10.1123/jtpe.2018-0264

Killingbeck, M., Bowler, M., Golding, D., & Sammon, P. (2007). Physical education and physical literacy. *Practice Matters*, 2(2), 20–24.

Longmuir, P. E., & Tremblay, M. S. (2016). Top 10 research questions related to physical literacy. *Research Quarterly for Exercise and Sport*, 87(1), 28–35. https://doi.org/10.1080/02701367.2016.1124671

Lounsbery, M. A. F., & McKenzie, T. L. (2015). Physically literate and physically educated: A rose by any other name? *Journal of Sport and Health Science*, 4(2), 139–144. https://doi.org/10.1016/j.jshs.2015.02.002

Meggs, J., Chen, M. A., & Koehn, S. (2019). Relationships between flow, mental toughness, and subjective performance perception in various triathletes. *Perceptual and Motor Skills*, 126(2), 241–252. https://doi.org/10.1177/0031512518803203

Mesquita, I., Farias, C., & Hastie, P. (2012). The impact of a hybrid sport education–invasion games competence model soccer unit on students' decision making, skill execution and overall game performance. *European Physical Education Review*, 18(2), 205–219.

Neiva, B. M. (2016). The transformative potential of the hours after school: Finding purpose through play. *Independent School*, 76(1), 1. http://www.nais.org/Magazines-Newsletters/ISMagazine/Pages/The-Transformative-Potential-of-the-Hours-After-School.aspx

Nyberg, G., & Larsson, H. (2014). Exploring 'what' to learn in physical education. *Physical education and sport pedagogy*, 19(2), 123–135.

O'Brien, W., Cuthbert, B., & McCarthy, N. (2018). Irish Case Study Conversation. In F. C. Chambers (Ed.), *Learning to Mentor in Sports Coaching: A Design Thinking Approach*. London: Routledge.

Parish, L. E., & Treasure, D. C. (2003). Physical activity and situational motivation in physical education: Influence of the motivational climate and perceived ability. *Research Quarterly for Exercise and Sport*, 74(2), 173–182. https://doi.org/10.1080/02701367.2003.10609079

Romar, J. E., Haag, E., & Dyson, B. (2015). Teachers' experiences of the TPSR (Teaching Personal and Social Responsibility) model in physical education. *Agora for Physical Education and Sport*, 17(3), 202–219.

Russ, S. W. (2006). Pretend play, affect, and creativity. In P. Locher, C. Martindale, & L. Dorfman (Eds.), *New directions aesthetics, creativity, and the arts* (pp. 239–250). Amytiville, NY: Baywood Publishing.

Seligman, M., & Csikszentmihalyi, M. (2000). Positive psychology: An introduction. *American Psychologist, 55,* 5–14. https://doi.org/10.1037/0003-066X.55.1.5

Shearer, C., Goss, H. R., Edwards, L. C., Keegan, R. J., Knowles, Z. R., Boddy, L. M., Durden-Myers, E. J., & Foweather, L. (2018). How is physical literacy defined? A contemporary update. *Journal of Teaching in Physical Education, 37*(3), 237–245. https://doi.org/10.1123/jtpe.2018-0136

Sierra-Díaz, M. J., González-Víllora, S., Pastor-Vicedo, J. C., & López-Sánchez, G. F. (2019). Can we motivate students to practice physical activities and sports through models-based practice? A systematic review and meta-analysis of psychosocial factors related to physical education. *Frontiers in Psychology, 10*(2115), 1–24. https://doi.org/10.3389/fpsyg.2019.02115

Sport Australia. (2020). Australian Physical Literacy Framework. Retrieved from https://www.sportaus.gov.au/__data/assets/pdf_file/0019/710173/35455_Physical-Literacy-Framework_access.pdf

Swann, C., Keegan, R. J., Piggott, D., & Crust, L. (2012). A systematic review of the experience, occurrence, and controllability of flow states in elite sport. *Psychology of Sport and Exercise, 13*(6), 807–819. https://doi.org/10.1016/j.psychsport.2012.05.006

Tremblay, M., & Lloyd, M. (2010). Physical literacy measurement – The missing piece. *Physical & Health Education Journal, 76*(1), 26–30. http://www.albertaenaction.ca/admin/pages/48/Physical%20Literacy%20Article%20PHE%20Journal%202010.pdf

Valentini, N. C., Rudisill, M. E., & Goodway, J. D. (1999). Incorporating a mastery climate into physical education: it's developmentally appropriate! *Journal of Physical Education, Recreation & Dance, 70*(7), 28–32. https://doi.org/10.1080/07303084.1999.10605683

Whitehead, M. E. (2010). *Physical Literacy: Throughout the Lifecourse.* London: Routledge.

Chapter 10

Thinking and feeling within/through physical education: What place for social and emotional learning?

Oliver Hooper, Rachel Sandford and Hannah Jarvis

Introduction

The potential of physical education (PE) has been widely lauded over the past decades, with much being claimed about the benefits that it might afford young people (Bailey et al., 2009; Beni, Fletcher, & Ní Chróinín, 2017). These various claims relate largely to the developmental capacity of PE, with reference to its potential to enhance learning across the psychomotor, cognitive and affective domains (Rossi & Jeanes, 2016; Green, 2020). Certainly, within the context of the United Kingdom, the Association for Physical Education (afPE) maintains that high-quality PE can foster the physical, social, emotional, moral, cultural and intellectual development of pupils (afPE, 2016). Whilst such assertions are not necessarily unfounded – though they are perhaps more firmly supported in certain domains (see Bailey et al., 2009) – there is much to be said of the subject's haste to justify its position within curricula on account of its 'unique' capacity to contribute to pupils' learning across these multiple domains. Within this chapter, we focus on the affective domain – specifically, social and emotional learning (SEL) – considering how learning within this domain might support more holistic outcomes within/through PE. Initially, we seek to examine the place of SEL within the context of PE, before exploring how SEL competencies have been framed more broadly within education. Subsequently, we present a reflective contribution from one of the authors – Hannah – who considers the place of SEL in PE from her own perspective as a practitioner. Following this, we explore models of/for developing SEL competencies within/through PE, focusing in particular on the Teaching Personal and Social Responsibility (TPSR) model. Finally, we consider how the notion of 'threshold concepts' might offer a useful means by which to (re)orientate how PE conceptualises and approaches learning and teaching around/through SEL.

Examining social and emotional learning within physical education

Educational institutions have long been considered pertinent places in which to shape the character, skills and values orientation of young people (McCuaig,

Marino, Gobbi, & Macdonald, 2015). Within this context, some subject areas are perceived to lend themselves more readily to practices and processes that emphasise the 'social' – with PE being one such subject. Research within the field certainly endorses the capacity of PE (and sport) to build character, develop 'life skills' and enhance socio-moral development (Rossi & Jeanes, 2016). Within their literature review examining values-based education in PE and school sport, McCuaig et al. (2015) consider what it is that makes the subject so well placed to influence such outcomes and argue that this can be attributed to three 'special characteristics' that are somewhat unique to the context: The subject matter, the learning environments and the facilitation of caring teacher-pupil relationships. Evidently, PE would appear to occupy a 'special place' within the school curriculum, in many ways, but perhaps particularly so with regard to its potential to contribute to the development of SEL competencies. PE provides a context within which there are many opportunities for young people to work collaboratively and constructively with one another and, in doing so, utilise and develop various interpersonal skills, such as communication, teamwork, and empathy (Bailey et al., 2009). These opportunities are contextualised within 'authentic' environments centred around motor skill performance and game play – which, often, involve positive interactions with peers. On this, Ciotto and Gagnon (2018, p. 28) highlight how 'the activities that take place in [PE] may elicit different emotions and feelings than those in the academic classroom,' further emphasising how uniquely positioned the subject is to support the development of SEL competencies.

Despite the evident potential of PE to contribute to the development of SEL competencies, this is an aspect of practice which some believe to be underdeveloped (Jacobs and Wright, 2014; Wright & Irwin, 2018). Wright, Gordon and Gray (*forthcoming*) contend that affective outcomes within PE – such as the development of SEL competencies – are deemed to be lower in priority than, for example, psychomotor outcomes. Similarly, Riolo (2019) argued that while social qualities are often deemed to be 'important' within PE contexts, they tend not to be perceived as 'powerful educational content' within a system that values more systematic and tangible educational experiences. Wright et al. (*forthcoming*) offer various reasons for this, among them the notion that PE teachers may not be as adept (or, at least, intentional) in their teaching for affective outcomes. It is interesting to note that this lack of intent may be counterproductive to the wider ambitions and aspirations of the subject, such as efforts to promote learning across multiple domains (Gagnon, 2016; Wright & Irwin, 2018). Whilst the development of SEL competencies within PE remains a somewhat underdeveloped aspect of practice, discussions around this topic within the educational field more broadly have made considerable progress.

Framing social and emotional learning competencies

Watson and Emery (2010) propose that there has been growing interest in – and emphasis on – social and emotional aspects of learning within recent years, though they note that 'there lacks consensus on what these capabilities are; what should be assessed or shown to have developed over time; and the most appropriate methods for doing this' (p. 767). Unsurprisingly, such a lack of clarity has resulted in SEL having been variously described within the literature – though there are several similarities between/across definitions. For example, Zins, Weissberg, Wang and Walberg (2004) suggest that SEL can be conceptualised as a process through which pupils are able to better manage their emotions and feelings and show care and concern for others whilst building positive peer relationships. Similarly, the Collaborative for Academic, Social and Emotional Learning (CASEL) consider SEL to be a process through which pupils 'understand and manage emotions, set and achieve positive goals, feel and show empathy for others, establish and maintain positive relationships, and make responsible decisions' (CASEL, 2019a, n.p.). It is interesting to note that both definitions highlight emotions, empathy, relationships and decision making as key features of SEL and, importantly, both conceptualise SEL as a *process*.

Building on their own definition, CASEL propose that SEL has five core competencies: self-awareness, self-management, responsible decision-making, relationship skills and social awareness (CASEL, 2017). CASEL (2017) situate these competencies within an integrated framework (see Figure 10.1) whereby the core competencies are situated at the individual level but surrounded by further levels spanning out to organisational (e.g. school) and community levels.

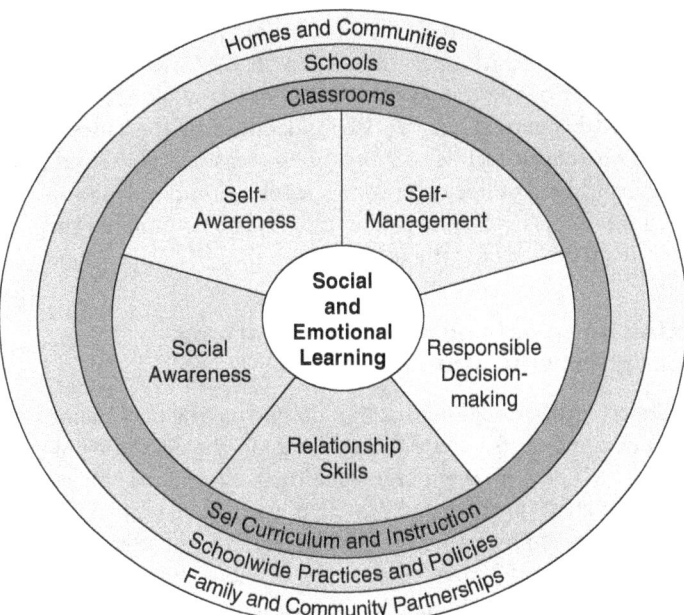

Figure 10.1 Social and emotional learning framework (*Source:* CASEL, 2017).

The framework's focus on the inter-relationships between individuals and social systems/settings can be seen to align with the sociological perspective of Pierre Bourdieu, particularly with his perception of the world as a multi-dimensional space comprising a network of interconnecting social fields (Bourdieu, 1985). These fields each have their own logic and structure, which is determined by the differentiation and distribution of various forms of capital, including social, physical and cultural capital (Bourdieu, 1986). Individuals thus strive to accumulate valued capital, which then serves to position them within the field and shape their practice (Bourdieu, 1990). It could perhaps be argued, in the context of this discussion, that the acquisition of SEL competencies can represent a valuable form of social capital for young people within the school context, facilitating effective practice by, for example, enabling productive communication with their peers, supporting the development of positive relationships and providing opportunities for shared experiences.

It has been suggested that by enhancing young people's SEL competencies within the school context, their capacity to utilise their knowledge, skills and experiences to effectively (and morally) negotiate day-to-day life (e.g. within their family and community contexts) will be improved – and there is mounting research evidence to support such claims (e.g. Durlak et al., 2011; CASEL, 2019b). For example, in their meta-analysis of 213 studies of school-based programmes designed to enhance SEL competencies, Durlak et al. (2011) noted positive outcomes in relation to behavioural referrals, academic performance and health and wellbeing. Meanwhile, a similar meta-analysis by Taylor, Oberle, Durlak, & Weissberg (2017) also purported that school-based programmes had positive outcomes in relation to health and wellbeing, with CASEL's (2019b) own research around the impact of the framework supporting claims in relation to all of the aforementioned benefits. Thus, with consideration of the current educational landscape – whereby academic pressures are increasingly perceived to negatively impact the health and wellbeing of young people – it is perhaps unsurprising that increased attention is now being paid to SEL and its potential to support positive outcomes within and beyond the school.

Reflecting on social and emotional learning within physical education practice

The discussion earlier would suggest that despite having made some progress, PE has not yet maximised its potential with regard to the development of SEL competencies – which perhaps represents something of a 'missed opportunity' for the subject. Wright et al. (*forthcoming*) note that it would be unlikely for a teacher to refute the benefits of promoting the development of SEL competencies through PE, but they acknowledge that 'what might be more challenging is to convince teachers that they have to change how they teach in order to develop such competencies' (p. 12). We take this statement as stimulus for discussion and, at this point focus our attention on the experiences of one of our authors – Hannah – a

PE teacher based at a secondary school in England. Hannah shares her thoughts on both the potential of PE to develop SEL competencies as well as the challenges faced in facilitating this as a teacher:

> PE, without a doubt, has the potential to promote SEL. As a PE teacher, I observe pupils' SEL competencies every day in my lessons, from getting themselves into groups during a warm-up, to working cooperatively to complete a skills practice, to managing their emotions during a small-sided game – especially if they're losing! Evidently, SEL competencies are inherent within PE, likely on account of the nature of our subject. As teachers, within PE, we have more agency to interact with learners – often on a one-to-one basis and/or through less formal interactions (i.e. in the changing rooms, walking out to a lesson taking place on the Astroturf, or during after-school clubs). These features are common across PE lessons, although the teacher, the school more broadly, and the wider community will affect the extent to which SEL takes place (or otherwise).
>
> On reflection, it is perhaps noteworthy that the examples I describe tend to have skill acquisition and/or health-related learning as a focus. This is because lessons – particularly at Key Stage Three (KS3) – are predominantly focused on the psychomotor domain. I am now in my fifth year of teaching and I find PE to be a very contested subject. I must meet the demands of my department, the demands of my school, and of course, the demands of the National Curriculum for PE (NCPE). In addition to this, I have to manage my own personal thoughts, feelings, and behaviours with regard to what my subject should be about. It is very hard – in my experience – to find a department where all teachers are on the same page with regard to what PE should (or could) be about. Arguably, this is no different to any other subject, but there seems to be less certainty in relation to PE specifically. Truthfully, as a teacher I get very little time to think about the 'wider' aspects of the subject, such as learning within the affective domain, and my pupils' SEL within my classes. The majority of my lessons, in KS3 at least, are determined by factors such as equipment and facilities, along with the characteristics of the pupils in the class I am due to teach – and what will be most educative and engaging for them. Supporting pupils to develop their SEL competencies may, therefore, not necessarily be a priority. That said, my own disposition means that I personally endeavour to promote SEL within my lessons. Whilst developing pupils' physically might be prioritised more broadly, learning cannot happen unless they are in the right 'place'.
>
> I would argue that PE is a really useful space to develop pupils' SEL competencies, but for that to happen more extensively (and more explicitly) there needs to be a fundamental shift in teaching philosophies and pedagogies. The nature of PE means it is well placed to foster SEL, but this can be hindered by several factors. Firstly, there is a (somewhat) necessary focus on psychomotor learning outcomes, on account of the requirements of the NCPE. Secondly, there are rather traditional views – from all involved – as to what PE should be about. My pupils themselves would likely struggle if I were to suddenly focus on affective learning outcomes, and I am not sure that I would feel entirely comfortable sharing with my

colleagues that I were focusing on such outcomes as opposed to psychomotor ones. Thirdly, demonstrating pupil progress in relation to affective learning outcomes is difficult – and this would be evident during formal observations of my teaching practice. It is much easier to deliver a lesson on tackling within rugby (for example) where at the end of the lesson it can be more easily demonstrated that pupils have made progress. As a teacher, I am judged on the progress of my pupils and this is linked to my own position and progression.

It is not a case of 'convincing' us teachers to change how we teach – many of us are unhappy with the way in which our lessons impact (or not) our pupils. Instead, it is a case of empowering us and equipping us with the knowledge and skills to better support pupils' holistic development within/through PE. The subject would evidently benefit from more specific guidance around the pedagogies that might be employed to promote SEL, stronger recognition of learning outcomes across multiple domains within the NCPE, as well as more subject-specific professional development. Further, there needs to be consideration of the wider pressures teachers face (e.g. planning requirements, attainment targets, evidencing progress) and the impact of these on our capacity to give our lessons the considered thought they require in order to ensure that they truly are educative across multiple domains.

Hannah's thoughts offer useful insight into a PE teacher's perspective on the development of SEL competencies within/through PE and, significantly, exemplify elements of the SEL framework outlinedearlier. It is interesting to note that she identifies how affective learning outcomes are typically positioned as secondary to psychomotor ones and are often not intentional/explicit within lessons. However, the influence of her own thoughts, feelings and behaviours in relation to promoting affective learning outcomes within PE is noteworthy and evidences – as Hannah notes – that teachers perhaps need not be 'convinced' of the value of SEL, but rather, 'empowered' and 'equipped' to work towards these. The challenges Hannah outlines are perhaps unsurprising, but these are important in considering how we might better support PE teachers in developing pupils' SEL competencies in order to enhance learning across multiple domains. To do so, we propose that we may need to reorientate how affective learning outcomes are approached within/through PE and as such consider existing models of/for developing SEL competencies.

Exploring models of/for developing social and emotional learning competencies within/through physical education

It is perhaps unsurprising – with PE being uniquely positioned to achieve learning outcomes within the affective domain (Ciotto & Gagnon, 2018) – that various approaches, models and programmes that embrace SEL have been developed and integrated within the contexts of PE and school sport (Sandford, Duncombe, & Armour, 2008; McCuaig et al., 2015). Such approaches often have, at their core, a desire to support learning across domains – not only within the affective domain (Riolo, 2019). One model that is perceived to be particularly pertinent when seeking to support social and emotional aspects of learning within PE is TPSR, initially developed by Don Hellison (1985) within the US context and now adopted by practitioners across the globe. Over the past decades, a growing body of research has sought to examine and outline the potential for TPSR to promote SEL within PE (e.g. Cecchini, Montero, Alonso, Izquierdo, & Contreras, 2007; Gordon & Doyle, 2015; Riolo, 2019). TPSR – sometimes referred to as the responsibility model – is an approach that seeks to support pupils as they learn how to be responsible for their own and others' wellbeing through physical activity and sport. The model is structured across five progressive levels (1 – Respect, 2 – Effort, 3 – Self-Direction, 4 – Caring and Leadership, and 5 – Outside the Gym) and it is framed around the teaching of constructive principles, both those associated with personal well-being (effort and self-direction) and social well-being (respecting others' rights and caring about others). These are seen to represent 'levels of awareness' through which young people progress, and which represent their growing sense of personal and social responsibility. It is interesting to note the emphasis on both personal and social skills here, as well as the perceived need to work on these, at times, individually. In this respect, the focus on transfer – as a key element of TPSR – helps to reinforce the ultimate need for self and social to be perceived as interlinked, with the recognition that, as Watson and Emery (2010) note, SEL is evidenced most clearly through the appropriate application of learning within different contexts.

TPSR was proposed as a 'set of ideas' rather than a rigid blueprint (Hellison, 1995), emphasising the need for a flexible approach that will facilitate practice which best fits the needs of learners within a particular context. As Hellison (1995) himself noted, TPSR does not mean practitioners getting inside pupils' heads but getting them inside their own heads. Interestingly, Riolo (2019) noted that this was not only true for pupils but also for practitioners, with teachers in his study acknowledging the 'rigorous reflective journey' they had undertaken in seeking to embed TPSR within their practice. Furthermore, he emphasised the relational nature of TPSR as being fundamental to this process, noting that 'teachers and students lived empowering, interactive and reflective experiences, which celebrated relationship building as well as inclusivity' (Riolo, 2019, p. 251). It has been argued that a practitioner can be a real catalyst for change when implementing models such as TPSR, but this is not a given and the development of pupils' SEL competencies is by no means guaranteed. Indeed, there is support for the view that teachers' own philosophies can play a role in determining the extent to which SEL is both instigated and advocated within PE practice – with Hannah herself noting that: *'my own disposition means that I personally endeavour to promote SEL within my lessons.'* Certainly, Riolo (2019) found that teachers with a positive disposition towards value-laden education could more readily 'bring out' social qualities within their teaching. However, the development of SEL is not purely the responsibility of those teachers (or schools or departments) who value these concepts, but rather the responsibility of all. Further, social and emotional aspects of learning should not be perceived as something pertaining only to PE – as Hannah comments: '*the teacher, the school more broadly, and the wider community will affect the extent to which SEL takes place.*' Rather, they should be embedded within a whole-school approach that facilitates a more holistic view of learning (Jacobs, Knoppers & Webb, 2013).

Social and emotional learning competencies as threshold concepts for physical education

Threshold concepts are regarded by Meyer and Land (2003) as being something that, when mastered, can affect a 'transformative' shift in a learner's perception of a particular field (such as PE). Meyer and Land (2005) posit that threshold concepts can be 'troublesome' for learners, as mastery requires them to navigate a liminal space, within which they must question existing knowledge/understanding and embrace new and (more) complex notions, which typically involves a process of mistake-making in pursuit of proficiency (Meyer & Land, 2006). Drawing on Bourdieu, we might conceptualise this as individuals' experiencing hysteresis – where there is a disconnect between habitus and the changing conditions of the field (Bourdieu, 1990).

Threshold concepts act as a bridge between content and skills, though they place emphasis on the latter. The content being learned is not the focus per se, but rather the means by which skills – such as SEL competencies – are developed, thereby facilitating 'deeper learning' for the individual (Meyer & Land, 2003). Noteworthy, perhaps, is the emphasis on the 'process' of learning – something that was noted earlier as being a key feature within definitions of SEL. Threshold concepts might be usefully adopted within PE, in order both to bring affective learning outcomes to the fore and to highlight their connections to/relevance for learning within broader domains (e.g. psychomotor and cognitive). By considering threshold concepts relating to SEL, PE teachers would be challenged to place emphasis on the skills (or perhaps rather, competencies) being developed within their lessons, which may empower them to step away from the more content-driven lessons to which they may be accustomed. Accordingly, it would enable lessons to move beyond what Hannah referred to as the '*necessary focus on psychomotor learning outcomes,*' facilitating the attainment of outcomes within the affective domain. Learning outcomes within the psychomotor and cognitive domains might also be better facilitated on account of this because, as Hannah comments: '*learning cannot happen unless [pupils] are in the right "place"*'.

Whilst threshold concepts may hold promise for enhancing practice within PE – particularly in relation to promoting the development of SEL competencies – endeavouring to outline what these might be is somewhat problematic. Unlike competencies within the psychomotor domain, those within the affective domain are much less certain and, as such, more difficult to 'bound.' As Hannah notes: '*demonstrating pupil progress in relation to affective learning outcomes is difficult.*'

Further, and as highlighted previously, there is no consensus as to what constitutes competencies with regard to the affective domain (Watson & Emery, 2010). However, with consideration of SEL specifically, we suggest that the five SEL competencies outlined within the SEL framework proposed by CASEL (2017) might offer a means of generating threshold concepts. Thus, we propose the following threshold concepts for PE, specifically in relation to SEL, and highlight (in brackets) how these might align to the five competencies within the SEL framework (CASEL, 2017):

1 PE requires learners to understand their emotions and demonstrate self-efficacy (Self-awareness).
2 PE requires learners to manage their emotions, remain motivated and work towards goals (Self-management).
3 PE requires learners to make decisions which impact on both themselves and others (Responsible decision-making).
4 PE requires learners to interact with one another cooperatively – often in pursuit of common goals (Relationship skills).
5 PE requires learners to recognise difference, respect diversity and be empathetic (Social awareness).

We posit that these threshold concepts could provide a foundation on which PE teachers – like Hannah – could base learning outcomes related to SEL. They would act as a means by which agreement could be reached with regard to what constitutes SEL within PE – which seems to be a notable challenge at present. However, the notion of threshold concepts does warrant consideration in relation to SEL within PE, as certain characteristics are somewhat problematic. For example, whilst we accept that the development of SEL competencies is likely to result in a relatively permanent change (a shaping of habitus), we question whether such competencies could ever truly be considered as 'mastered.' Further, whilst threshold concepts may help to address the lack of consensus as to what constitutes SEL in PE, they do not facilitate the 'measurement' of these, as SEL competencies are themselves rather intangible.

The work of Watson and Emery (2010) is particularly useful in this regard – as they themselves sought to establish a set of guidelines that would support practitioners in their efforts to teach and assess pupils' achievements across what they term 'social and emotional dispositions and skills' (SEDS). Drawing on the work of Bourdieu, they note that SEL competencies are perceived to be products of the 'social milieu' – identifiable as dispositions or strategies that are developed as a result of engagement in a context but which 'cannot be readily observed, only inferred from behaviours' (Watson & Emery, 2010, p. 777). Evidently, whilst SEL competencies might not be able to be measured per se, their development could be inferred in relation to pupils' behaviours. However, Watson and Emery (2010) also debate whether SEDS should be considered as fixed or transferable, linking this to traditional arguments of acquisition versus participation in terms of learning (i.e. knowledge as gained/owned by an individual or as evident in action/interaction with others and in response to contexts). They suggest that there can be an objectification of SEDS over time but that this can also be understood as a result of appropriate (socially accepted) performances being reinforced by individuals within different communities of practice. Ultimately, this further emphasises the need to recognise the socially embedded and situated nature of SEL. As Hannah notes: 'SEL competencies are inherent within PE,' but for the subject to maximise its potential for developing these, affective outcomes need to be brought to the fore – and threshold concepts might provide a useful means of facilitating this.

Conclusion

Within this chapter, we have explored the affective domain within PE, focusing in particular on SEL. We have outlined the considerable potential of the subject in this regard but acknowledged the challenges faced in relation to promoting affective learning outcomes within/through the subject. Ultimately, we concur with Wright et al. (forthcoming) that further progress can and should be made in this area. In this respect, 'threshold concepts' could act as a useful means by which to (re)orientate how the subject conceptualises and approaches learning and teaching around SEL. Yet, there are evident tensions here, as competencies are clearly more difficult to 'bound' in the affective domain than, for example, in the psychomotor domain. Nonetheless, threshold concepts could provide a foundation on which teachers – like Hannah – can base learning outcomes related to SEL. However, doing so requires both (explicit) intent and (sustained) implementation within practice and may also require as Hannah suggests: 'a fundamental shift in teaching philosophy and pedagogy.'

References

afPE. (2016). Outcomes of PE. Retrieved from http://www.afpe.org.uk/physical-education/wp-content/uploads/Outcomes-of-PE-Poster-September-2016-web-version.pdf (Last accessed January 03, 2020).

Bailey, R., Armour, K., Kirk, D., Jess, M., Pickup, I., & Sandford, R. (2009). The educational benefits claimed for physical education and school sport: An academic review. Research Papers in Education, 24(1), 1–27.

Beni, S., Fletcher, T., & Ní Chróinín, D. (2017). Meaningful experiences in physical education and youth sport: A review of the literature. Quest, 69(3), 291–312.

Bourdieu, P. (1985). The social space and the genesis of groups. Theory and Society, 14(6), 723–744.

Bourdieu, P. (1986). The forms of capital. In J. Richardson (Ed.), Handbook of Theory and Research for the Sociology of Education (pp. 241–258). New York, NY: Greenwood Press.

Bourdieu, P. (1990). The Logic of Practice. Stanford, CA: Stanford University Press.

CASEL. (2017). SEL Core Competencies. Retrieved from https://casel.org/core-competencies/ (Last accessed January 03, 2020).

CASEL. (2019a). Overview of SEL. Retrieved from https://casel.org/overview-sel/ (Last accessed January 03, 2020).

CASEL (2019b). *SEL Impact.* Retrieved from https://casel.org/impact/ (Last accessed January 03, 2020).

Cecchini, J., Montero, J., Alonso, A., Izquierdo, M., & Contreras, O. (2007). Effects of personal and social responsibility on fair play in sports and self-control in school-aged youths. *European Journal of Sport Science, 7*(4), 203–211.

Ciotto, C., & Gagnon, A. (2018). Promoting social and emotional learning in physical education. *Journal of Physical Education, Recreation and Dance, 89*(4), 27–33.

Durlak, J., Weissberg, R., Dymnicki, A., Taylor, R., & Schellinger, K. (2011). The impact of enhancing students' social and emotional learning: A meta-analysis of school-based universal interventions. *Child Development, 82*(1), 405–432.

Gagnon, A. (2016). Creating a positive social-emotional climate in your elementary physical education program, *Strategies, 29*(3), 21–27.

Gordon, B., & Doyle, S. (2015). Teaching personal and social responsibility and transfer of learning: Opportunities and challenges for teachers and coaches. *Journal of Teaching in Physical Education, 34*(1), 152–161.

Green, K. (2020). Physical education and school sport: Is there a wider social role? In S. Capel, & R. Blair (Eds.), *Debates in Physical Education* (2nd ed., pp. 18–35). Abingdon: Routledge.

Hellison, D. (1985). *Goals and Strategies for Physical Education.* Champaign, IL: Human Kinetics.

Hellison, D. (1995). *Teaching Responsibility Through Physical Cctivity.* Champaign, IL: Human Kinetics.

Jacobs, F., Knoppers, A., & Webb, L., (2013). Making sense of teaching social and moral skills in physical education. *Physical Education and Sport Pedagogy, 18*(1), 1–14.

Jacobs, J., & Wright, P. (2014). Social and emotional learning policies and physical education, *Strategies, 27*(6), 42–44.

McCuaig, L., Marino, M., Gobbi, E., & Macdonald, D. (2015). *Taught not Caught: Values based education through physical education and School Sport: Literature Review.* AIESEP Partners for WADA, ICSSPE, IOC, Fairplay & UNESCO.

Meyer, J., & Land, R. (2003). *Threshold Concepts and Troublesome Knowledge: Linkages to Ways of Thinking and Practising within the Disciplines* (ETL Project, Report 4). Retrieved from http://www.etl.tla.ed.ac.uk/docs/ETLreport4.pdf (Last accessed January 03, 2020).

Meyer, J., & Land, R. (2005). Threshold concepts and troublesome knowledge (2): Epistemological considerations and a conceptual framework for teaching and learning, *Higher Education, 49*(3), 373–388.

Meyer, J., & Land, R. (2006). Threshold concepts and troublesome knowledge: Issues of liminality, In J. Meyer, & R. Land (Eds.), *Overcoming Barriers to Student Understanding: Threshold concepts and troublesome knowledge* (pp. 19–32). New York, NY: Routledge.

Riolo, I. (2019) *A Journey towards value-laden education. Understanding teacher's perceptions of the social domain within the Maltese PE context.* Unpublished Doctoral Thesis. Loughborough University.

Rossi, T., & Jeanes, R. (2016). Education, pedagogy and sport for development: Addressing seldom asked questions, *Sport, Education and Society, 21*(4), 483–494.

Sandford, R., Duncombe, R., & Armour, K. (2008). The role of physical activity/sport in tackling youth disaffection and anti-social behaviour. *Educational Review, 60*(4), 419–435.

Taylor, R. Oberle. E. Durlak, J., & Weissberg, R. (2017). Promoting positive youth development through school-based social and emotional learning interventions: A meta-analysis of follow-up effects. *Child Development, 88*(4), 1156–1171.

Watson, D., & Emery, C. (2010). From rhetoric to reality: The problematic nature and assessment of children and young people's social and emotional learning. *British Educational Research Journal, 36*(5), 767–786.

Wright, P., & Irwin, C. (2018). Using systematic observation to assess teacher effectiveness in promoting personally and socially responsible behavior in physical education, *Measurement in Physical Education and Exercise Science, 22*(3), 250–262.

Wright, P., Gordon, B., & Gray, S. (*forthcoming*). Social and emotional learning in the physical education curriculum. In M. He & W. Schubert (Eds.) *The Oxford Encyclopaedia of Curriculum Studies.*

Zins, J, Weissberg, R. Wang, M. & Walberg, H. (2004). *Building academic success on social and emotional learning: What does the research say?* New York, NY: Teachers College Press.

Part III

Lessons learned: Threshold concepts for physical education

Chapter 11

Threshold concepts for physical education

David Aldous and Fiona C. Chambers

Introduction

As highlighted in Chapter 2, we have a significant issue in physical education (PE) which has compounded the lack of status of our subject and our profession. It is this – it appears that PE has not claimed any threshold concepts. As a starting point, Chapters 1 and 2 explored the nature of PE. This led to the conclusion that PE was a cross discipline and, within the taxonomy of cross-disciplines, it is termed an interdisciplinary profession. This shows the disciplinary complexity of PE. Moreover, it points to the uniqueness of PE being informed (a) by threshold concepts from all disciplines which contribute to it and (b) having its own threshold concepts which reside in a third space (Bhabha, 1994), an interstitial space (Figure 11.1), between all such disciplines.

Methodology

Case studies

As evident within section two, the seven exploratory case studies used the Chambers (2018) design thinking approach to address a design challenge to identify threshold concepts in PE. Writing pods, comprising academics and practitioners examined the following areas of human movement: gymnastics, dance, parkour, outdoor education, martial arts, Gaelic games and netball. Writing pods drew on their (a) research, (b) experiences of teaching children and young people and (c) educating current and future PE teachers. These contributions were also shaped by writing pod authors' own biopedagogies (Armour & Fernandez-Balboa, 2001).

Data analysis

Data analysis (DA) involved two iterative phases: (1) dialogic analysis (Matusov, Marjanovic-Shane, & Gradovski, 2019; Lambert & Penney, 2020) with discourse analysis and (2) knowledge mapping (Raiker & Procter, 2012). This was conducted by the editors through the online Concept Board tool, guided by the following principles,

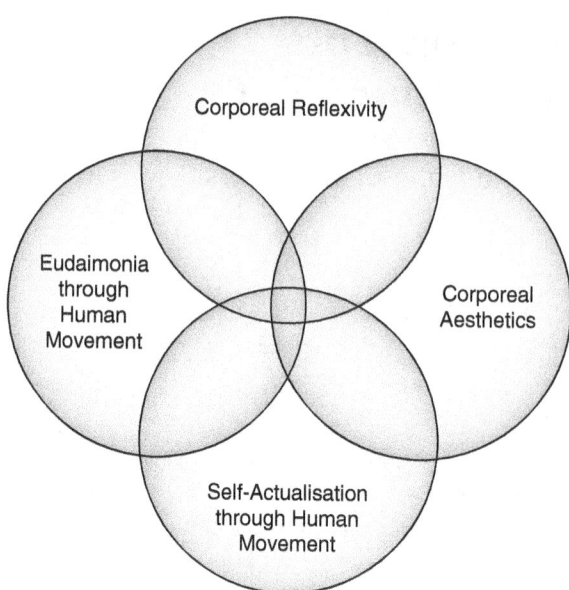

Figure 11.1 Diagram illustrating the interstitial spaces between threshold concepts.

a   *Dialogic analysis*: Matsusov et al. (2019) claim that dialogic analysis is an interpretative methodology which closely analyses spoken or written utterances or actions for their embedded communicative significance. In this case, it is interrogating the consumption and production of knowledge of writing pod members. We employed sensitising questions to support the dialogic analysis. This involved the heart and mind of the researcher to try to reveal and deepen the meanings of the studied phenomena by addressing and replying to the diverse research participants, other scholars, and anticipated readers.

b   *Discourse analysis*: According to Hall and Chambers (2012), discourse analysis is the study of texts. Texts are what people say and what people write, and include multimodal texts incorporating a combination of visual, print, image and audio texts. Furthermore, they posit discourse analysis does two things simultaneously as it both draws attention to the language used and to the social dimension of its use.

Hall and Chambers (2012) further highlight how those who analyse discourse, identify both the:

> preferred or intended meaning a text seeks to convey and, crucially, they also identify the linguistic devices used to construct that preferred meaning …. They seek to establish the dominant version of reality that is brought into

life via the text … By showing how a text achieves its desired effects, i.e., how we are persuaded to read it as the author intends us to read it, the discourse analyst renders something of the process visible. Thus, the text is opened up for deeper scrutiny and review and, in the process, alternative readings to the preferred or intended reading can be offered (p. 296–297).

In reading, we were interested in *'what the taken-for-granted, insider scripts and discourses are, and how they might enable and constrain what is doable, sayable and thinkable [which is] never innocent or neutral. It is always partial, always from a position, shaping and shaped by society'* (Hall & Chambers, 2012, p. 298). So, when engaging in DA, we began with the speaker's intended meaning first i.e. 'reading with the grain.' Then, we moved to 'reading against the grain,' highlighting the issues with which they might disagree. This resulted in a collection of concepts which were added to a movement 'concept sandbox' through a process of knowledge mapping. This involved: (i) creating mind-maps of connected concepts (nodes) from the concept sandbox and (ii) developing linking statements between each concept (node). The process led to the identification of four threshold concepts for PE, each of which demonstrated Land et al.'s (2005) eight key characteristics of threshold concepts, i.e. transformative; performative; irreversible; integrative; bounded; troublesome; reconstitutive and discursive (see Chapter 2).

These four agreed threshold concepts for PE are: (1) Corporeal reflexivity; (2) corporeal aesthetics; (3) self-actualisation through human movement and (4) Eudaimonia through human movement. The chapter now begins to outline the initial construction of threshold concepts that are unique to PE. In the findings section, we will define, outline and begin to unpack some of the key characteristics of each. The examples provided are not intended to be prescriptive, but rather a point where readers can begin to formulate their own ideas as a starting point of creativity.

Findings & discussion: Generating four threshold concepts for physical education

Corporeal reflexivity

Analysis of the case studies highlighted an implicit and explicit focus on the role of the body. Given the focus on movement within these case studies, the presence of the body should come as no surprise. Indeed, the sociology and philosophy of education has continually highlighted the role of the body in learning across a number of different movement contexts, including dance and choreography (Wellard et al., 2007) and martial arts (Brown, 2013) as well as PE. Such work, resonating the corporeal turn within social theory (Shilling, 2005; 2012), has often reinforced the notion of the role of the body as being 'layered, complex, contradictory and contested' (Kirk, 2004, p. 64). Yet, despite the plethora of critical scholarship regarding the body in education, as Evans (2004) there comments:

the discipline's capacity and pedagogical responsibility to work on, effect changes in, develop and enhance **'the body's' intelligent capacities** for movement and expression in physical culture, in all its varied forms, **has been displaced** (Evans, 2004, p. 96)

Such displacement of professional interest in the body, is reflective of the continued need for physical educators' attention being centred on what Evans (2004, p. 96) notes as 'just about everything other than that which is distinctive and special about itself and its subject matter.' This is in response to a multitude of dominant health, sport and performance discourses (Evans et al., 2004; Webb et al., 2004; Evans et al., 2008) that have suppressed focus on the subjective and affective corporealism of the body, advocated by sociological lenses. As a consequence, PE in schools and (more worryingly) in Physical Education Teacher Education (PETE) **has become a disembodied subject,** in which the body exists as somewhat of an elusive omnipresence, which discourages educators creating movement understanding and practices that are complex, multidimensional and which foster learner autonomy. As a result, an understanding of the body that transcends learning domains and curricula focus is rare and is clearly in need of renewed attention. Thus, a threshold concept that encourages practitioners to focus on the body as a vehicle for learning within the micro-level of the classroom seems to not only be important but necessary for the future interdisciplinarity of PE. Corporeal reflexivity puts the 'body' back into focus in PE, not only as a vehicle and site for learning, but as a catalyst for learning. Learners who enjoy corporeal reflexivity have the following qualities.

The data analysis process brought us toward a knowledge map, illustrated in Figure 11.2 that places a more explicit focus on the role of the body in the knowledge and practice of movement. Such nodes resonate with the work of Ochs (2015, p. 277), who summarises corporeal reflexivity as involving:

> displays of awareness of one's body as both an embodied, experiencing subject and an embodied physical object accessible to the gaze of others. In displays of corporeal reflexivity, the embodied, experiencing subject turns its attention to its physical body, re-visioning it as an object of scrutiny, usually under the normative gaze of others.

Whilst PE has been recognised as an educative space where the complexity of the body is constructed (Webb et al., 2008) our development of the term corporeal reflexivity aims to draw attention to support educators and learners to become more knowledgeable regarding the body and embrace the complexity of the body within the praxis of PE. This enables the body to become both an embodied and experiencing subject; emphasising the lived, physical and environmental dimensions of the body. Doing so, builds upon the work of Evans et al. (2010) whose focus on the corporeal device focused on the body *'not just as a discursive construction, a conduit for the relay of messages outside itself – but as a*

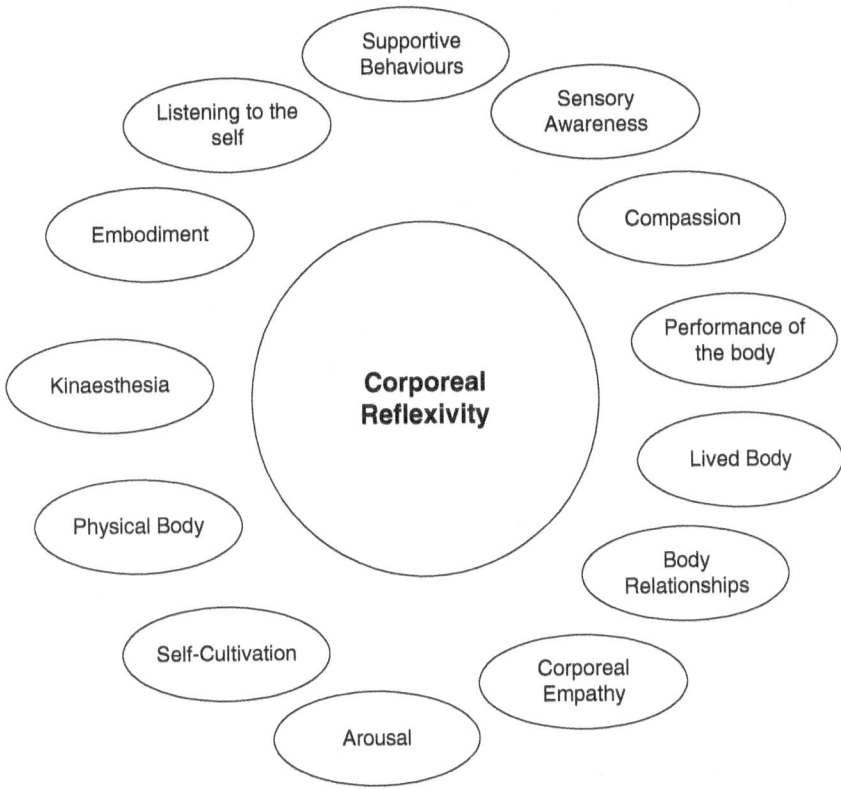

Figure 11.2 Knowledge map – Threshold concept for PE: Corporeal reflexivity.

biological body, a material relay of and for itself' (p. 179). In doing so, it could be construed that corporeal reflexivity is **troublesome** in that it enables the learner to become aware of how *their* body is both an object of scrutiny but also a source of creative and generative power. In many respects, our use of the concept, as an educative catalyst, is intended to be **transformative** in the sense it encourages the learner to become reflexively aware of how the body is surveyed by others (Webb et al., 2004). Furthermore, the nodes evident within Figure 11.2, are intended to enable learners to become aware of the reflexive potential of their own bodies in relation to others. As such, it is hoped that by focusing on the reflexive nature of the body, learners can in time also learn to be critical of the existing surveillance practices and associated assumptions about the body that have seen to lead to a number of health related problems (Evans et al., 2010). As such, it is evident that corporeal reflexivity has a number of elements that can be characterised as being **reconstitutive.**

The emphasis on enabling learners to become reflexively aware of their body points to the need for PE to provide a space from where people are able to become aware of the interconnectedness between their self, the physical body and the world around them; a critical element in the cultural relay/transformation of knowledge into forms of movement practices (see Quennerstedt, Ohman, & Ohman, 2011). Thus, in many respects the focus provided by the multi-dimensional focus of corporeal reflexivity has a number of **irreversible and bounded** qualities; in the sense that once a learner becomes reflexively aware, they may then develop a sense of agency over their experience of movement.

One nodal concept that has emerged through our discussions has been how a potential focus on **self-cultivation through the body** may influence learners' knowledge and practice of movement. Evident as a key principle with Eastern movement forms (see Jennings, Brown, & Sparkes 2010), self-cultivation places distinctive orientation on uniting the body, mind and spirit through forms of physical practice (Brown, 2013). As noted by the Japanese philosopher Yuasa (1987, cited in Brown, 2013, p. 2), self-cultivation is a practice that, 'that attempts, so to speak, to achieve true knowledge by means of one's total mind and body.' The focus on true knowledge exemplifies how the concept of self-cultivation has both **irreversible** and **transforming** qualities that would sensitise *both* educators and learners to teaching and experiencing PE as a way of cultivating and enhancing spirituality through the physical body and not merely as a series of corrective techniques that perhaps are evident within some forms of westernised PE curricula. Such points also resonate with the work of Garfinkel (2006) in the sense that PE must focus the development of movement by ensuring that the concept of corporeal reflexivity is applied in a way to enable young people to have the knowledge and ability to develop a critical understanding of their body and those of others. This moves beyond reading the body but also understanding how the body can be read and interpreted in a human movement context.

Therefore, whilst we would exercise some caution in making too many claims regarding the potential of corporeal reflexivity, we do believe that as a concept it reflects the eight characteristics of a threshold concept. Accordingly, it does offer a way of further encouraging educators and learners to acknowledge the role of the body in a more prominent and imaginative way within PE. Our encouragement is also exemplified in the development of the concept corporeal aesthetics.

Corporeal aesthetics

The data analysis process of the case studies highlighted the importance of the interplay between (a) action, (b) cognition and (c) experience of being, within movement, which led to the threshold concept of corporeal aesthetics (Figure 11.3). The principles behind this concept strongly resonate with the viewpoint of Dyer (2009, p. 108) who notes how:

> Movement aesthetic values emerge from personal and communal morals and ideals as well as social mores of the body, which create **contextual lenses for experiencing**, interpreting, and making meaning of movement vocabularies created and perpetuated in dance communities.

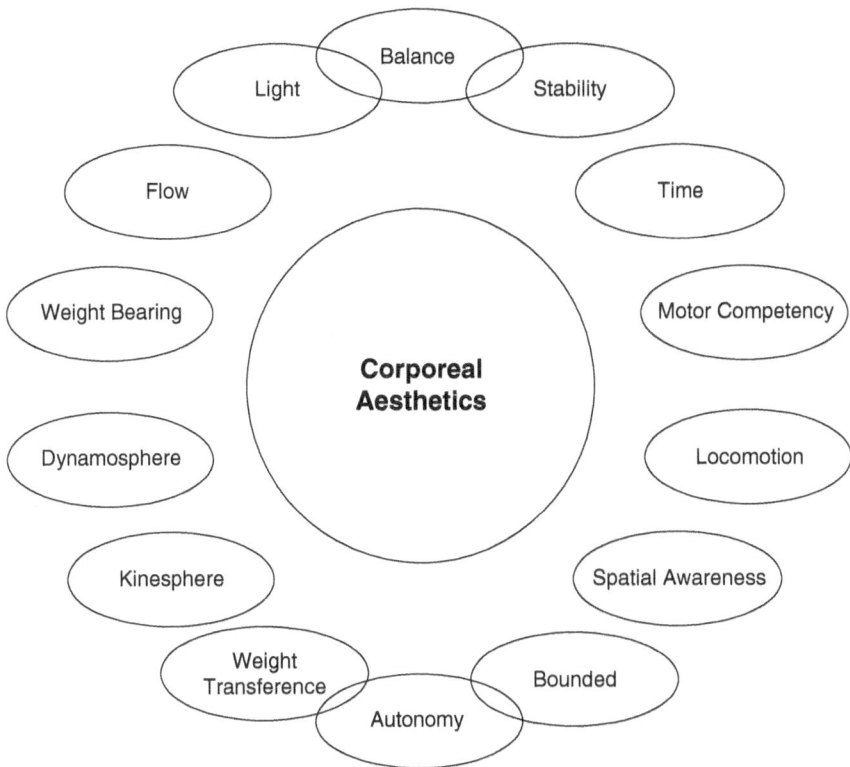

Figure 11.3 Knowledge map – Threshold concept for PE: Corporeal aesthetics.

Building on the work of Dyer, we posit that this threshold concept will help phys-ical educators to harness the dynamic relationship between the biological, physi-ological and cognitive elements that occurs in all movement contexts.

Harnessing this dynamic relationship exemplifies how corporeal aesthetics may be **troublesome**. This resonates with the viewpoint of Hoogland (2003), who describes the power of the embodied experience:

> Taking the existential condition of any subject's being-in-the-world approach the practice of [physical education] as in Braidotti (2002) words, an 'embod-ied' and 'embedded' practice of becoming, that is to say, as an ongoing process of making and doing that is indispensable to the continual co-production of both human beings and their variously interconnected material and socio-symbolic outsides.

Mastering such power enables educators and learners to engage with movement experiences that focus on the **integrative** connections between the sensual, phys-ical and emotional elements of movement. This resonates with Dewey's theory of experience. In describing the impact of an aesthetic experience, Hoogland (2003) has this to offer:

> [It is] neither intellectual, cognitive, nor even spiritual, but primarily affective: at once perceptual and sensual, physical, and emotional. They had been touched at a level that, in a slightly different perspective, might be located at the interface between the corporeal and the incorporeal … is the very down-to-earth quality of aesthetic experience, its phenomenal immediacy and undeniably embodied nature (p. 4)

Consequently, a focus on Corporeal Aesthetics of movement enables further understanding of what Bell (2009) points to the potency of aesthetic movement as a **discursive** space for learning to be human: 'Activities that are so physical, aesthetic, and established appear to play a particularly powerful role in shaping human sensibility and imagination' (p. 137). Furthermore, in highlighting how the learner may wrestle with aesthetic experiences Dewey is further accentuating the **transformative** and **irreversible** elements of corporeal aesthetics. He purported '*The aesthetic harmony and tension emerges out of the interaction between the experiencer and the environment*' (Haskins, 2020, p. 453). This describes the multi-domain engagement with the aesthetics of a given **performance** in PE. Haskins refers to embodied aesthetics or the aesthetics of embodied life (ibid, p. 453) which might help to give credence to the notion of corporeal aesthetics.

Corporeal aesthetics comprises concept nodes that resonate extensively from the work of Laban and Bartenieff movement analysis (Maletic, 1987; Payne, 2017) *and* those principles found with more scientific orientated languages such as motor competency (see Logan et al., 2018). As evident within case studies, the work of Laban and later Bartenieff places focus on analysing relationships that aim to demonstrate connectivity between the body, space, effort and shape. Furthermore, case studies emphasise the importance of weight transference, weight bearing and balance when engaging in movement learning experiences in PE. Such concepts invoke a focus on the buoyancy, effortlessness and intensity of movement. In addition, concept nodes associated with weight, space, time and flow reinforce the importance of what Laban referred to as the dynamosphere (Kikhia et al., 2014). In the same way, concept nodes point to the importance of having an understanding of what Laban referred to as the Kinesphere. This being the 'reach space' around the body is to the teaching and understanding of movement. Collectively, these concept nodes highlight the **reconstitutive** nature of corporeal aesthetics.

Our Concept nodes also include a focus on locomotion. Whilst locomotion is also an embryonic term that contains many components (see Medved, 2001), its focus on understanding the actions by which 'the body as a whole moves through aerial, aquatic and terrestrial spaces' (Medved, 2001, p. 1) makes it a critical component in the focus of understanding the flow of the body through spaces as an integral element to the teaching of movement.

Whilst undeniably influential, on their own these terms, only convey a one dimensional understanding and practice of movement. As Chapter 9 illustrates, critical to a multi-dimensional and connective understanding of the aesthetics of movement is the focus on movement found within the languages of motor competencies and fundamental movement skills. Whilst beyond the capacity of our initial ruminations regarding the aesthetics through movement concept to cover in-depth the multitude of terms and foci that motor competencies generate (see Logan et al., 2018 for a comprehensive account), the key focus on goal-directed and **performative** elements of movement is highly valuable in informing practitioners knowledge and practice of movement. As such it should be a critical element of the languages of movement repertoire but *only* if it is taught in a way that connects the internal language syntaxes to the creation of pedagogical practices that enable learners to retain a sense of autonomy in the aesthetical appreciation and practice of movement.

Separately, concept nodes of the **Corporeal Aesthetics** have made an extensive contribution to the advancement of knowledge and practice of movement across a range of PE, dance and physical activity contexts. **Corporeal Aesthetics** emphasises the following for practitioners (a) the value of interweaving Laban's Movement Analysis framework, motor competency and physical literacy literature. Such synergistic relationships empower the learner to critique their movement in the context of the movement environment and (b) the powerful symbiotic relationship between corporeal reflexivity and corporeal aesthetics.

Self-actualisation

In 1943, Abraham Maslow proposed his hierarchy of needs theory in the field of psychology. These have been derived from the most rudimentary needs of human beings i.e. those of Maslow (1943) (a) our biological needs as individuals; (b) our need to coordinate our actions with others; and (c) the need of groups to survive and flourish. This outlined the five basic human needs in the form of a hierarchy, also called the Hierarchy of Human Needs. The five needs that were originally enlisted were physiological, safety, love and belonging, esteem and self-actualisation. Maslow further expanded self-actualisation into four needs, namely: cognitive, aesthetic, self-actualization and self-transcendence. Maslow regarded the drive towards self-actualisation as being a core benefit to society leading to solidarity, compassion, care, problem-solving and altruism. Arnold summarised Maslow's (1954) view of self-actualised people as follows:

> [They] are marked by their more than usually efficient perception of reality; their acceptance of self and others; their spontaneity; their lack of ego-centeredness; their non avoidance of privacy; their autonomy; their ability to derive inspiration and strength from the ordinary experiences of life; their ability to have frequent peak experiences; their feeling for

mankind by way of sympathy and identification; their ability to form deep personal relationships; their democratic character-structure in that they can form relationships irrespective of class, education, race, and religion; their ability to differentiate between ends and means; their sense of humor; their creativeness; their relative detachment from the culture in which they are immersed that they are more readily able to discover their growth needs or being values (p. 92)

This compelling description illustrated in Figure 11.4, draws attention to the complexity of the self-actualised state, which could be construed as **troublesome** for the learner as he/she learns to enact and **integrate** a myriad of abilities. Further, it points to the **transformative** nature of self-actualisation, should it be realised. Moreover, it is clear that there is an **irreversible** quality to it, as the person experiences the feeling of being truly self-actualised. In Chapter 2, we outlined how PE was an interdiscipline within the taxonomy of cross-disciplines – As such PE has a central role to play in educating learners to be self-actualised. It was

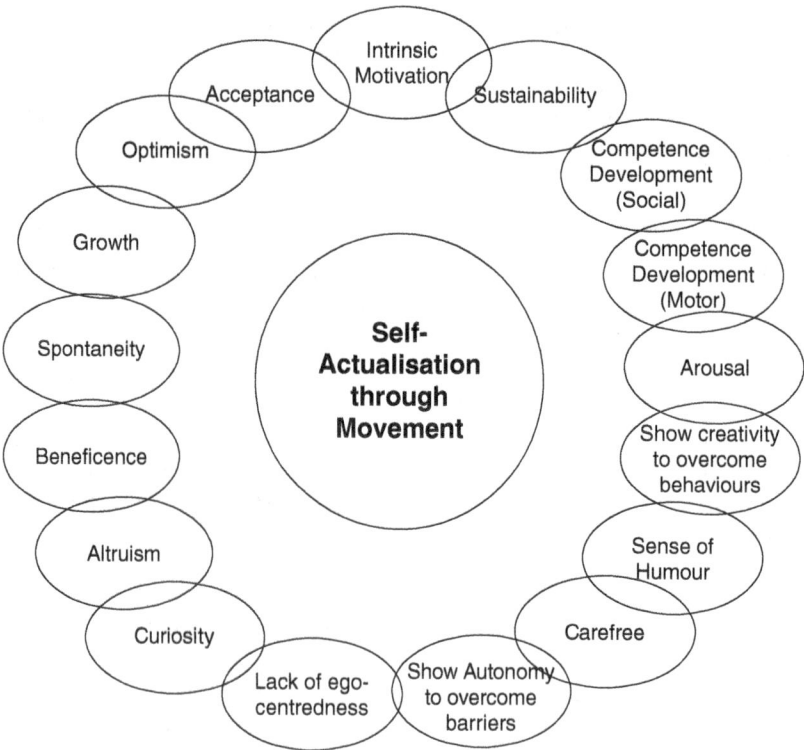

Figure 11.4 Knowledge map – Threshold concept for PE: Self actualisation through human movement

Allen & Fahey (1977) who pointed to the fact that physical activities provide a locus for such 'being values'. Peter Arnold (1979) supports this view:

> One aim of education, therefore, is to provide a range of activities that when entered into, are likely to bring about actualized states of being which can be enjoyed for their own sake. These will, of course, include so-called 'practical' subjects as well as 'academic' ones. In terms of self-actualization the most worthwhile subjects will be those which when engaged upon will bring about the most complete or most intense states of being which are found in themselves valuable. Clearly in such a scheme physical education, made up as it is from games, swimming, gymnastics, athletics, outdoor pursuits, dance and the like, has a part to play (p. 92)

Once more, this shows a context for self-actualisation *within* PE. This highlights the **performative** nature of this self-actualisation and that it can be perhaps **bounded** within PE in this respect. The self-actualised learner's use of language changes as he/she articulates the feeling of self-actualisation through human movement – the **discursive.** Such experiences of self-actualisation are often found in peak or flow states where 'being values' are omnipresent, linked to prior knowledge. In this way learning to be self-actualised is **reconstitutive.** Maslow (1968) description is helpful here:

> an episode, or a spurt in which the powers of the person come together in a particularly efficient and intensely enjoyable way, and in which he is more integrated and less split, more open for experience, more idiosyncratic, more perfectly expressive or spontaneous, or fully functioning, more creative, more humorous, more ego-transcending, more independent of his lower needs, etc. He becomes in these episodes more truly himself, more perfectly actualizing his potentialities, closer to the core of his being, more fully human. (p. 97).

It is clear that self-actualisation incorporates all eight characteristics of a threshold concept. We therefore claim 'self-actualisation through movement' as a core PE threshold concept.

As Self-actualisation through human movement is underpinned by 'being values' it can be taught using a model of values based education (VBE). Physical Education is a space for VBE (McCuaig et al., 2015; Chambers & Sandford, 2018). Research shows that learning in PE can help children and young people to build character, develop 'life skills,' engage in positive youth development, develop as socio-moral citizens, contribute to community development and learn how to resolve conflict (Rossi & Jeanes, 2016). In this respect, McCuaig et al. (2015) notes that PE has three unique affordances: the subject matter, the learning environments and the caring teacher-student relationships. Learning to be **self-actualised through human movement** is a complex endeavour, but with a thoughtful pedagogical approach, it can be attained.

Eudaimonia through human movement

Wellbeing can be construed as either **hedonistic** or eudaimonic. Hedonia centres on happiness, '*the emotional state associated with full engagement or optimal performance in meaningful activity*' (Averill & More, 2004, p. 664). In contrast, **eudaimonia** focuses on living life in a full and deeply satisfying way (Deci & Ryan, 2008; Houge Mackenzie & Hodge, 2020). Bullough & Pinnegar (2009) state that happiness (hedonia) ensues when (activity) is found (to be) intrinsically rewarding, morally upstanding, purposeful, appropriately challenging and fully supportive of the learning and development of the people involved (p. 246). Hedonia and eudaimonia are two sides of the 'wellbeing coin.' Here, the focus is on eudaimonia (Figure 11.5).

Huta & Ryan (2010) describe how self-actualisation and eudaimonia are the catalysts for human endeavour, but flow is particularly associated with eudaimonia (Csikzentmihalyi, 1997) (See Chapter 2). Eudaimonia is a combination of an uplifting feeling of skill mastery, mental happiness, enhanced self-esteem, transcendence, ecstasy and euphoria (Cooper, 1998). Chatfield (2012) describes it as

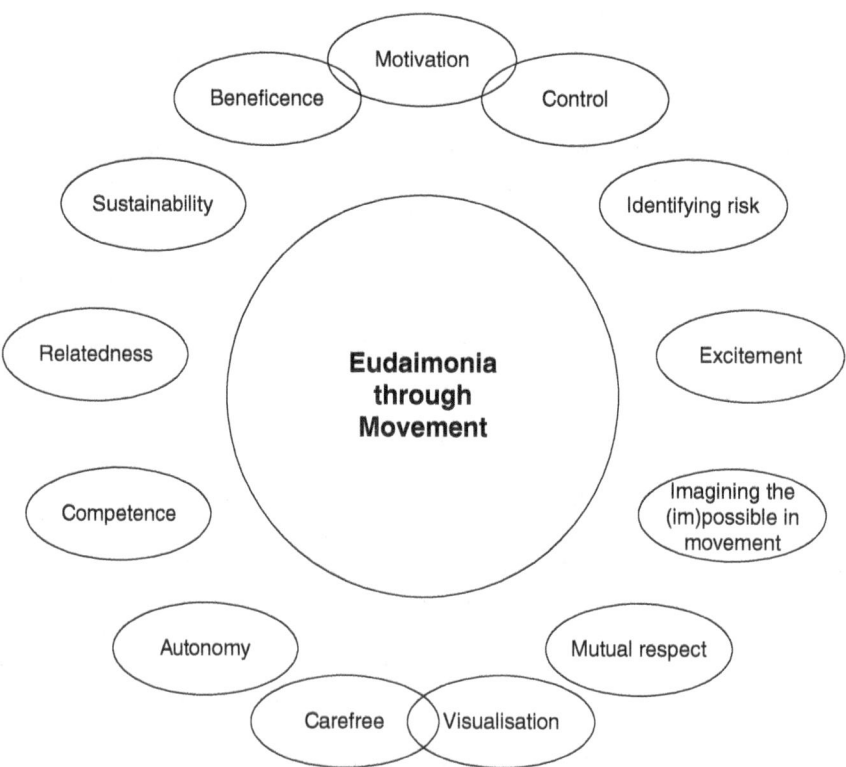

Figure 11.5 Knowledge map – Threshold concept for PE: Eudaimonia through movement

human thriving and flourishing. Freeman (2000, p. 280) spoke about the fact that being human implies that we all have innate potential which needs to be nurtured so that we can fulfil this potential:

> If everything has a purpose there has to be a final end (telos) of any organism to which its form is directed. For a fish it might be to swim well. Therefore, every move of the form is toward making it swim well. It grows fins, a tail, a means of breathing without air, so that it can fulfill its potential. Aristotle argues that the human 'substance' is shaped toward the state of eudaimonia, well-being, the state of flourishing as a human.

It is clear that eudaimonia emerges for learners in those moments when they are fully engaged in meaningful activities in PE, when they sense what they are doing represents their best performance, their fullest expression of the goodness of human movement.

The features of eudaimonic subjective wellbeing are purpose and life satisfaction (Houge Mackenzie & Hodge, 2020). These are actualised through via the satisfaction of the three basic psychological needs for autonomy, competence and relatedness as outlined in Self Determination Theory (SDT), as well as the recently proposed fourth basic need for beneficence (Martela & Ryan, 2016; Martela, Ryan, & Steger, 2018). In sum, based on research on self-determination theory, basic psychological needs, and prosocial impact, Martela & Riekki (2018) suggest that:

> There are four psychological satisfactions that significantly shape meaningfulness across cultures: autonomy (sense of volition), competence (sense of efficacy), relatedness (sense of caring relationships), and beneficence (sense of making a positive contribution) (p. 1).

All of these dimensions indicate that it is a **performative** endeavour, which is also **troublesome** as it demands simultaneous learner confidence and competence. This leads to a **transformative, irreversible** and **bounded** within human movement (PE) where the learner scaffolds his her learning **reconstituting** and **integrating** it in light of this new eudaimonic experience, so that it becomes part of his/her discourse **(discursive)**.

Self-determination theory provides a valuable framework for examining motivationally supportive PE experiences through satisfaction of three basic psychological needs: autonomy, competence and relatedness. By using the Schwartz Continuum of Values (2012) (see earlier in this chapter), the learner is challenged to begin to move toward beneficence as a fourth aspect of eudaimonia.

In helping students to become producers and consumers of knowledge (Cook-Sather & Luz, 2015) or as Chambers (2019) terms it, prosumers of knowledge, skills and attitudes. Empowering the learner in this way disrupts the traditional student–teacher relationship and can contribute towards further epistemological maturity, which can clear to autonomy and competence and a greater sense of agency. Mezirow terms this as transformative learning, which involves exploring, trying on, building competence in, and integrating new roles and relationships. The first step in this is self-awareness which means becoming: 'critically aware of the cultural and psychological assumptions that have influenced the way we see ourselves and our relationships and the way we pattern our lives' (Mezirow 1978, p. 101). The use of the flipped classroom can be one way to PE nurture this. Zainudden & Perera (2019) assert that the flipped classroom helps develop student autonomy and empower the learner.

Conclusion

The eclectic range of movement languages, and concepts evident within the case studies of Section 2 reinforces our belief that PE is a cauldron of interdisciplinary learning each of which contribute to the conceptual and empirical understanding of movement. Such eclecticism can only be a positive catalyst in enabling PE to be able to continually evolve and become more creative in its response to what design thinkers term a range of 'wicked problems.' However, as we have also highlighted within this chapter, unless such eclecticism is harnessed, it may also contribute to the displacement of the focus on the critical relationship between body, mind and spirit that are central to the sustainable experiences of movement within PE.

Such eclecticism might also play a role in deterring educators in engaging with the principles of each concept; critical in the creation of their own conceptual languages of movement. With this in mind, our chapter has focused on beginning to map out what we believe to be four key threshold concepts that can be used by educators in the creative development of movement within PE. Augmenting the work outlined in Chapters 1 and 2, what we have hoped to achieve is addressing Rowbottom's (2007) critique around the ambiguity of threshold concepts. To do so, we have used the model illustrated in Figure 11.6 a means from where we can critically discuss the nature of 'concepts' in order to provide clarity around the meaning of threshold concepts and their connectivity to the pedagogical context of movement.

In our adapted model, the threshold concepts are representative of internal languages of movement. As we have emphasised in Chapter 1, we believe that such languages should be comprised of a weak grammatical syntax and be used in a non-reductionist manner. Retaining this weak grammatical syntax enables the threshold concepts to be interactive. The external languages of movement are generated from the threshold concepts and orientated towards empirical understanding of movement within pedagogical contexts such as Parkour, Gymnastics, Outdoor Education and Dance.

Aligned with the design thinking that has influenced our thinking throughout this book, we intend for these ideas as a starting point to be put into practice. By no means do we feel that the concepts presented are absolute. Nevertheless,

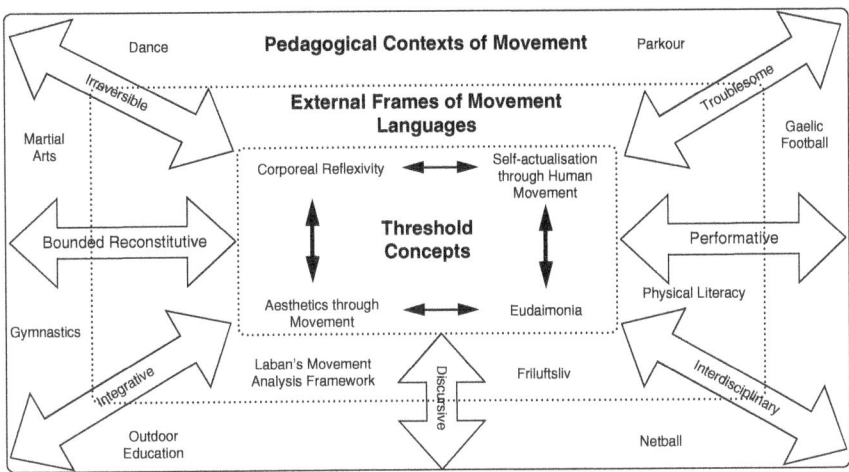

Figure 11.6 Diagram to illustrate the sociological construction of threshold concepts for movement (MkI).

Source: Adapted from Morais & Neves, 2001.

the illustration presented should be considered a heuristic/sensitising device from where practitioners from different cultures/backgrounds might generate their own concepts/frameworks that are specific to their own pedagogical contexts.

Our proposed initial generation of *Threshold Concepts for Physical Education* have attempted to take a holistic and organic approach. What should be immediately evident is the dialectical interconnection between each of the concepts. Such interconnectivity is central to enabling practitioners transcend their knowledge and practice across assemblages that necessitate multiple interpellations that transcend the four cognitive, affective, psychomotor and social domains so prevalent within the learning and practice of PE. In presenting the concepts in this manner, whilst we have also attempted to retain a sense of their weak grammatical structure, we fully acknowledge that at this stage, there is also a danger of creating an internal language of description that conceptual language that is in danger of not being able to be transformed to inform practice within specific pedagogical contexts. Consequently, what is required is for the concepts to now be overtly planned to inform 'rich learning outcomes' (Dennehy & Chambers, 2019). These rich learning outcomes take account of the preliminal, liminal and postliminal states. By unpacking rich learning outcomes physical educators can identify the threshold concepts which the learner must attain to achieve this rich learning outcome.

Clearly, the characteristics of each presented threshold concept offer only a brief introduction to our initial thinking. By our own omission, there remains much to do beyond the chapter and book. For example, we are acutely aware of both the lack of empirical research on how such concepts might already exist within practice but also how practitioners may now translate and create their own concepts in relation to the exigencies of their own context. Furthermore, we also acknowledge the significant gap in understanding how such concepts could be used within pedagogical contexts. It is with this point in mind that we turn our attention towards such considerations in Chapter 12.

References

Allen, D. J., & Fahey, B. W. (1977). *Being Human in Sport*. Philadelphia: Lea & Febiger.

Aristotle, (Ed.) (1943). Nicomachean ethics, book two. *Aristotle: On Man and The Universe*. Roslyn, NY: Walter J. Black.

Armour, K. M., & Fernandez-Balboa, J. M. (2001). Connections, pedagogy and professional learning. *Teaching and Teacher Education*, *12*(1), 103–118.

Arnold, P. (1979). *Meaning in Movement, Sport and Physical Education*. London: Heinemann.

Averill, J. R. & More, T. A. (Eds.) (2004). Happiness. *Handbook of Emotions*. New York: Guilford Press.

Bullough R. V. Jr., & Pinnegar, S. (2009). The happiness of teaching (as eudaimonia): Disciplinary knowledge and the threat of performativity. *Teachers and Teaching*, *15*(2), 241–256.

Bell, C. (2009). *Ritual: Perspectives and Dimensions*. Oxford: Oxford University Press.

Bhabha, H. K. (1994). *The Location of Culture*. New York: Routledge.

Braidotti, R. (2002). *Metamorphoses: Towards a Materialist Theory of Becoming*. Oxford: Blackwell.

Brown, D. (2013). Seeking spirituality through physicality in schools: Learning from 'Eastern movement forms', *International Journal of Children's Spirituality*, *18*(1), 30–45. doi:10.1080/1364436X.2013.776521

Chambers, F. C. (ed.) (2018). *Learning to Mentor in Sports Coaching: A Design Thinking Approach*. Oxon, Ox: Routledge.

Chambers, F. C. (2019). Developing the values compass. In F. C. Chambers, A. Jones, O. Murphy, & R. A. Sandford (Eds.) *Design Thinking for Digital Wellbeing: Theory and Practice for Educators*. London: Routledge.

Chambers, F. C. (2019). Implementing the values compass: Application to values dilemmas. In F. C. Chambers, A. Jones, O. Murphy, & R. A. Sandford (Eds.), *Design Thinking for Digital Wellbeing: Theory and Practice for Educators*. London: Routledge.

Chambers, F. C., & Sandford, R. A. (2018). Learning to be human in a digital world: A model of Values Fluency Education for Physical Education. *Sport Education and Society*, *24*(9), 925–938. doi: 10.1080/13573322.2018.1515071

Chatfied, T. (2012). *How to Thrive in a Digital Age*. London: Macmillan.

Cook-Sather, A., & Luz, A. (2015). Greater engagement in and responsibility for learning: What happens when students cross the threshold of student–faculty partnership. *Higher Education Research and Development*, *34*(6), 1097–1109.

Cooper, A. (1998). *Playing in the Zone: Exploring the Spiritual Dimensions of Sports*. Boston, MA, USA: Shambhala Publications.

Csikszentmihalyi, M. (1997). *Finding Flow: The Psychology of Engagement With Everyday Life*. New York, NY: Basic Books.

Deci, E. L., & Ryan, R. M. (2008). Hedonia, eudaimonia, and well-being: An introduction. *Journal of Happiness Studies*, *9*, 1–11.

Dennehy, N., & Chambers, F. C. (2019). *Connected Curriculum: Principles of Assessment.* University College Cork.

Dyer, J. (2009). Merging traditional technique vocabularies with democratic teaching perspectives in dance education: A consideration of aesthetic values and their sociopolitical contexts. *The Journal of Aesthetic Education, 43*(4), 108–123.

Evans, J. (2004). Making a difference? Education and 'ability' in physical education. *European Physical Education Review 10*(1), 97–108.

Evans, J., Rich, E., & Holroyd, R. (2004). Disordered eating and disordered schooling: What schools do to middle class girls. *British Journal of sociology of education, 25*(2), 123–142.

Evans, J., Rich, E., Davies, B., & Allwoood, R. (2008). Education, disordered eating and obesity discourse. *Fat Fabrications.* London: Routledge.

Evans, J., Davies, B., & Rich, E. (2010). Bernstein, body pedagogies and the corporeal device. In G. Ivinson, B. Davies, & B. Fitz (Eds.), *Knowledge and Identity: Concepts and Applications in Bernstein's Sociology,* (pp. 176–90). London: Routledge.

Freeman, C. (2000). *The Greek achievement.* New York: Viking.

Garfinkel, H. (2006). *Seeing Sociologically: The Routine Grounds of Social Action.* Boulder: Paradigm Publishers.

Hall, K., & Chambers, F. C. (2012). Discourse analysis. In K. M. Armour & D. Macdonald (eds.), *Research Methods in Physical Education and Youth Sport.* London: Routledge.

Haskins, C. (2020). Dewey's art as experience in the landscape of twenty first century aesthetics. In S. Fesmire (Ed.), *The Oxford Handbook of Dewey.* Oxford: Oxford University Press.

Hoogland, R. C. (2003). The matter of culture: Aesthetic experience and corporeal being. *Mosaic: An Interdisciplinary Critical Journal, 36*(3), 1–18.

Houge Mackenzie, S. & Hodge, K. (2020). Adventure recreation and subjective well-being: A conceptual framework. *Leisure Studies, 39*(1), 26–40.

Huta, V., & Ryan R. M. (2010). Pursuing pleasure or virtue: The differential and overlapping well-being benefits of hedonic and eudaimonic motives. *Journal of Happiness Studies, 1,* 735–762.

Jennings, G., Brown, D. H. K., & Sparkes, A. C. (2010). It can be a Religion for you if you want it to be: An ethnography of a Wing Chun Kung Fu's Club as a Body-Self Transforming Cultural Practice. *Ethnography, 11*(4), 533–557.

Kirk, D. (2004). Towards a critical history of the body, identity and health: Corporeal power and school practice. In J. Evans, B. Davies, & J. Wright (Eds.). *Body knowledge and control: Studies in the Sociology of Physical Education and Health* (pp. 52–68). London: Routledge.

Kikhia, B., Gomez, M., Jiménez, L., Hallberg, J., Karvonen, N., & Synnes, K. (2014). Analyzing body movements within the Laban effort framework using a single accelerometer, *Sensors, 14,* 5725–5741. doi: 10.3390/s140305725

Lambert, K., & Penney, D (2020). Curriculum interpretation and policy enactment in health and physical education: Research teacher educators as policy actors, *Sport, Education and Society, 25*(4), 378–394.

Land, R. et al., (Ed). (2005). *Threshold concepts and troublesome knowledge (3): Implications for course design and evaluation.* Improving Student Learning Oxford, Oxford Centre for Staff and Learning Development.

Logan, S. W., Ross, S. M., Chee, K., Stodden, D. F., & Robinson, L. E. (2018). Fundamental motor skills: A systematic review of terminology. *Journal of Sports Sciences, 36*(7), 781–796.

Luttrell, S., & Chambers, F. C. (2013). *Pathways for Teacher Implementation: Senior Cycle Physical Education Curriculum and Instructional Models*. Dublin: e-print.ie

Luttrell, S., & Chambers, F. C. (2013). *Learning Wall: A Cauldron of Curriculum and Instructional Models*. Dublin: e-print.ie

Payne, H. (2017). The psycho-neurology of embodiment with examples from authentic movement and Laban movement analysis. *American Journal of Dance Therapy*, 39, 163–178.

Maletic, V. (1987). *Body-Space-Expression: The Development of Rudolf Laban's Movement and Dance Concepts*. New York: Mouton de Gruyter.

Martela, F., & Ryan, R. M. (2016). The benefits of benevolence: Basic psychological needs, beneficence, and the enhancement of well-being. *Journal of Personality*, 84, 750–764.

Martela, F. et al. (2018). Meaningfulness as satisfaction of autonomy, competence, relatedness, and beneficence: Comparing the four satisfactions and positive affect as predictors of meaning in life. *Journal of Happiness Studies*, 19, 1261–1282.

Martela, F. & Riekki, T. J. J. (2018). Autonomy, competence, relatedness, and beneficence: A multicultural comparison of the four pathways to meaningful work. *Frontiers in Psychology*, 9(1157).

Maslow, A. H. (1954). *Motivation and Personality*. New York: Harper.

Maslow, A. H. (1968). *Towards a Psychology of Being*. Princeton, N.J.: Van Nostrand.

Matusov, E. Marjanovic-Shane, A., & Gradovski, M. (2019). *Dialogic Pedagogy and Polyphonic Research Art: Bakhtin by and for Educators*. doi: 10.1057/978-1-137-58057-3. New York: Palgrave Macmillan.

McCuaig, L., Marino, M., Gobbi, E., & Macdonald, D. (2015). Taught not Caught: Values based Education through physical education and School Sport: Literature Review. AIESEP Partners for WADA, ICSSPE, IOC, Fairplay & UNESCO.

Medved, V. (2001). Measurement of Human Locomotion. *Kinesiology*, 33(2), 5–19.

Mezirow, J. (1978). Perspective transformation. *Adult Education Quarterly*, 28(2).

Morais & Neves, (2001). Pedagogic social contexts: Studies for a sociology of learning. In A. Morais, I. Neves, B. Davies, & H. Daniels (Eds.). *Towards a Sociology of Pedagogy: The Contribution of Basil Bernstein to Research*. New York: Peter Lang.

Ochs, E. (2015). Corporeal reflexivity and autism. *Integrative Psychological Behaviour*, 49, 275–287.

Quennerstedt, M., Ohman, J., & Ohman, M. (2011). Investigating learning in physical education–A transactional approach. *Sport, Education and Society*, 16(3). 159–77.

Raiker, A., & Procter, R. (2012). Threshold concepts and their use in the professional development of mathematics teachers: A methodology for collaboration across four European countries. British Educational Research Association Annual Conference (BERA), Manchester, UK, 4–6 September 2012. Manchester: BERA, paper 0231.

Rossi, T., & Jeanes, R. (2016). Education, pedagogy and sport for development: addressing seldom asked questions. *Sport, Education and Society*, 21(4), 483–494.

Rowbottom, D.P. (2007). Demystifying threshold concepts, *Journal of Philosophy of Education*, 41(2), 263–270.

Shalom H Schwartz, S.H., Cieciuch, J., Vecchione, M., Davidov, E., Fischer, R., Beierlein, C.,... Konty, M. (2012). Refining the theory of basic individual values, *Journal of Personality and Social Psychology*, 103(4), 663–688.

Shilling, C. (2005). The rise of the body and the development of sociology. *Sociology*, 39(4), 761–767.

Shilling, C. (2012). *The Body & Social Theory* (3rd ed.). London: Sage Publications.

Webb, L., McCaughtry, N., & MacDonald, D. (2004). Surveillance as a technique of power in physical education. *Sport, Education and Society*, 9(2), 207–222. doi: 10.1080/1357332042000233949

Webb, L., Quennerstedt, M., & Öhman, M. (2008). Healthy bodies: construction of the body and health in physical education, *Sport Education & Society*, 13(4), 353–372.

Wellard I., Pickard, A., & Bailey, R. (2007). A shock of electricity just sort of goes through my body: Physical activity and embodied reflexive practices in young female ballet dancers. *Gender and Education*, 19(1), 79–91,doi: 10.1080/09540250601087793

Wisniewski, T. et al. (2018). Supporting students through role redefinition: A self-determination theory perspective. *Education as Change*, 22(1), 23.

Yuasa, Y. (1987). *The Body: Toward an Eastern Mind/Body Theory*. Albany, NY: State University of New York Press.

Chapter 12

Threshold concepts for physical education: From conceptual possibilities to pedagogical realities

Anna Bryant, David Aldous and Fiona C. Chambers

Introduction

The possibilities offered by the enactment of a transformative agenda for 21st Century physical education (PE) have compelled educators to engage with an increasingly more complex approach to the designing of curricula and enactment of pedagogical and assessment strategies within the micro-level of the classroom. Notable examples of such developments include those found within the translation and enactment of the Australian (see Brown & Penney, 2017) and Swedish PE Curricula (Larsson & Nyberg, 2016) both of which place a focus on the principles and pedagogical possibilities of movement. Importantly, for these curricula to become enacted necessitates that academics and practitioners to be encouraged to 'make the familiar strange' (Evans and Davies, 2004), to remain curious about the interdiscipline of PE and continue to develop their sociological and pedagogical imaginations.

Keeping the views of Evans and Davies in mind, the four threshold concepts for PE presented in Chapter 11 ('**Corporeal Reflexivity**', '**Corporeal Aesthetics**', '**Self Actualisation through Human Movement**' and '**Eudaimonia through Human Movement**') need to be translated into praxis. In essence, they must be translated from aspirational possibilities into the messy and complex pedagogic realities (Brown and Penney, 2017, p. 123) that 'by definition encompasses **decisions**, **planning** and **action** associated with curriculum and assessment of teaching PE within the micro-level of the classroom.'

Through our experiences of working with practitioners in a period of curriculum transformation in Wales and in Ireland, we are also acutely aware that for many practitioners who have been trained within a system that (through political necessity) has orientated around forms of performative and technocratic forms of pedagogical and assessment practice, making the 'leap' to the pedagogical realities that are informed by complex threshold concepts may at times seem quite daunting. It is important to note that simply calling out the eclectic range of languages and threshold concepts (as we have done in Chapter 11) will not support educators in their planning or actions *nor* will it benefit the learner within the micro-level of the classroom – change in praxis requires a deeper engagement.

With this in mind, we are cognisant of Tinning's (2004) perceptive point that in encouraging practitioners to become increasingly unorthodox, necessitates more than offering just a series of concepts and what is required is further mapping of these threshold concepts against curricula, pedagogical and assessment principles and practices.

In what follows, this chapter outlines how these threshold concepts may be used in the mapping of curricula, pedagogical and assessment of movement using a series of principles which guide pedagogical and assessment approaches. To begin with we outline some suggested pedagogical principles for educators to ensure the complexity of threshold concepts is retained and not lost in translation. We also invite the educator to bear in mind flexible roles of educator and learner, as constructivists who can engage with authentic forms of movement. In the latter part of the chapter, we provide an illustrative example of mapping such pedagogical principles for threshold concepts onto the new Welsh curriculum's Health and Well-Being Area of Learning and Experience. This is intended to help physical educators to learn how to implement the mapping process to their own praxis.

Threshold concepts: Connecting conceptual possibilities to pedagogic realities

The movement case studies presented in this book illustrated a number of pedagogical practices and principles used to generate meaning and understanding of movement. In summary, these included a prominent focus and use of Laban's Movement Analysis Framework (Chapter 4 and 5); Motivation theories and 'developing a goal orientation task mastery as the practitioner' (Chapter 6); Teaching Games for Understanding (Chapter 8), principles from physical literacy (Chapter 9) and Social and Emotional Learning Framework (CASEL, 2017) (Chapter 10). What is notable within the majority of these case studies is the focus on using constructivist principles to co-construct but also capture empirically the experiences of movement with the learner. Yet, what is promising is how these case studies were able to retain a sense of complexity by embracing the role of learners as being flexible and autonomous

Furthermore, the case studies also illustrated a number of other broader pedagogical principles that transcend PE context. These include, 'the influence of music to alter movement' (Chapter 5); 'allowing time for experimentation' (Chapter 5); Using culturally relevant frameworks e.g. Friluftsliv from Norway (Chapter 7); and an important focus on the social values of PE (Chapter 10). Collectively, the frameworks and principles outlined within the case studies bear testament to the complex and often messy mixture of pedagogical languages within PE (see Chapter 1). These concepts and principles have acted as a rich source of ideation and have helped us to begin further mapping out some key pedagogical and assessment principles that might be useful in helping practitioners begin to make the leap from conceptual possibilities to pedagogical realities.

In many respects, it also illustrates a number of pedagogical possibilities that, if encouraged and supported, may be used by educators in their enactment of threshold concepts of movement.

Thus, whilst we acknowledge that there might be other pedagogical principles that are orientated towards empirically understanding changes to PE praxis, we feel that what is also required are a set of principles that may support educators in beginning to translate concepts into forms of pedagogic realities. In doing so, we have drawn upon Calvino's six memos (2016) for the next millennium to formulate Pedagogical Principles of Translation to guide the translation of conceptual possibilities:

1 **Lightness**: Educators are required to be agile in their thinking regarding the possibilities for conceptual translation as well as the needs of the learner.
2 **Quickness**: Educators require a sense of vivacity, energy and feeling in beginning the translatory process.
3 **Exactitude**: In development of pedagogical practices and principles, educators are required to be precise and accurate in their translation of concepts and use of pedagogical practices.
4 **Visibility**: Educators need to be nurtured to develop their imagination to ideate pedagogical possibilities and explore what is possible within the pedagogical reality they reside.
5 **Multiplicity**: In coming to imagine the connections between concepts and pedagogic practice, educators should be encouraged to look beyond the conventional disciplinary boundaries.
6 **Carelessness**: Educators should be provided with time and space from where they might engage with playfulness with the view of enabling their own pedagogical practices to feel more authentic.

These Pedagogical Principles of Translation are intended to augment those traditional principles used currently by physical educators. This is important as we are cognisant of Tinning's (2004) wise words i.e. we do not want to create a sense of unorthodoxy for the sake of being unorthodox. That said, in beginning to play with these principles ourselves, we do believe that the six principles, if used sensitively, may begin to enable educators to make the interconnections between conceptual possibilities and pedagogical practices. In a way, they might be seen as the building blocks that can be used with the following more recognisable considerations for conceptual-pedagogic translations:

1 Educators should be provided with the **time and space** to develop 'spaces of pedagogical action' to enable the enhancement of experimentation and creativity (Penney, 2013).
2 Educators should be provided with the tools and resources to foster 'generative creativity' and reconnect with their own **pedagogical dispositions** (Brown & Penney, 2017).

3 Educators should **engage in a design thinking process** that is respectful, sensitive and rooted in activity, context and culture (Jones & Turner, 2006) in which they practice.

It also goes without saying that alongside the need for pedagogical principles, the translation of conceptual possibilities also necessitates that educators place particular focus on considering what these principles might look like in practice. However, in line with the thoughts of Backman et al. (2012), we believe that such principles are important to encourage educators to move beyond the rigid orthodoxies prevalent within the teaching and assessment of movement in PE and to seek solutions beyond established boundaries. Such thoughts build on the ideas of Murray et al. (2020, p. 282) who comment that 'how we structure space for student variation and begin to listen and look for student understanding' is crucial in formulating the pedagogical realities of PE. Moreover, the principles outlined above are intended to inform pedagogical and assessment practices that both enable the translation of the Threshold Concepts in a way that ensures that the autonomy of learners is retained. Moreover, they are intentionally designed to advocate what Penney (2013) notes as the important role 'spaces of pedagogical action' play in nurturing their own understanding and practice of the four threshold concepts presented in Chapter 11. In light of what we are proposing within this chapter and the book, the illustrated 'Pedagogical Principles of Translation' are particularly important in what Brown et al. (2017) note as practices that sensitively socialise practitioners to engage with a creative process that may appear unsettling and at times a little chaotic.

Finally, it is also important to recognise that the Pedagogical Principles of Translation outlined should not be considered exhaustive but are intended to act as a heuristic set of sensitising principles that can be conceptualised within assemblages that provide interconnections between concepts and pedagogic realities. They provide stepping stones to further consideration of how educators might engage with a transformative process in which they are able to make the connections between threshold concepts and pedagogical realities. In what follows, we provide an illustrative example of how such principles of translation, bounded within a design-thinking process (see Chapter 3), may be used to bring curricula to pedagogical practice.

Illustrative example: Mapping conceptual possibilities within the pedagogic realities of the new Welsh Health and Well-Being Area of Learning and Experience (AoLE)

Here we provide an illustrative example from the context of Welsh curriculum development. For those unfamiliar with this context, Wales has been engaged with a series of curricula reforms since 2015. Whilst it is beyond the context of this chapter to provide a comprehensive overview of these reforms (see Aldous, 2018), significant for Welsh Physical Educators has been the design of the new Health and Well-Being Area of Learning and Experience (HWB AoLE) (Welsh Government, 2017). A key feature of the new AoLE is a series of What Matter Statements (WMS) that are connected and interdependent across a the 4 learning domains (Welsh Government, 2020),

- Developing physical health and well-being has lifelong benefits.
- How we process and respond to our experiences affects our mental health and emotional well-being.
- Our decision -making impacts on the quality of our lives and the lives of others.
- How we engage with social influences shaped who we are and affect our health and well-being.
- Healthy relationships are fundamental to our well-being (Welsh Government, 2020, p. 74–75).

Another key structural feature of the new curriculum for Wales is the inclusion of what is termed principles of progression (Welsh Government, 2020). These principles, designed to enable educators to have agency over their choice of pedagogical and assessment practice, have been based on more broader pedagogic principles outlined within the Donaldson Report (Donaldson, 2015; Morgan, 2018). However, as recognised within some of our initial exploratory research (Eynon & Aldous, 2019), secondary physical educators in Wales are in need of further support in developing appropriate forms of pedagogical and assessment practices that enable the sustainable and independent translation of the principles of the new HWB AoLE. With this in mind and in relation to our work outlined in the book to date, we provide a series of six design thinking steps, to support the design of a hypothetical unit of work that could be situated used to deliver the new welsh curriculum to a class of 11–12 year old learners in their first term in secondary school. These steps are informed by the Chambers (2018) model of design thinking (See Chapter 3).

Phase 1: Compassion

Within the first element of the design-thinking process, educators would be encouraged to reflect and empathise upon the social, cultural, educative and biological needs of their learner. Key to nurturing the reflective and empathic abilities of the educator would be the focus on embedding the Translatory Pedagogical Principles of **space and time** for reflection (see Lamb, Lane & Aldous, 2013 Lamb and Aldous, 2016). Underpinning this sense of compassion requires educators to engage with what Schon (1987) notes as a series of 'reflective conversations' based on their previous experiences of teaching PE. Such reflective conversations (see step 3 below) could also be augmented through initial engagement with a number of selected concepts. Generating this space and time would enable educators to begin considering what concepts might also be used to further their empathetic connection with the learner. These would then be developed through a process of ideation.

Phase 2: Ideation

Central to the development of pedagogic realities would be allowing educators the space and time to engage with a process of purposeful ideation. Such ideation would be guided to focus on considering what concepts might be useful in addressing the needs of the learner and to begin making the interconnections between curricula, conceptual and pedagogical principles.

As we have illustrated elsewhere (Egan et al., 2019a & 2019b), central to the ideational phase is again the provision of **time and space** to provide educators with the opportunity to engage with a range of resources and Threshold Concepts that might be used. Such ideation might be provided through inspiration drawn from the experiences of other educators but also from readings and observations of a) the learners, b) curriculum and c) threshold concepts. However, again echoing the thoughts of Penney (2013) the ideation phase might involve educators generating 'spaces for pedagogical action' in which educators are given the space from where to ideate regarding the multitude of possibilities the concept can generate and also what type of pedagogical principles these might be connected with.

For example, for the purpose of this illustration, educators might select to make interconnections between **'Corporeal Reflexivity'** and the first two WMS of the new Welsh AoLE, namely: 'Developing physical health and well-being has lifelong benefits' and 'How we process and respond to our experiences affects our mental health and emotional well-being'. In this example the concepts of **'Corporeal Reflexivity'** that appear most evident (but not the only or exclusive WMS) to WMS 1 and 2 include, **'sensory awareness,' 'listening to self,' 'performance of the body,' 'corporeal empathy'** and **'corporeal compassion.'** In doing so, educators are provided with the space from where to explore all of the possible synergies that integrate all threshold concepts as well as the WMS and acknowledge that the next block of lessons might focus on other combinations of the WMS.

Underpinning the educators experience of the ideation phase are the Translatory Pedagogical Principles of **lightness** and **visibility.** For example, educator engagement within the pedagogical spaces of action will only be valuable if educators are required to be agile in their thinking regarding the possibilities for conceptual translation and are also nurtured in developing their imagination in the ideation of pedagogical possibilities. In reflection of Chapters 1 and 11, this again emphasises the necessity and value of languages of description that at their centre are largely composed of weak grammatical syntaxes (Bernstein, 1999) that enable educators to draw on principles beyond the traditional conceptual boundaries of PE.

The final suggested element of the ideational phase is the generation of learning outcomes that act as a connector between the conceptual, curricula and pedagogical principles being addressed. Again, for the purposes of illustration, the following learning outcomes (LO) could be used,

LO 1: To understand the feeling of the body through movement

LO 2: To understand empathy and compassion

LO3: To understand the interconnections of the feelings of body through movement with empathy and compassion

Although, it may be argued that generating learning outcomes somewhat narrows the focus, such focus is crucial in enabling the translation of concepts into pedagogical practices. It also provides a strong focus for the next phase of the development process: Prototyping using pedagogical tools.

Phase 3: Prototyping

Within the prototyping phase, educators and learners would then begin to explore the use of different pedagogical tools and resources that would enable the translation of concepts into forms of pedagogical practice. What is also important to recognise is that whilst it may be aspirational in the long-term to ask educators to generate their own tools within the prototyping phase, we are also acutely aware of not reinventing the wheel and harnessing what tools may already exist and are available to educators. For example, educators may be inclined to explore the frameworks and lenses that are evident within this book. For example, as readers will now recognise, central to the work evident in the case studies has been the influence of Laban, Physical Literacy, Lloyd's Function – Flow Framework and the SOLO taxonomy. Such frameworks and principles should be used in a manner that fosters **generative creativity** but also that reflects the translatory principle of **Exactitude**. In what follows, we briefly outline some of the key characteristics of two examples of such pedagogical and assessment resources; that of the SOLO Taxonomy in PE and the use of a movement conversation.

SOLO taxonomy in PE

In Chapter 2, we introduced the SOLO taxonomy (Structure of the Observed Learning Outcome) (Biggs & Tang, 2011), which helps to inform the process of devising an assessment rubric. Previously, the work of Dudley has highlighted the use of the SOLO framework in 'A Quality and Health Optimising Physical Education Assessment Framework' as a means to be used within the assessment of learning within PE (Dudley, Goodyear, & Baxter, 2016) and within physical literacy (Barnett et al., 2019; Keegan et al., 2019). The SOLO framework shows five key stages from the Prestructural, Unistructural, Multistructural, Relational, with a significant leap to 'extended abstract'. This framework breaks down the task so that the learner can clearly see what is required for that 'leap' across the threshold i.e. from performative to proactive conception. As a reminder (Table 12.1) provides a visual representation of the SOLO framework, specifically that adapted by Dudley Goodyear, & Baxter (2016) for a quality health PE context.

The principles of the framework outlined above exemplify how the pedagogical principle of **Exactitude** may be translated into forms of pedagogical practice. The strength of the SOLO framework lies in its ability to provide educators and learners with clear and precise guidance on how to guide learners through the process of developing understanding and practice of movement. This is further exemplified within the example of a 'curriculum planning tool' (see Table 12.2). Here, we have built upon Dudley, Goodyear & Baxter,(2016) 'quality and health optimising PE assessment framework' in three key ways. Firstly, we have adapted it to become a curriculum planning tool by shining a light on the curriculum focus, the four PE threshold concepts of **'Corporeal Reflexivity,' 'Corporeal Aesthetics, 'Self Actualisation through Human Movement'** and **'Eudaimonia through Human Movement'** along the left hand column. In doing so, we have removed the reference of the four learning domains (physical, cognitive, affective and social) from the left hand column and made reference to them in the right hand column. Secondly, we have mapped Meyers & Land (2005) 'pre liminal (extended abstract)' to postliminal Space' and their eight key characteristics of threshold concepts i.e. Transformative; Performative; Irreversible; Integrative; Bounded; Troublesome; Reconstitutive and Discursive (see Chapter 2) to this framework. Thirdly, we have unpopulated the framework and added some key questions and considerations around the focus of this illustrative example, **'Corporeal Reflexivity'** in and the new HWB AoLE in Wales.

It is important to reiterate that the intention of this tool is to not provide a diagnostic approach to movement but to guide both educator and learner in their ability to engage with **Multiplicity** and imagine the connections between concepts and pedagogic practice. Finally, we hope that the sophisticated (and iterative) continuum, evident within the table acts as a mechanism from where to stimulate visibility within the prototyping phase of the significant leap that the learner needs to make from the 'relational' to the 'extended abstract' phase to obtain the threshold concept and if necessary provide further insight that can be used within the ideation phase of curricula development.

Individual and Peer feedback movement conversation

Our second example of a pedagogical tool that could be developed within the prototyping phase is an example of what we have termed a **'pupil movement conversation.'** Drawing upon Schon's (1987) principles of 'reflective conversations' and Lloyd's (2015; 2016) notion of a 'movement conversation,' we have developed a tool that provides opportunities to awaken the imagination, curiosity, and deepen connections with the learning environment for both educator and learner alike. The integration of Lloyd's principles are also important as it integrates the

Table 12.1 A quality and health optimising PE assessment framework

Progression	'Prestructural'	Unistructural	Multistructural	Relational	Progression Threshold	Extended Abstract
All Learning Domain	The acquisition of unconnected information, which have no organisation and makes no sense	Simple and obvious connections are made, but their significance is grasped	A number of connections may be made but the meta connections between them are missed, as is their significance for the whole	The student is now able to appreciate the significance of the parts in relation to the whole		'The student is making connections not only within the given subject area, but also beyond it, able to generaliSe and transfer the principles and ideas underlying the specific instance. Student have exceeded the cognition, affective, social or psychomotor, expectations of the developmentally appropriate standards'
Learning Context	No apparent learning observed	Learning progression evident across all learning domains, with significant learning noted in Extend Abstract phase.				

Source: Adapted from Dudley Goodyear, & Baxter, 2016; 2016, p. 328

Table 12.2 Physical education threshold concept curriculum planning tool

				Pre liminal Space	Threshold (liminal space)	Postliminal Space
Progression These are guided by rich learning outcomes				Encounter with troublesome knowledge	Integration Discarding ontological and epistemic shift **Reconstitutive**	Transformation Irreversibility Crossing conceptual boundaries Changed discourse **Consequential**
Physical Education Threshold Concepts	'Prestructural' The acquisition of unconnected information, which have no organisation and makes no sense	'Unistructural' Simple and obvious connections are made, but their significance is not grasped	'Multistructural' A number of connections may be made but the meta connections between them are missed, as is their significance for the whole	'Relational' The student is now able to appreciate the significance of the parts in relation to the whole	**Threshold (liminal space)**	**Extended Abstract – Postliminal Space** **The Threshold Concept** 'The student is making connections not only within the given subject area, but also beyond it, able to generalise and transfer the principles and ideas underlying the specific instance. Student have exceeded the cognition, affective, social or psychomotor, expectations of the developmentally appropriate standards.'

(Continued)

Table 12.2 (Continued)

				Pre liminal Space	Threshold (liminal space)	Postliminal Space
Corporeal Reflexivity 'displays of awareness of one's body as both an embodied, experiencing subject and an embodied physical object accessible to the gaze of others. In displays of corporeal reflexivity, the embodied, experiencing subject turns its attention to its physical body, re-visioning it as an object of scrutiny, usually under the normative gaze of others' (Ochs, 2015, p. 277).	How can you support the learner to... Learn how and what to observe? Learn how to ask questions? Learn how to give feedback?	How can you support the learner to.... Learn how to frame feedback? Learn how to sandwich feedback? Describe their performance? Describe how they are feeling during movement?	How can you support the learner to... Provide accurate and more detailed feedback? Explain and begin to self evaluate their performance? Explain how they are feeling during movement? Understand how others are feeling during movement?	How can you support the learner to Provide evaluative feedback e.g. make a point, evidence and elaborate? Analyse and evaluate their performance Analyse and evaluate how they are feeling during movement and identify triggers for their feelings? Appreciate and understand how others are feeling during movement Consider the impact of their own actions on others?	How can you support the learner to … Performing a Rich task? Complexity Application Evaluation and Synthesis Top end of the taxonomy…. More socially responsible? Altruism? to advocacy	**The Learner has learned Corporeal Reflexivity. This is demonstrated by the learners grasp of the following interconnected concepts, which will be evident across all four learning domains** -Body relationships -Supportive behaviours -Lived body -Kinaesthesia -**Corporeal empathy** -**Corporeal compassion** -**Sensory Awareness** -**Listening to the self** -Physical body -**Performance of the Body**

Corporeal Aesthetics	How can you support the learner to...	How can you support the learner to...	How can you support the learner to...	How can you support the learner to...	The Learner has learned Corporeal Aesthetics. This is demonstrated by the learners grasp of the following interconnected concepts, which will be evident across all four learning domains
'Movement aesthetic values emerge from personal and communal morals and ideals as well as social mores of the body, which create contextual lenses for experiencing, interpreting, and making meaning of movement vocabularies created and perpetuated in dance communities' (Dyer, 2009, p. 108).					Stability -Times -Balance -Motor competency -Locomotion -Spatial Awareness -Bounded -Weight Transference -Kinesphere -Dynamosphere -Weight Bearing -Light Flow

(Continued)

Table 12.2 (Continued)

	Pre liminal Space	Threshold (liminal space)				Postliminal Space
Self Actualisation through human movement Arnold summarised (Maslow's (1954) view of self-actualised people as follows: [They] are marked by their more than usually efficient perception of reality; their acceptance of self and others; their spontaneity; their lack of ego-centeredness; their non-avoidance of privacy; their autonomy; their ability to derive inspiration and strength from the ordinary experiences of life; their ability to have frequent peak experiences; their feeling for mankind by way of sympathy and identification; their ability to form deep personal relationships; their democratic character-structure in that they can form relationships irrespective of class, education, race, and religion; their ability to differentiate between ends and means; their sense of humor; their creativeness; their relative detachment from the culture in which they are immersed that they are more readily able to discover their growth needs or being values (p. 92)	How can you support the learner to…	How can you support the learner to…	How can you support the learner to…	How can you support the learner to…	How can you support the learner to…	**The Learner has learned Self Actualization through human movement This is demonstrated by the learners grasp of the following interconnected concepts, which will be evident across all four learning domains** Intrinsic Motivation Sustainability Competence development (social) Competence development (motor) Arousal Show Creativity to overcome barriers sense of humour, carefree Show Autonomy to overcome barriers Lack of ego-centredness **Curiosity [with four sub-categories] (Merck, 2018)** · Deprivation sensitivity · Joyous exploration · Stress tolerance · Openness to people's ideas altruism beneficence acceptance spontaneity Growth Optimism

		How can you support the learner to…	How can you support the learner to…	How can you support the learner to…	How can you support the learner to…	**The Learner has learned Eudaimonia through Human Movement**
Eudaimonia through Human Movement Eudaimonia is a combination of an uplifting feeling of skill mastery, mental happiness, enhanced self-esteem, transcendence, ecstasy and euphoria (Cooper, 1998). Chatfield (2018) describes it as human thriving and flourishing.						**This is demonstrated by the learners grasp of the following interconnected concepts, which will be evident across all four learning domains** Motivation Control Identifying Risk Excitement Imagining movement that is possible Respect – mutual Visualisation Carefree Autonomy Competence Relatedness Sustainability Beneficence
Learning Context Learning is observed and assessed through a designated physical activity and physical education experience.	No apparent learning observed in a physical education context, no development towards concepts of the threshold concept	Development and improve in proportion to learning progression and context. Quality indicators could include, listening and looking for student understanding of Knowledge moving from concrete to abstract. Refinement and growing sophistication in the use and application of skill. Learners becoming more socially responsible, as they progress from primarily considering oneself to considering the impact of their own actions on others at a local, national and global level. Learners will progress from feelings of caring and respecting others to the capacity of advocacy on behalf of others (Welsh Government, 2020, p. 76) Over time demonstrate increased self-regulation.				

Source Adapted from Dudley Goodyear, & Baxter, 2016, p. 328

domains of knowledge and attempts to take the learner and educator from what they are familiar with to the more unfamiliar through 'function, form, feeling and flow.' However, we do acknowledge that there are an eclectic range of framework-questions that practitioners might draw upon to help facilitate the learners' movement conversation. The following movement conversation is guided by a series of steps and prepared questions adapted from Lloyd (2015) as a basis for individual and peer feedback.

- Firstly, the learners should be placed into pairs and should film each other in a movement/activity (for example, dance or gymnastics).
- Secondly, the learners should find a suitable space for a movement conversation between each other once the videos have been taken.
- Thirdly, the learner should give each other some space to read the guiding questions, while rewatching the clips.
- Fourthly, the learner should jointly watch the videos and engage in the movement conversation – the learner should then take it in turns (interviewer) to guide the conversation through the pre-prepared questions on 'Function to Flow' that have been adapted from Lloyd (2015) and are illustrated below. Following this, the learner should answer the questions and provide feedback on their peers' performance. Moreover, a block (2–4) of lessons around **Corporeal Reflexivity** provides the learner with an opportunity to progress through and build upon their movement conversation. Although not the focus of this illustrative case study, this pedagogical tool also lends itself to support the development of **Corporeal Aesthetics**.
- **Function**: Tell us about your movement in the video clips. What do you notice? Probe: How happy are you with your performance?
- **Form**: What does your movement look like? (describe shape, body parts, face, etc.) probe: How are you physically positioned? How in control are you? Probe: can you explain? What would you like it to be?
- **Feeling**: What does your movement feel like? (feeling in your muscles, mood, level of energy, etc.) What does your movement sound like? Do you feel anything from within? If so how can you explain that feeling? What triggered that feeling?
- **Flow**: When viewing the video, what animal best describes your movement and why? (Adapted from Lloyd, 2015, p. 576)
- Finally, the learner engages in a **'reflexivity moment'** by answering the following individual questions – How might you improve your performance? How did you find the 'movement conversation process'? 'What did you learn about your partners' feelings around their performance?' 'How might you support your partner to help them develop their performance and their 'movement conversation' in the future?

Again, similar to the example of the pedagogical framework outlined above, the movement conversation is not intended to be prescriptive but rather to act as a trigger from where both educators and learners are able to nurture individual **visibility** and to an extent provide a bounded sense of carelessness in their exploration and development of movement. This type of activity might be relevant to all types of learners but particularly those in the 'prestructural' and 'unistructural' phase who struggle to make any sense of, or grasp the significance of their movement experiences (Biggs & Tang, 2011).

Following the thoughts of Ivinson (2012, p. 495), in beginning to consider the different types of tools and resources that might be needed we also 'seek to recognise learners not as those who reproduce existing signs, but rather as active sign-makers involved in dynamic processes.' Thus, the resources and tools are not intended for prescriptive use but as a means by which the learning of both learner and educators may be empowered to a point by where they are able to vividly engage with the translation of concepts into forms of practice within their specific pedagogical realities. Furthermore, in focusing on the assemblages of such principles, we hope (eventually, with time) to encourage educators to be spontaneous, encourage engagement with a trial and error process and enable them to ride waves of unpredictability that often arise within the interactions of PE contexts.

Step 6: Implement and Evaluate

The notion of evaluation being part of the process of a project (in this case curriculum planning) rather a product is a more formative approach, one also shared by Rossi et al (2004). Having assessed the following facets of the curriculum: purposes of evaluation, programs structure and circumstances (i.e. stage of development) and resources available for evaluation (Rossi et al., 2004), it is recommended that we adopt a formative approach to the evaluation of the curriculum plan. In order to this, we select appropriate evaluation methodologies to support this approach. The WK Kellogg Foundation refers to theory-based evaluation. A simple way of looking at this is to think of it as the link between the rationale behind the curriculum plan and the logic that links the activities and outcomes of the curriculum plan. Weiss (1995) outlines the four main purposes of Theory-Based Evaluation approach:

1 It ensures that the evaluation focuses on key aspects of the curriculum
2 It allows evaluation results to combine to feed into a broad theoretical base
3 It asks educators to reach consensus on assumptions about what they are doing and why, and
4 Evaluations based on theoretical assumptions carry more weight.

The qualitative Theory-Based model of evaluation in the intended curriculum plan. This will be done using a 'map' of curriculum, also called a Theory of Change Logic Model (Weiss, 1995). This is a model of change that outlines the assumptions on which the curriculum is to be evaluated (Weiss, 1995). In simple terms it shows why we think the curriculum will succeed and it explains the changes we intend to make by creating a pathway through the life of the curriculum. A Logic model illustrates the rationale and processes of the programme. Rossi et al., (2004) recommend that Theory-based evaluation using the Logic Model should judge the quality of the curriulum's performance under the following headings: (1) need for curriculum, (2) the curriculum design, (3) its implementation and service delivery (4) it's impact or outcomes and (5) its efficiency.

Conclusion

To conclude, what we have hoped to have provided is a dynamic, relevant and thought provoking illustration of how the conceptual possibilities outlined within the threshold concepts can be translated into the pedagogical realities of where movement occurs within PE. In doing so, we have been acutely aware that such a process is not without its challenges and will require sensitive guidance and an experimental space from where educators and learners may creatively nurture their understanding and practice of movement together. Despondently, our own experiences have highlighted how such spaces are continually squeezed within schools and more worryingly Higher Education. Nevertheless, we are also enthused by the ongoing work by colleagues in Sweden and Australia that have placed emphasis on developing forms of pedagogical resources that support educators in the creative interpretation and enactment of transformative curricula. It is hoped that our ideas outlined within this final chapter may provide further inspiration, discussion and support for educators who are beginning to engage with their own development of curricula.

With educators in mind, we have also provided some pedagogical and assessment principles and examples of pedagogical and assessment approaches that may be used as a starting point from where to engage with the messiness of curricula enactment. We have acknowledged the eclectic range of framework and tools that might be drawn upon to help learners embrace the liminal spaces that arise through the connection between concepts and practice. It was not our intention to be prescriptive but rather to use these frameworks and tools as a means of exemplifying one way in which design thinking can be used to translate conceptual possibilities into forms of pedagogical realities within the context of PE.

References

Aldous, D. (2018). Working towards understanding the possibilities and constraints of contemporary curriculum reform within Welsh Secondary Physical Education. Oral Presentation to British Education Research Association (BERA) Annual Conference, Manchester, UK, September, 2018.

Barker, D., Bergentoft, H., & Nyberg, G. (2017). What would physical educators know about movement education? A review of literature, 2006–2016, *Quest*, 69(4), 419–435.

Barnett, L. M., Dudley, D. A., Telford, D., Lubans, D. R., Bryant, A.S., Roberts, W. M., ... Keegan, R.J. (2019). Physical literacy in young people: Guidelines and recommendations for the selection of measures in schools. *Journal of Teaching in Physical Education (JTPE)*, 38(2), 119–125.

Bernstein, B. (1999). Vertical and horizontal discourse: An essay. *British Journal of Sociology of Education*, 20(2), 157–173.

Biggs, J. B., & C. Tang. (2011). *Teaching for Quality Learning at University*. Berkshire: Open University Press.

Brown, T., & Penney, P. (2017). Interpretation and enactment of senior secondary physical education: pedagogic realities and the expression of Arnoldian dimensions of movement. *Physical Education and Sport Pedagogy*, 22(2), 121–136.

Calvino, I. (2016). Six memos for the next millennium. Pengiun Books, London, UK.

CASEL. (2017). *SEL Core Competencies*. Retrieved from https://casel.org/core-competencies/ (Last accessed January 03, 2020).

Chambers, F. C. (ed.) (2018). Learning to mentor in sports coaching: A design thinking approach. Oxon, Ox: Routledge.

Cohen, S. A. (1987). Instructional alignment: Searching for the magic bullet. *Educational Researcher*, 16(8), 16–20.

Donaldson, G. (2015). Successful futures: Independent review of curriculum and assessment arrangements in Wales, Crown Copyright, OGL.

Dudley, D., Goodyear, V., & Baxter, D. (2016). Quality and health optimizing physical education: Using assessment at the health and education nexus. *Journal of Teaching in Physical Education*, 35, 324–336. doi:10.1123/jtpe.2016-0075

Egan, D., Aldous, D., & Bryant, A. (2019a). Curriculum development through professional enquiry: Developments in Wales, retrieved from: https://www.bera.ac.uk/blog/curriculum-development-through-professional-enquiry-developments-in-wales

Egan, D., Bryant, A., Gordon, B., Aldous, D., Clement, J., Edwards, L., Loudon, G., & Mitchell, G. (2019b). Undertaking Professional Enquiry: An introduction for Lead Enquirers, Welsh Government. Retrieved from https://hwb.gov.wales/storage/aeb2810d-f670-4718-87a1-299696ce5156/guide-to-undertaking-professional-enquiry.pdf

Eynon, L., & Aldous, D. (2019). Understanding the impact of Health & Well-Being curricula reform on the dimensions of pedagogic practice within secondary Physical Education in Wales, *Oral Presentation to British Education Research Association (BERA) Annual Conference*, Manchester, UK, September, 2019.

Evans, J., & Davies, B. (2004). Pedagogy, symbolic control, identity and health. In J. Evans, B. Davies, & J. Wright (Eds.). *Body Knowledge and Control: Studies in the Sociology of Physical Education and Health* (pp. 4–17). London: Routledge.

Ivinson, G. (2012). The body and pedagogy: Beyond absent, moving bodies in pedagogic practice. *British Journal of Sociology of Education*, 33(4), 489–506.

Jones, R., & Turner, P. (2006). Teaching coaches to coach holistically: Can Problem Based Learning (PBL) help? *Physical Education and Sport Pedagogy*, 11(2), 181–202.

Keegan, R.J., Dudley, D. A. Telford, D. Lubans, D. R. Bryant, A.S., Roberts, W.M., ... J.R. Barnett, L.M. (2019). Defining and operationalizing physical literacy: A modified Delphi method, *Journal of Teaching in Physical Education (JTPE)*, 38(2), 105–118.

W.K. Kellogg Foundation (1998). W.K. Kellogg Foundation Evaluation Handbook. W.K. Kellogg Foundation.

Lamb, P., Lane, K., & Aldous, D. (2013). Enhancing the spaces of reflection: A buddy peer-review process within physical education initial teacher education. *European Physical Education Review*, 19(1), 21–38.

Lamb, P., & Aldous, D. (2016). Exploring the relationship between reflexivity and reflective practice through Lesson Study within Initial Teacher Education. *International journal for lesson and learning studies, 5*(2), 99–115.

Larsson, H., & Nyberg, G. (2016). It doesn't matter how they move really, as long as they move.' Physical education teachers on developing their students' movement capabilities, *Physical Education and Sport Pedagogy, 22*(2), 137–149.

Lloyd, R. J. (2015). The 'Function to Flow' (F2F) Model: An Interdisciplinary Approach to Assessing Movement Within and Beyond the Context of Climbing. *Physical Education and Sport Pedagogy, 20*(6), 571–592. doi: 10.1080/17408989.2014.895802

Lloyd, R. (2016). Becoming physically literate for life: Embracing the functions, forms, feelings and flows of alternative and mainstream physical activity, *Journal of Teaching in Physical Education, 2016, 35*(2), 107–116

Morgan, K. (2018). Making sense of the pedagogical principles in Donaldson's 'Successful Futures': A Welsh Physical Education perspective. Physical Education Matters, Spring.

Ochs, E. (2015). Corporeal Reflexivity and Autism. *Integrative Psychological Behaviour, 49,* 275–287.

Penney, D. (2013). Points of tension and possibility: boundaries in and of physical education, *Sport Education and Society, 18*(1), 6–20.

Rossi, P. H., Freeman, H. E., & Rosenbaum, S. (2004). Evaluation: A Systematic Approach. *Contemporary Sociology, 36*(4).

Schon, D. A. (1987). *The Reflective Practitioner: How Professionals Think in Action.* New York: Basic Books.

Tinning, R. (2004). Ruminations on body knowledge and control and the spaces for hope and happening. In J. Evans, B. Davies & J. Wright (Eds.). *Body knowledge and control: Studies in the Sociology of Physical Education and Health* (pp. 218–238). London: Routledge.

Weiss, C. H. (1995). Nothing as practical as good theory: Exploring theory-based evaluation for comprehensive community initiatives for children and families. In J. P. Connell, A. C. Kubisch, L. B. Schorr, & C. H. Weiss (Eds.). *Approaches to Evaluating Community Initiatives* (pp. 65–92). New York, NY: Aspen Institute.

Welsh Government (2017). Education in Wales: Our national mission. Education Wales. Welsh Government.

Welsh Government (2020). Curriculum for Wales Guidance. Welsh Government.

Chapter 13

Endnote: Final thoughts and future directions

Fiona C. Chambers, David Aldous and Anna Bryant

Introduction

This book was written at a very interesting moment in history; at the cusp of normal day to day life and the Covid19 global pandemic. Against this backdrop, it has caused our community to critique the nature of our subject area during a rapidly changing and dynamic situation. Globally, the pandemic has forced the physical education (PE) community to galvanise and to engage in this critical dialogue. Adding to Dr Risto Martinnen's Podcast 'Playing with Research in Health and Physical Education,' over the past number of months, the following online professional initiatives have been launched: PHE Canada's 'Cross Country Check in,' the SHAPE America online discussion boards, ACHPER Online Learning Programmes and the #AIESEPConnect Series. Our professional community is connecting across the globe to share critical insights on the nature of PE during Covid19, what it may look like in a post-Covid19 world and the power of the PE professional community in the proactive design of meaningful PE.

Design thinking begins with a problem statement (Liedtka, 2015), which focuses on the end-users i.e. the physical educator and the learner. Therefore, the problem statement at the heart of this book was:

Problem Statement:

Description: As a profession, we do not appear to have an agreed matrix of threshold concepts for PE.

Learning Need: PE educators need to identify threshold concepts for PE so that they can plan implement and assess learning in and through PE.

Insight: The absence of agreed threshold concepts in PE leads to ambiguity and a weakening of the perceived value of PE in the curriculum and also impacts the status of our profession.

This is a truly wicked problem, which calls for a human-centred approach to innovation i.e. design thinking. We see this book as timely. Written for physical educators, this edited book used a design thinking approach to analyse seven movement case studies in the following areas of human movement: gymnastics, dance, parkour, outdoor education, martial arts, Gaelic games and netball. The process involved writing pods using design thinking to (a) interrogate liminality (transformative learning) in PE and furthermore, (b) to put forward their proposed threshold concepts for PE and (c) suggested curriculum, pedagogy and assessment approaches to support the learning of their proposed threshold concepts for PE. The editors further dialogic and discourse analysis of these outputs led to (i) the four agreed threshold concepts for PE – Corporeal Reflexivity; Corporeal Aesthetics, Self-actualisation through Human Movement and Eudaimonia through Human Movement; and (ii) the presentation of principles of pedagogical translation and a comprehensive user-friendly praxis matrix for the curriculum pedagogy and assessment for such threshold concepts.

In learning to embrace design thinking, it is clear from this process that our professional community must and can remain curious and agile. We believe that physical educators are more than 'knowledge-brokers' (Macdonald, 2015). We are designers and are ideally placed to iterate solutions to the wicked problems in PE as and when they present themselves. In addition, this process adopted in this book highlighted the premise that PE is not content driven, it is threshold concept driven. As such, physical educators need to be competent and confident in a range of activity contexts to experiment and 'play' with threshold concepts in the first place. If we are to begin thinking about physical educators as designers, we need to consider how might we use the 'concept sandbox' to influence the learners' engagement in preliminal, liminal and postliminal spaces as they grapple with the threshold concepts for PE.

Future directions

We contend that we are standing on the shoulders of giants in our field and that this book has augmented some of this seminal work. However, for us a number of design questions remain for consideration:

1 What does it mean for pedagogy if we have to consider all four threshold concepts when planning for learning?
2 Is it possible to plan for one threshold concept in isolation?
3 What are sustainable assessment strategies for threshold concepts?
4 How can we continue to map and validate new threshold concepts for physical education?
5 How can physical educators work together in virtual and real settings to galvanise our profession as a learning community?
6 What does the Covid19 pandemic mean for future offline/online/blended iterations of physical education and physical education teacher education?
7 How can our professional community continue to do meaningful research during and post pandemic?
8 What are the most agile ways of conducting and disseminating our research such that it impacts praxis?

References

Liedtka, J. (2015). Perspective: Linking design thinking with innovation outcomes through cognitive bias reduction. *Journal of Product Innovation Management, 32*(6), 925–938.

Macdonald, D. (2015). Teacher-as-knowledge-broker in a futures-oriented health and physical education. *Sport, Education and Society, 20*(1), 27–41.doi: 10.1080/13573322.2014.935320

Index